ACHIEVING INVISIBILITY

ACHIEVING
INVISIBILITY

THE ART OF ARCHITECTURAL VISUALIZATION AND RENDERING

ADAM CRESPI

FAIRCHILD BOOKS

New York

DIRECTOR OF SALES AND ACQUISITIONS: Dana Meltzer-Berkowitz

EXECUTIVE EDITOR: Olga T. Kontzias

ACQUISITIONS EDITOR: Joseph Miranda

SENIOR DEVELOPMENT EDITOR: Jennifer Crane

ART DIRECTOR: Adam B. Bohannon

PRODUCTION MANAGER: Ginger Hillman

ASSOCIATE PRODUCTION EDITOR: Jessica Rozler

EDITORIAL SERVICES: Newgen-Austin/G&S

COMPOSITION: Barbara J. Barg

Library of Congress Catalog Number: 2007934596

ISBN: 978-1-56367-541-6

GST R 133004424

Printed in the United States of America

TP09

Contents

Extended Contents

Acknowledgments

To my wife, Michelle, and daughters, Keilani and Makena, thank you for letting Daddy work long nights and the occasional mornings; the couch will recover, I am sure. To Larry Richman, Academic Director of Media Arts and Animation at the Art Institute of California—Orange County, and Ronni Whitman, Academic Director of Interior Design at the Art Institute of California—Orange County, for allowing me the privilege of teaching so many students in multiple majors. To my fellow instructors at DigiPen Institute of Technology, thank you for expecting me to be the point man on all things computer-generated. Thank you to Dr. Ralph Knowles, one of my early instructors at the University of Southern California, for teaching me to thank about the Sun as an inhabitant in a building. To Miriam Tate and everyone at Miriam Tate Company, for teaching me how to look at color and design with a critical eye. For Victor J. Michael, ASID, for letting me model some of the more amazing retail spaces I have been privy to see, and for pushing my lighting exploration as only a demanding client can. Finally, thank you to my father, for passing on his attention to detail and rational thought to me. Without his influence, I would not be where I am today.

CHAPTER **1** Philosophy and Psychology
of Modeling

SECTION A: WHY BUILD A MODEL?

"**W**hy should I produce a rendering of this?" Whether you are self-employed as a rendering artist, a specialist at a firm, or a student learning the ropes, this is the first question that should go through your mind when asked to produce a rendering or an illustration of a building, structure, or interior. As with so many things in this world, like triple bacon cheeseburgers, giant Hummer SUVs, and pink poodles, just because we can does not always mean we should. Although computers have become faster, more powerful, and cheaper over the years by orders of magnitude, considerable effort is still involved in modeling, lighting, texturing, and rendering an image or an animation.

A common misconception applies to computer-generated renderings. People—especially clients, but this may also include family, friends, and most other Earth dwellers—assume that the use of a computer speeds up the creation of a rendering through some sort of built-in intelligence. This is simply not true. While computers are terrific at performing repetitive tasks or automating functions, they are still inherently dumb. The human at the keyboard must still create the model that produces the rendered image. Countless times, someone has asked me point-blank if I took a picture of what they wanted and "scanned it in" to create a rendering, or they assumed that I had a few magic buttons labeled House and Furniture in some program I used. This leads us to one of the central tenets of client relations: Don't laugh in their face. Remain in control even when your insides are doing quivering back flips at the depths of their delusion. Keep that (iron-jawed) professional demeanor until you can let it out somewhere safe, like in your car or over a stiff glass of Attitude Adjustment with trusted coworkers later.

To continue with the computers are fast-yet-dumb line, what the increases in power have done is allow us to explore more ways of presenting the desired information within the same timeframe. Along with the hardware developments have come galactic leaps in software. We now have at our disposal tools so amazingly evolved that they have transcended being mere replacements for handcrafted illustrations and are new, legitimate art forms with new attendant methodologies, theories, and -isms. (Think of any rabidly preached philosophy, such as Deconstructionism, Realism, Post, Post-Post, and Post-Post-Post Modernism, and so on.) Decisions that had to be made at the outset of a hand rendering, such as exact placement of the view, lighting conditions, or even color choices in wall paint, can now be made far later in the process. The new art form of the digital rendering allows design concept sketching to occur in three dimensions, in true light, true color, and real scale.

This brings us back to the central question of this section, why build a model? The answer is simple: communication. We build a model to live up to the old saw that a picture is worth a thousand words. We model and render to communicate design intent. We model and render images because we designers communicate among ourselves in a dialect foreign to lay ears. Renderings are the translations of our ruminated ramblings into something the masses can understand.

SECTION B: HOW TO USE A MODEL

A model is primarily useful in two main areas: design concept sketching and design presentation. In this vein, I am talking specifically of a surface model as we will produce in 3ds Max. For the purposes of this book, we will ignore solid models as used by our comrades in engineering and industrial design, as well as building information models used for construction design and planning. Our model is about perceived size and volume, the relationship of elements, the perception of space, color as a mood, and the dancing of light.

The first purpose, design concept sketching, is a slippery one. I design in 3ds Max. I do not possess even moderately adequate drawing skills; after untold effort and frustration, I have concluded that I am simply not hardwired for it. However, I have found that my sense of volume, my ability to design in space, is quite robust. I have made my Cartesian world my canvas, and this is where I draw. Sketching in 3ds Max requires both knowledge of the toolset available and fluency with the tools combined with fluidity of workflow to allow the design to emerge. It has taken me years to achieve this synergy; however I believe that by learning from and avoiding many of my mistakes, you will scale the learning curve more quickly.

Some of you may read the preceding paragraph and discount 3ds Max, or any 3D package for that matter, as too costly in time and effort for anything but rendering a finished design. What may persuade you otherwise is an idea of how to use 3ds Max to sketch out the forms and details of the design in true light and color; we will cover techniques to explore the design before it is finalized. Frequently, a client or supervisor has given me a quick outline of the major forms, and said, "Go to it. Develop it as much as you need to present a rendering." I have often used the process of building a 3D model to find out what will or will not work in the design—essentially designing as I go. Think of 3D in this situation as a group of people trying to figure out what to eat. Everyone may shrug and say they don't know, or whatever sounds good; however once they head toward a particular restaurant, making choices about what to eat is far easier. Sketching in 3D starting from nothing can be daunting; sketching based on some direction is absolutely achievable.

The second main purpose of design visualization is presentation. Every profession has its own language, technical terms, syntax, and subtle exclusion of those not in the know. Architecture and interior design are no different; we have our endless terms, volumes of high-minded theoretical book cover filler, a dedicated press orbiting our microcosm, and so forth. Added to this, we have our own visual language for the display of building and construction information, using lines and notations to dissect a structure into nearly unrecognizable parts. The average person on the street, or for that matter, the average client, cannot read these drawings without help. Additionally, said Person-Who-Signs-the-Check often cannot assemble the presented drawings into a coherent whole in his or her mind. Hence, to overcome this defect, designers have drawn renderings to communicate the future structure since man started repositioning rocks in his cave.

Until comparatively recently in the history of architecture, renderings have always had a certain stylization, largely dependent on the artist and the medium used. Although often quite beautiful to look at, unfortunately, these renderings were more a suggestion of the final product rather than a detailed immersion of the viewer in the space. Today's digital models allow us to place true camera viewpoints into or around a space or building, construct the building as it would really be built, apply the specified materials, and finally light the design in true sun or from true luminaries. We render digitally to reduce the ambiguity in the client's perception about the final design; to communicate in a universal language of pictures the exact nature of the future in that particular locale on the planet.

SECTION C: SUNBEAMS ARE SEXY

When I teach modeling and rendering, at any level, one of the first things I do is to discuss why we should render. I also list the five core tenets of design visualization, and enjoy the giggles and deer-in-the-headlights looks I get from my class. Remember these central principles:

1.   Sunbeams are sexy.

2.   People like shiny objects.

3.   Clients are rich and stupid.

4.   Don't make the audience seasick.

5.   Show them the money.

I'll say it again. Rule 1: *Sunbeams are sexy.* Clients love to see sun coming through windows and spilling across floors and walls. We as a species feel good when we see sunlight, even in a picture. To put this in perspective, think of every nasal decongestant ad shown on television, and most every allergy relief pill as well. Each commercial fades out on scenes bathed in a golden light, to symbolize the user's return to normal breathing. In architectural and interior design magazines, interiors are always shown during daytime, with sunlight pouring through any available window. Retailers get in on the act, too. Any catalog of home furnishings, dècor, appliances, rugs, electronics, personal computers, or food is bound to feature some if not all of its products bathed in sunlight. We humans, as well, like the way we look in the sun; we also like how our stuff looks in the sun.

The upshot of all this is to let the sun dance in your renderings. However you do it, create a warm sun that streams through the windows or whatever openings you have, and let it reach as far as it can into your space. If you are showing an outside scene, use the sun to your advantage. You won't have the warm glow of an interior, but rather a method to showcase all of your crisp shadow lines, reveals, overhangs, eyebrows, sills, and canopies.

How you add this sun is as important as why you add it. When placing a sun for an interior rendering, angle it so that the sunbeams come in diagonally from two directions, such as top and left, or plan and elevation. Sunbeams should cascade through the window, spill across the floor, and caress the opposite or adjacent wall, in exactly those romantic of terms. If you are using this rendering to communicate design intent, either for development or presentation, nothing sells a space like sunbeams. Sun is your tool to add depth, warmth, contrast, sparkle, and importantly, the phenomena we associate with dynamic lighting, such as dazzling the camera. People want to believe your rendering as a picture; help their perception along by adding things that everyone on the planet expects to see, such as sun. Figures 1.1 and 1.2 show two examples of sunlight in a space, the first placed badly, the second placed correctly. The incorrectly placed sun is stifled, the patterns generated on the floor barely noticeable, and the space lacks contrast. In the image with the correctly placed sun, the floor sings with light, and the geometry of the adjacent wall is highlighted by the differing angles of the sun.

Rule 2: *People like shiny objects.* Yes, I realize that most of you will either giggle or bristle at this observation. I am not reducing most of humanity to drooling idiots, content to gaze into mirrors and waxed floors, though some clients may fit that description every so often. What I mean by this tenet is that you will invariably encounter a situation where you have spent days modeling a scene, more days texturing and lighting, and even more days rendering. Upon presentation, what is the first thing the client notices? The floor is reflecting everything else in the room. One flat polygon, with a simple texture applied jumps ahead of all of your hard work, and to add insult to injury, most of the heavy lifting was done by the computer. I can count on all of my fingers, my toes, and some borrowed fingers the number of times this has happened to me, either with a firm or on my own.

FIGURE 1.1
*An incorrectly
placed sun adds
little character to
a room.*

FIGURE 1.2
*A correctly placed
sun lets light stream
across the floor
and up the wall,
adding contrast
and warmth to
the image.*

You should learn a couple of things from this situation, and believe me, you will encounter this sort of reaction regularly. While it may not always include a polished terrazzo floor or even opposing bathroom mirrors, be prepared mentally for the viewers of your image to notice things that are secondary to what you intended to show. Like it or not, people are not in your head; what appears to be crucial or a matter of professional pride to you may be invisible to them.

The second major lesson to be learned is that people do in fact like shiny objects. However, and this is a big however we'll encounter again in Chapters 9 through 13, people expect *shiny* objects to be, well, shiny. What spoils the illusion of a rendering is when everything is shiny, or everything is dull. Too often, novices will make everything shiny and hence reflective, even things that shouldn't be. This can lead to unnatural lighting, blown-out lighting instead of soft lighting, huge render times, and most importantly, a loss of believability in the final image. Remember, the viewer should mentally place him- or herself in the space you are showing, dissolving the barrier between an interpretation of a design and a picture of it. Too many or too few shiny objects spoil the illusion and add viewer-perceived distance from the design.

There is a twist to this caveat, provided by the very nature of what we are usually rendering: we are digitally showcasing new architecture and interior design. Ideally, once all is said and built, a good deal of a new or freshly remodeled edifice should be shiny. We use the phrase "shiny new whatever" in our language for precisely this meaning: new things are often shiny. When viewers look at an image, they want to feel that the building or room is just finished, scrubbed, untouched by anyone else, and ready for them. People, on a more general level, want to feel special; this makes it much easier for them to buy into the design. So, give the people what they want—shiny objects. Just make sure that they are shiny within the context of what should be shiny, and in contrast to things that are not shiny.

Rule 3: *Clients are rich and stupid.* This is another general rule that always draws a laugh from my students. Once, a client was in the classroom when I said this. The client approached me on a break after I had explained the rule and told me I wasn't charging enough for the knowledge I had, and that I was right! What does this mean then, you may be asking? Do I actually walk up to my clients and call them stupid to their faces and then thank them for the check they hand me? No. I am occasionally close to, but not quite that foolish. What "clients are rich and stupid" means is this: as a practitioner of architectural visualization and wrangler of large computers, you are a Person-in-the-Know. Your clients depend on you to synthesize your knowledge of building with your expertise of rendering; probably conjure up some black magic, or at least tastefully charcoal-shaded magic; and show them exactly what they are thinking.

Your clients are relying on you as the expert. As a visualization professional, you should to assume that your clients made their money in something other than design or visualization. Starting from the time someone says that he or she has a project for you to check out, you will need to guide the client through pronouncing all of what he or she wants. People will get a vague notion that they need some kind of computer-generated rendering, and so they will come to you. Beyond that, you can safely assume that they are stupid. In reality, these people are probably reasonably smart; the simple fact is that every step of the way, you will need to help them pronounce what they want, and then you will need to reply to it.

Rule 4: *Don't make the audience seasick.* This seemingly innocuous phrase actually ties into many of the previous rules for design visualization, and very closely to camera placement and animation. You are constructing a model in real space, in true light, with true materials, and viewing it (unless you are rendering elevations) from a true camera perspective. Your job as a visualization artist is to immerse the viewer in the picture or animation to the point where disbelief is suspended and the viewer sees from in the space. Remember this rule when studying camera placement in Chapter 2; there is usually no place for a classic Hitchcock Dutch tilt camera angle or handheld fisheye camera in visualization. A shooting style à la *The Blair Witch Project* will not communicate the design well in an animation.

Rule 5: *Show them the money.* This last rule ties together the concepts of "sunbeams are sexy," "people like shiny objects," and camera placement. You rightfully assume that your clients have no idea about where to site a camera to show a design. However, the client will have a very certain idea about where the money is being spent on this project. Your mission as a visualization professional is to site your camera to pat the clients on the back and congratulate them on money well spent. It is perfectly acceptable to understatedly compliment their taste and suggest featuring prize fixtures, views, furniture, and so on as a focal point in the imagery.

It will take a bit of dexterity on your part to ferret out the best view in some situations. As an example, a client may have paid a great deal of money for an ocean view lot, or a hilltop pad, or some other prized condition. Optimally, the design of the building or house should take advantage of said view as much as possible. Your imagery should showcase that view as seen from the most important or grand space within the building. If you are rendering an exterior, the aforementioned stunning view should be a backdrop for the structure. What you may encounter is a situation where the largest amount of money spent besides on the view is in the kitchen overlooking the family room and grand view, but to feature the kitchen means turning your virtual back on the windows.

A smart visualization artist will parlay this possible crisis into an opportunity for more work. As illustrated in Figure 1.3, two images may be the best way to show the design. One image features the kitchen in all of its shiny detail, while the other places the viewer in the kitchen, enjoying that million-dollar view. Two things will come of this solution: more work for you, which you can charge more for, and clients pleased with your services as you are so sensitive to their design (read: you give good ego stroke).

SECTION D: WHAT IS AN INVISIBLE MODEL?

Your job, in essence, is to do the exact opposite in your visualizations that Hollywood directors do: don't leave your mark. Many movies are advertised as having the stamp or style of a particular person on them. "Coming soon, from the director of . . ." We've all seen or heard the ads promoting movies bearing someone's distinct directorial persona. In placing your camera, be neutral. The picture is not about you, it *is* about the design. Your job is to remove yourself from the picture—or at least your style should not show as far as the client is concerned.

Besides removing your persona from the camerawork, one of the most important rules of thumb is to *not* interpret and stylize the design. You are being paid as a visualization professional to craft the model of the building per the architect's or interior designer's specifications. In doing so, it is imperative to adhere to the design as closely as humanly possible. If the client wanted you to design the building, he or she would have asked you directly to place your signature on it. In practical terms,

FIGURE 1.3

Camera locations
for kitchen and
window views.

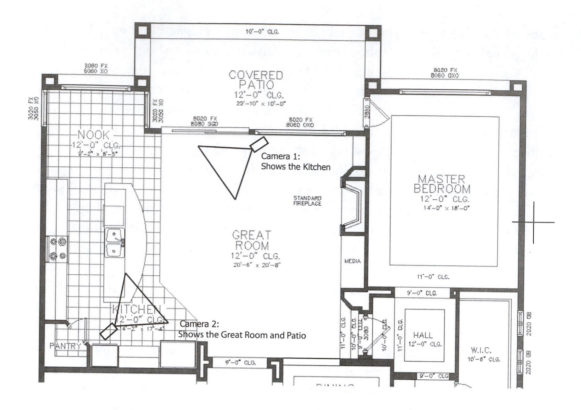

this means we as professionals must be faithful to the dimensions of the design and the style that was intended.

This brings up, on a broader level, the issue of modeling accurately the things we expect to see. Manufacturers go to great lengths to design their wares, and they often post specification sheets with dimensions on their Web sites. Follow those dimensions to the letter if you are crafting a specific assembly or product. Additionally, even some generic objects have standard sizes, and it is your responsibility to find out what those are before modeling them. For example, residential garage doors come in standard sizes of 8′ × 7′ for a single-car garage, and 16′ × 7′ for a two-car garage. Unless a garage door is drawn to very odd-looking proportions, you can be assured that the doors are that size when modeling them. People will also expect to see the typical garage doors they are familiar with, so if your door is 18′ × 6′, it will look odd in everyone's mind. When people look at your rendering, they should not notice all of the details individually, because they look exactly as they are supposed to look. Common items' realism or accuracy should not be called into question. The individual parts of the rendering should be invisible, leaving the overall design to stand out.

SECTION E: CONCLUSION

The art of being a visualization professional is to not let your art show. Wearing the hats of psychologist/bartender, artist to the king or queen, and technical wizard behind a curtain, your job is to produce renderings that your clients will love. The stumbling block in all this is that you are also a teacher, salesperson, and hacker/manipulator of human networks. You must tell your clients what it is they in fact want, but make them think it was their idea all along. The visualization artist plays god, directing the sun and heavens, but must be as faceless as a stranger in a crowd, transparent to the overall cause. Nonetheless, bringing building designs to life so they may be blessed and be built is a noble job. If you can do this while choosing your battles and your words carefully, and let the sunlight spill through the windows, you will have done your job well.

CHAPTER **2** Beginning Model Construction

SECTION A: PRE-VISUALIZATION TECHNIQUES

One of the biggest decisions facing architectural rendering artists, and animators and environment artists in general, is not what to model, but what not to model. With time and effort, almost anything can be visualized; one needs only to watch any recent film to see the fruits of bleeding-edge research and development. Whole digital armies do battle, giant storms swallow ships, and huge beasts roam the cyber-steppes. However, these feats are accomplished at tremendous cost, both in time and money. Dozens if not hundreds of people work on the visual effects in these films, often under titles that mean nothing to the layperson. Outside of the movie industry, a Render Wrangler or an Illumination Engineer is an unknown quantity; the art of unwrapping the UWV coordinates of a model has little contextual ground to stand on in any other arena.

Unfortunately, you as an architectural rendering artist or an environment artist do not have the film industry's luxury of time, money, and toolset customization at your disposal. In a more realistic scenario, you will be asked to produce a rendering for a client who wants it yesterday, on a shoestring budget, and with very little rendering power to spare. If you are lucky, you'll have a couple of weeks to work—but Murphy's Law seems to be always in effect, thus most of the products, fixtures, finishes, and furniture will not be found in your library. This will leave you feeling like you are modeling the known universe and speculating on what year you may actually be able to start lighting and rendering.

All is not lost—however, most of it is creatively misplaced. The big deal is to nail down exactly what you need to see *before* you start modeling. Most beginners want to model the world and figure out how to show it later. I have watched students modeling the rivets on a character's blue jeans, or chamfering every edge on an Eames bookshelf, without knowing what angle and distance this object was going to be seen from. Clients are equally terrible at telling you what they want, usually voicing a desire for something cool and little else. It is up to you, then, to guide them as to what they should have you produce. You are the expert at this, or so the money they are paying you says.

FIGURE 2.1

*Proposed retail
store with cameras
sketched on plan.*

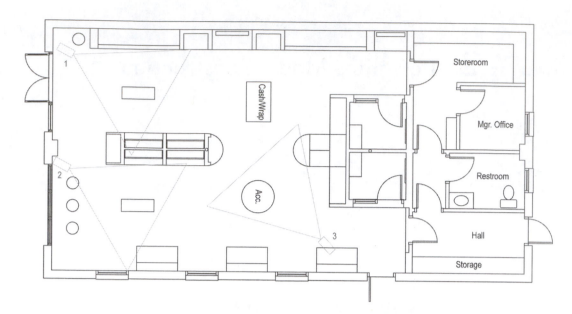

One of the first things to do when starting a new project, or even in the bid phase as I do with my clients, is to sit down with a building plan and figure out what will give clients the most bang for the buck. Typically, I'll talk clients through vocalizing what they think is the most important piece or area of the building or space. I'll write letters on the plan to denote still camera locations, then draw approximate field of view outlines and focal points (more on this in Section B).

For example, say a design firm has requested two images of a planned retail store to show its client the proposed design. I've placed cameras 1 and 2 on the plan: camera 1 shows the store from the entry, and camera 2 focuses on the cash/wrap (see Figure 2.1). As we discussed in Chapter 1, visualizations should show clients where their money is being spent. Camera 1 is a look-and-feel shot, capturing the overall mood, fixtures, finishes, and lighting of the store in the longest view possible. Camera 2 is a closer shot of the cash/wrap, as this piece, like reception desks, is often a signature statement about the design or place. Equally if not more important, camera 2 also highlights the retail store's logo and name behind the cash/wrap; in commercial work, sensitivity to the client's brand image cultivation and marketing thrusts will win major points for you as a rendering specialist. Camera 3 looks back at the center full-length display as well as the accessories counter and cash/wrap, plus it gives a closer view of the expensive chandelier in the center.

SECTION B: PLACING CAMERAS

Placing cameras is actually quite easy for both still images and animations. As we are just beginning, we'll focus mainly on still images; in many cases the still camera placement can be a fine starting or ending point for an animated camera. What I'll mainly focus on here is how and where to place a still camera to showcase a design, often referred to as a beauty shot. Occasionally, I have worked on projects where my client only wanted one beauty shot but wanted four or five view shots. A view

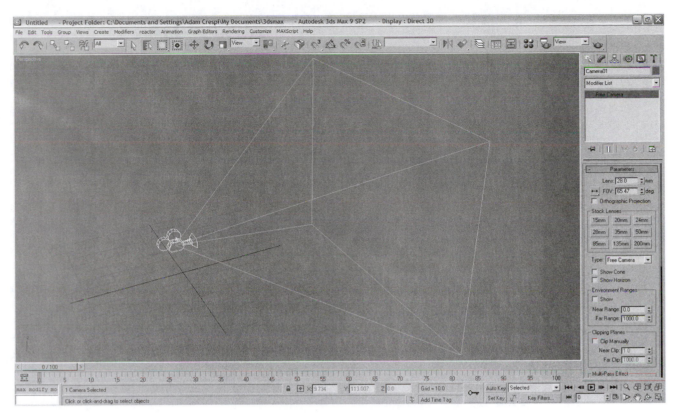

FIGURE 2.2

A camera in 3ds Max as seen in the Perspective viewport.

shot is often used to show what part of a proposed construction will or will not be seen from a neighbor's house, patio, driveway, living room, and so forth. As the placement of view shots is predetermined by said neighbors and rarely showcases the best features of the design, I'll ignore them for the moment.

A camera in 3ds Max is simply a viewpoint placed at a single coordinate in space. What this view shows is constrained by the simulation of perspective, distortion, lens, and field of view of a real camera. (Note: Yes, shutterbugs, I purposefully did not mention aperture, exposure, f-stop, or film speed. Those are render and lighting-centric functions that will be covered in Chapters 9 and 10. Don't panic.) What I look for when I am placing a camera is the longest view possible in a space. As shown in Figure 2.2, the camera's field of view is a pyramid extending away from the camera icon.

Figure 2.3 illustrates what you get with a badly placed camera. This gallery looks rather ho-hum in this view. Figure 2.4 shows the difference a well-placed camera can make. You can see from the plan view in Figure 2.5 that camera 01 corresponds to the view shown in Figure 2.3 and camera 02 corresponds to the more dynamic view of the gallery in Figure 2.4.

I try to abide by several general guidelines when setting up a camera. The first is to keep the camera at what will be perceived as a person's height. People come in all sizes, of course, but I have found that between 5′4″ and 6′0″ seems to work best. Above or below that range and things start to distort oddly; remember, you are

FIGURE 2.3

A sample scene with a badly placed camera. In this view, the camera does not show the extent of the space by standing in the middle looking squarely at the window.

FIGURE 2.4

The same scene with a properly placed camera. The full space is shown, with a much more dynamic camera placement. The scale of the space and complexity of the geometry is highlighted as well.

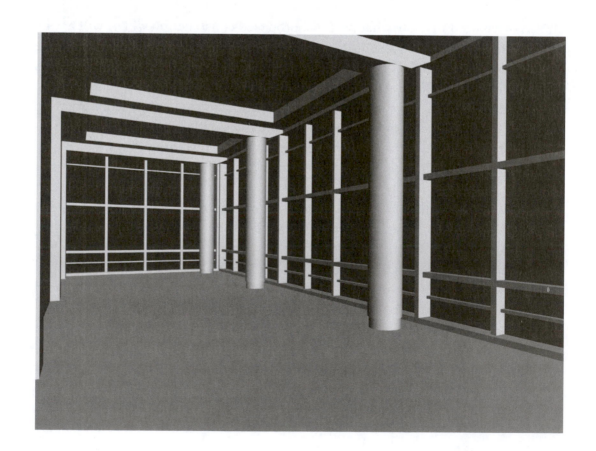

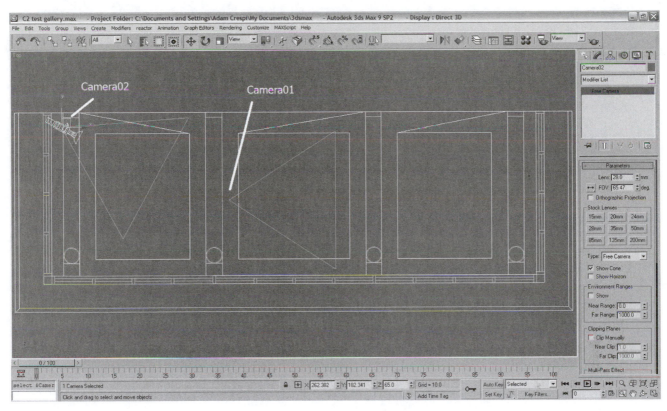

FIGURE 2.5

A plan view of the test gallery showing the camera locations and fields of view. Note that the field of view is shown to the default target distance of 160 inches rather than the full length of the space.

not making a horror movie, but instead highlighting a design. Figure 2.6 shows the ceiling and floor coverage you can achieve in this range. For exterior shots, there is a bit more latitude, heading up toward 8′0″ off the ground, but use this extra height with discretion.

The second guideline for camera placement, as mentioned in the retail store example, is to take the longest view of a building or a space. Referencing rule 5 of visualization found in Chapter 1, "show them the money," cameras should be placed to provide the longest view possible. As you saw in Figure 2.2, the field of view from a camera extends out in a pyramid shape from the camera center. In a non-camera viewport, this field of view helps frame the shot; in the view from the camera, perceived room size is lost because some of the floor and ceiling is outside of the field of view (see Figure 2.7). Keep in mind as you suggest and place cameras that this image may be the deciding factor in selling a design, or a home for that matter. Views should look as spacious as possible. A nice feature of working virtually is that the camera itself has no volume; it is simply a coordinate in space. Hence, you can stuff the camera much farther into a corner than in reality in order to get the shot you need.

The third major guideline for camera placement is to place your camera so that you do not appear to be hiding something. The camera view shown in Figure 2.8

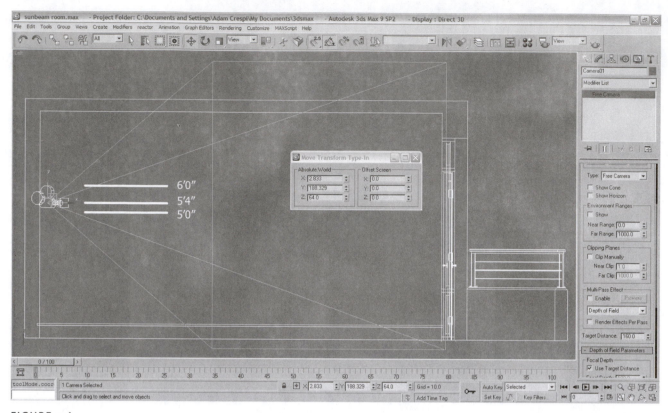

FIGURE 2.6

Camera placement height range from finish floor.

FIGURE 2.7

In plan, the camera appears to show the whole room. In elevation, roughly a third of the length is lost behind and above or below the field of view.

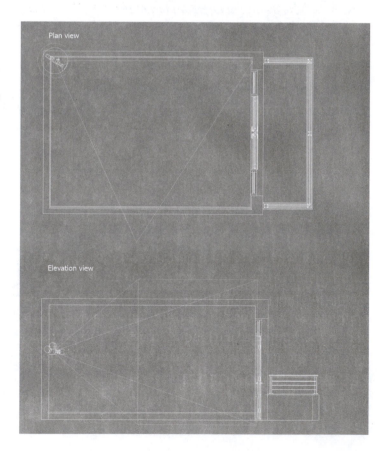

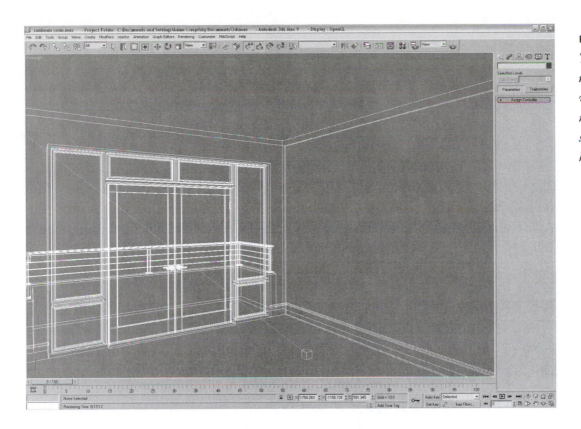

FIGURE 2.8

The camera does not show the left wall; the viewer may perceive that something is being hidden purposely.

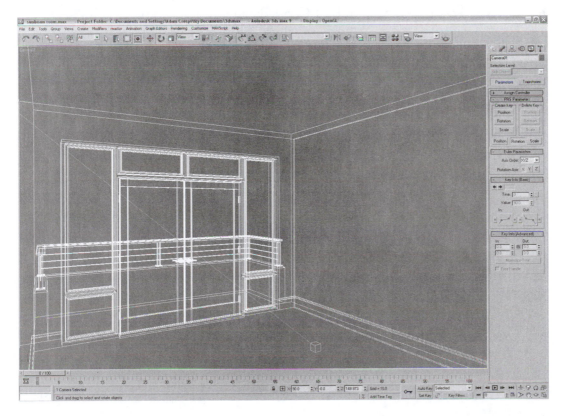

FIGURE 2.9

The camera is rotated slightly to include the left wall; it is now apparent that the whole space is being shown.

is taken from the location shown on the plan in Figure 2.7. In this picture, the left side wall is completely hidden. Although the plans show that it is just a straight wall, people seeing only this image will unconsciously assume that something to the left is not being shown purposely. It would be better to pull the camera out of the corner slightly, and rotate it so that just a sliver of the left side wall is visible (see Figure 2.9). By showing both corners of the wall with the doors and windows, the camera, and therefore the design, makes the statement that there is nothing to hide.

So to recap, when deciding where to place a camera, first, keep it in the range of a person's height, or up to 8'0" off the ground for exterior shots. Second, place the camera where it will provide the longest view possible. And third, make sure your camera placement does not suggest to the viewer that you are trying to hide something. These same rules apply for exterior views as well.

SECTION C: CHOOSING TIME OF DAY

When do we render an image or an animation? Aside from the obvious answer—when we are done modeling, texturing, lighting, animating, and testing them—we must consider the time of day that best shows the building. One of the computer's biggest strengths in design visualization is its ability to generate multiple images of a structure at different times of day. We can even animate a whole day's passage from dawn to dusk or longer, showing the building in the changing light and color.

That last phrase is the key to choosing the time of year, month, and day. Every location has subtly different daylight intensity and color. A brassy winter afternoon in Los Angeles, with golden light that slants in through west windows, would produce twilight in Seattle. An East Coast dawn glimmering on a high-rise would leave a West Coast house in darkness. Besides the general lighting of a structure from a particular direction, we need to think about the color of the light as applied to the colors of the materials at a certain time of day. That brassy winter afternoon in Los Angeles will add a golden tint to everything in the scene; this is fine for gold-flecked Jerusalem stone but may detract from crisp white walls.

Counterparts of the color and direction of the light are the color and direction of the shadows. Long sunbeams reaching across a space at dusk are wonderful for caressing the nuances of geometry in a model, however, they leave long dark shadows cast from objects. Strong sunlight will show roof details and shadow lines on trim in terrific contrast, but it will also bounce into large shadows just enough to leave them lacking depth.

Before choosing a time of day to show a model, recite the number one rule of architectural visualization, *Sunbeams are sexy*. Once you have picked the windows and doors where the sun will enter for maximum effect, then it is time to choose the time of day. Whether you are planning to use the new mental ray daylight system or simply approximate a time of day, it is important to decide on a date and time. Even if the rendering shows an approximate time of day, remember that you are the professional here. Your clients are relying on you to take care of the details and make their building look pretty. Being able to suggest a time of day and a date will give everyone common ground from which to think about the quality of the model—and make you look smart in the eyes of the clients, as this is probably something they hadn't begun to think about.

SECTION D: SCENE UNITS

Three-dimensional space is essentially limitless. We do not need to scale a model to fit our viewport or reduce the physical size of a building to be able to render it. We will, to all intents and purposes, never run out of space. Hence, we should build everything at real size. As we'll see in Chapter 10 on rendering, as well as in mapping coordinates for materials, accurate size is absolutely crucial to global illumination and other physically accurate phenomena.

How to view the size of things, the scene units we use, is a matter of personal preference. The default scene unit in 3ds Max is a generic unit, set by default to inches. Thus, by entering 60 in a field of an object's parameters, you are entering 60 inches. Personally, I find that this default works quite well, as many of the measurements I deal with are in fractions of inches that I have memorized the decimal value for, such as 0.125 (⅛″), 0.25 (¼″), 0.625 (⅝″), and so on. Additionally, 3ds Max will convert feet to units (or inches) in a field, thus if 36′ is entered, 3ds Max will convert it to 432.

It does not really matter what units you choose to work in, as long as things are the correct size. If feet and inches is your bag, go for it. Should you need to work in the metric system, 3ds Max will easily handle that as well. For the purposes of this book, all dimensions will be given in generic scene units, assuming that the scene units are set to inches per the default.

To set the scene units should you desire to work in something other than generic units, choose Customize > Units Setup from the top menu, and choose the units you like.

SECTION E: IMPORTING PLANS

Quite often as visualization professionals, we are asked to work from CAD drawings of various flavors. Thankfully, most CAD programs can write several different formats for export, and 3ds Max can read many different file types as well. As Autodesk's AutoCAD and 3ds Max are seamlessly compatible, import of DWG files is painless and relatively quick. Perhaps the biggest hurdle when importing plans is knowing what to use and where to use it, and when to hide or delete it. People all too often make the mistake of viewing the AutoCAD drawing as the model, thinking they can simply extrude the walls up and slap a ceiling on. Yes, this can be done, but no, it should not. For a design visualization professional, the CAD drawings are the template to build on. Additionally, the organization needed in a CAD drawing is quite different from that of a 3D model. In a CAD drawing, all of the walls of all of the plans and elevations may be on a single layer, which may import as a single object or as several hundred objects. There is also data that is of no use to a model, such as hatch patterns, points, notes, and so on.

When I import a CAD file, I assume that the creator knew nothing of what I was going to do with it and spend a minute or three poking around. I'll load up the file in Autodesk's DWG TrueView (a free utility that can be downloaded from Autodesk), which has less system overhead than AutoCAD. Because much of the work I do is at a very early stage of design, the architect or interior designer may not have set up views in the Layout view. When exploring a drawing, it is usually safe to assume that it has not been set up for print, and so looking at the Model view first is a good idea. Additionally, 3ds Max imports from the Model Space, so having a grasp on the drawing there may help avoid drama and confusion later on in 3ds Max.

EXERCISE 1   Importing and untangling a CAD drawing

For the purpose of this tutorial and for later use in this book we will be using CAD drawings of a historically patterned building undergoing a rehabilitation and renovation into a restaurant. Also, we will assume AutoCAD is not available for manipulating files; hence we will use the free Autodesk DWG TrueView utility available at http://www.autodesk.com.

1.   In DWG TrueView, go to File > Open or press Ctrl + O and open the *retail renovation.dwg* file in the Source Files folder on the CD (see Figure 2.10).

FIGURE 2.10

The Retail Renovation. dwg as viewed in Autodesk DWG TrueView, with the Layers menu open. Note the hidden Electrical, Soffit, Lighting, and Switches layers.

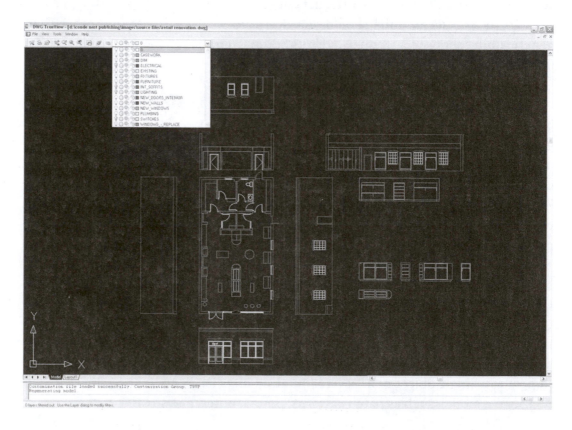

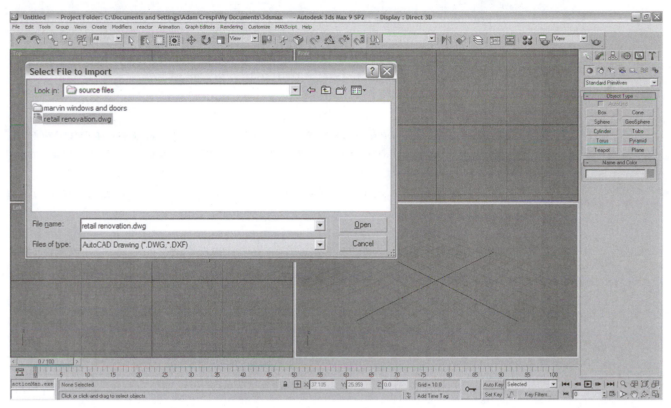

FIGURE 2.11

The Import dialog.

2. Take a moment to familiarize yourself with the drawing by turning off and on the layers. Learn what layers contain various objects, and be sure to look at elevations, plans, details, ceilings, anything that helps you get acquainted with the building. As an example on this drawing, the full height display casework lines up perfectly in the drawing with the soffits. Only by examining the interior elevations and by turning off and on casework and soffit layers would this become apparent.

3. Once you have gotten the lay of the land, so to speak, open 3ds Max. On the top menu, choose File > Import, and browse to the Assets folder for this chapter on the CD. Change the File of Type menu to DWG if necessary, and select the *Retail Renovation.dwg* file (see Figure 2.11).

4. 3ds Max and AutoCAD talk very well together, not surprising since they are made by the same company. A Proxy Objects Detected dialog may pop up; it is usually safe to click Yes and proceed. When the AutoCAD DWG/DXF Import Options dialog pops up, uncheck all of the Geometry import options except External references in the Include section (see Figure 2.12). Generally, a ton of organizational baggage comes in with AutoCAD drawings that you simply do not need. Additionally,

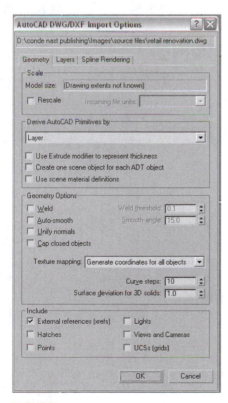

FIGURE 2.12

DWG import options.

as you may not know how the drawing was created, lines or polylines may have heights assigned that will spawn walls all over your drawing, or worse. The idea is to have the drawing come in as whole splines, just splines, and nothing but the splines—no hatches, no points, and no strings attached.

Note:

3ds Max does support a link between AutoCAD and itself, allowing you to externally reference an AutoCAD drawing. This tends to slow 3ds Max down, as it looks for drawing updates. Furthermore, you cannot snap to an externally referenced AutoCAD drawing, which creates an unacceptable lack of precision. Some of you out there may label me a 3ds Max zealot or anti-AutoCAD; but I am not. (Well, okay, I am a diehard Max-head.) I believe that it is better to import the drawing and be able to snap to it, paying the small price of re-importing any updates. I also use this method as a check to verify any changes for myself and with the client, generating an itemized list before modifying a model.

5. When the drawing comes in, all of the layers should import in and be visible on the Layers palette (see Figure 2.13). There may be occasional objects named Block_XYZ or otherwise as well. The drawing should come in at the same size as the model in AutoCAD; however, sometimes they do not. First, organize and check the size of things, and scale if necessary. Switch back to DWG TrueView and find a long dimension that is as even as possible. Look for dimensions that are exact feet, such

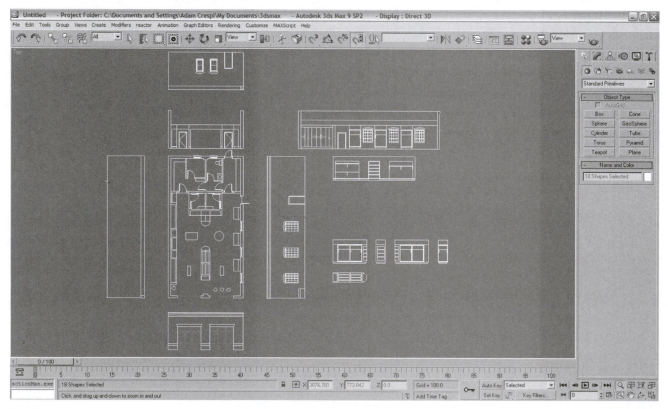

FIGURE 2.13

The imported drawing.

as the long side wall, which is 60′0″. This will be the reference for scaling. Choose Create > Helpers > Tape Measure from the top menu, or go to the Create tab on the Command panel, then to the Helpers button, and choose Tape Measure. Click and drag from one outside corner of the long wall to the other.

6. The Tape Length on the Modifier reads 1524.0, in scene units, which are inches. As 60′0″ is 720 inches, this drawing is a little off in size, unless sixteen-foot tall doors are normal in your city. Given the length we have, and the length we need, we can calculate a scale percentage to scale the drawings by, and end up with the right length. This percentage is 720 (the size we want) divided by 1524 (the actual size) times 100 (to yield a percent). If the actual size is smaller than the desired size, divide the desired size by the actual size instead. For us, this equation yields a scale percentage of 47.2440944. Click on the Layer Manager button on the Main Toolbar to access the Layer Manager.

7. In the Layer Manager, turn on all of the hidden layers by clicking on the Hidden icons, and unfreeze any frozen layers as well (see Figure 2.14).

8. Select all of the objects in the viewport, right-click, and choose the dialog box next to Scale on the quad menu. In the Offset:Screen field, enter 47.2440944 and press Enter (see Figure 2.15).

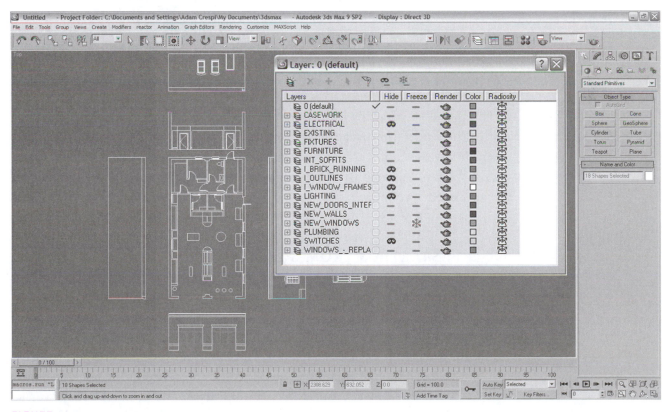

FIGURE 2.14

The Layer Manager.

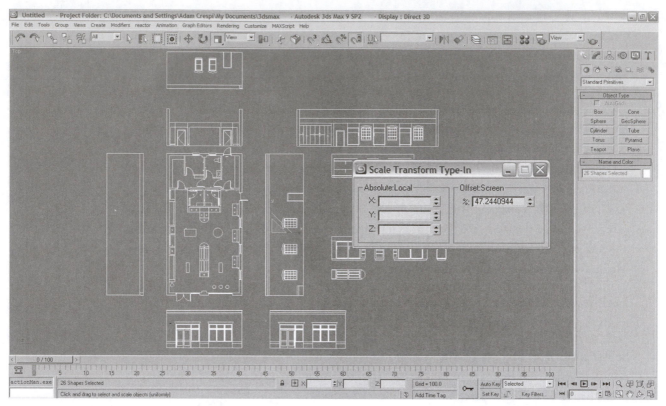

FIGURE 2.15

Scaling the drawing.

9. The drawings should all be the right size now. Create a new Tape Measure and measure the long wall again. On the Modifier panel, Tape Length should be 720.00.

10. At this point, the drawing is ready for use as a model. Depending on the organization of the model, this usually has layers that span plan and elevations; I will most often simply select all of the objects and group them. Select all of the objects, and choose Group > Group from the top menu. Name this group DWG - Plans and elevations. Save your file.

SECTION F: STARTING FROM SCRATCH

Starting from scratch is fairly easy; just open 3ds Max and go, right? Almost. A few organizational tasks will make life easier down the line, and a couple of key concepts will streamline workflow. When first starting a new model, either set the project or save the scene in an existing project. In 3ds Max, a project is simply a designated folder that has subfolders for all of the components of a scene or a project. This Project folder will contain any project-specific referenced files, such as maps, externally referenced scenes, custom material libraries, and so forth. However, it is important to keep the project project-specific. A goal at all times should be to build up your library of products, objects, and finishes. Keep non–project-specific items in a folder on your network, or in a place where they can be easily found and used. As an example, the following is a rough table of the directory structure in my shop. All of the files are located on a partition on my server for access by multiple computers.

P:\ on server BigDog
\Projects *(the main projects directory, organized chronologically)*
    \2007001 Black Mountain Retail – Opal clothing store *(the main directory for each project)*
        \admin *(all of the documentation)*
            \transmittals
            \received files
            \contracts
            \reference photos
        \2007001 – Opal *(the 3ds Max Project directory)*
\R&D *(ongoing research projects and product development)*
\Maps *(libraries of texture maps)*
        \Woods
        \Masonry
        \Stone
        \Tile
        \Fabrics
\Libraries *(building products, categorized by type and cross-referenced by manufacturer)*
    \Lamps
        \Pendant
        \Table
        \Exterior
    \Tables
        \Side
        \End
        \Sofa
        \Dining
    \Chairs
        \Dining
        \Lounge

Once you have set up the organizational structure, it is time to begin modeling. Really, you can place models anywhere in 3D space and they will work just fine. However, I usually try to start a model around 0,0,0. That way, as I switch views from front to left to right, objects created in those views are not flung out in space relative to the model. Additionally, when no objects are selected, 3ds Max will arc-rotate the viewport around 0,0,0. If the building is there, it will not fly off the screen during viewport rotation.

The last thing to remember when starting a new model is to keep the main finish floor at 0′0″. The designer usually draws it this way as well. This allows heights of objects or vertical placement to be accurate without subtracting any variable factor. For example, I often draw the ceiling in a top or bottom view as a flat surface and then move it into position. Having the finish floor at 0′0″ allows me to input the absolute, or world, placement precisely and easily.

SECTION G: CONCLUSION

Take time at the onset of any project to plan and get organized. Think through the general guidelines outlined in this chapter. It is far better to take an extra hour to set up a structure than to jump into modeling and have to fix and patch later. The mark of the professional, in the client's eyes, is someone who has gone through this enough to anticipate the pitfalls and walk them through it all unscathed. Finally, remember that the goal is to show the building, always.

SECTION A: SPLINE-BASED MODELING OVERVIEW

In this series of exercises, we will explore spline-based modeling techniques for constructing common building materials and objects. One of the strengths of 3ds Max is its precision in object creation and movement; this is especially useful when creating small, expected details in architecture.

Splines developed from naval architecture, when a thin wooden strip, or spline, was bent around weights called knots to describe a curve. The modern language of the spline in computer graphics uses control handles to describe the influence of vertices on their adjoining segments. This technique was pioneered by Pierre Bezier, a mathematician working for Renault, the French automobile manufacturer in the 1960s.

We are jumping into spline modeling for two primary reasons. First, we need doors, windows, molding, and walls to construct our buildings. Spline-based modeling will let us quickly generate a detail library and a building shell, ready for furniture, fixtures, and equipment. The second reason is that I want you to start thinking in a language of detail, crisp surfaces, elegant construction, and efficient modeling that will save time and rendering power later.

SECTION B: DOORS

EXERCISE 1:   Building a simple doorjamb and casing

In this exercise, we will construct a doorjamb and casing using Editable Splines and the Bevel Profile modifier. Throughout this and succeeding exercises, we will cover various tools available as part of Editable Splines and illustrate elegant modeling techniques.

1. Open 3ds Max, or save and reset your current application so you have a clean slate. Each of the exercises in this chapter will serve as the foundation for your detail library. Starting with a clean file for library building ensures that objects and materials aren't accidentally deleted or overwritten.

2. In a Top view, roughly around 0,0,0, draw a Rectangle. The size of the rectangle does not matter, as we will resize it. This can be done in several ways:

    a. On the Command panel, choose the Create tab, and then select the Shapes button, then choose Rectangle (see Figure 3.1).

    b. On the Top menu, choose Create > Shapes > Rectangle (see Figure 3.2).

    c. In the viewport, hold Ctrl 1 RMB, and choose Rectangle from the Modeling quad (see Figure 3.3).

FIGURE 3.1
Creating a Rectangle from the Command panel.

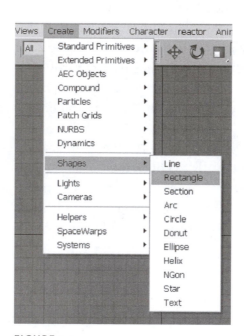

FIGURE 3.2
Creating a Rectangle from the Top menu.

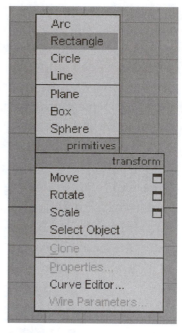

FIGURE 3.3
Creating a Rectangle from the Modeling quad.

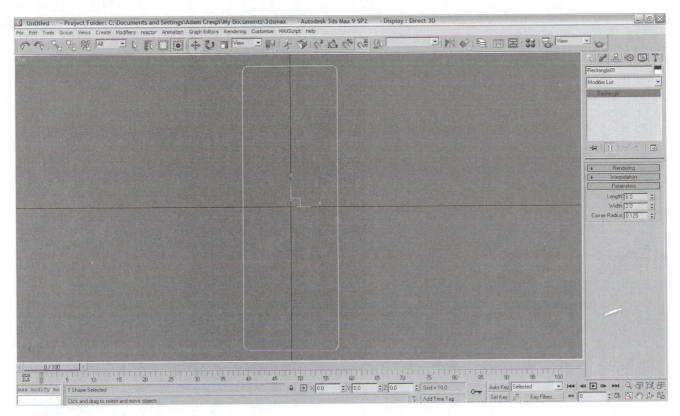

FIGURE 3.4

The Rectangle at proper size.

3. From the Command panel, go to the Modifier panel and resize the rectangle to a length of 6″ and a width of 2″, with a corner radius of 0.125″ (see Figure 3.4). This will form the casing on both sides of the door, spaced for a 2 × 4 framed wall with ¾″ drywall on each side.

4. Clone the rectangle by either pressing Ctrl + V, or right-clicking and choosing Clone. In the Clone dialog, choose Copy as the object type (see Figure 3.5).

5. On the Modifier panel, change the parameters of the new rectangle to a length of 5″ and a width of 0.125″, with no corner radius. This will form the exposed edge of the jamb, and add a shadow detail.

6. Turn on the Selection Lock by hitting the spacebar. Snap on one of the right side vertices of the small rectangle, and move it on the X axis to snap onto the left-most top vertex of the larger rectangle (see Figure 3.6).

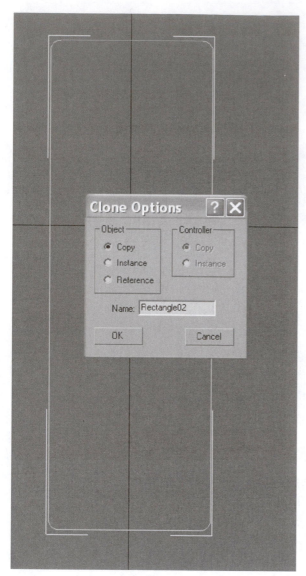

FIGURE 3.5
Cloning the Rectangle.

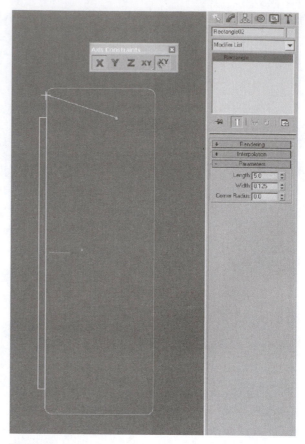

FIGURE 3.6
The cloned Rectangle snapped onto the original.

7. Clone the rectangle by either pressing Ctrl + V, or right-clicking and choosing Clone. In the Clone dialog, choose Copy as the object type.

8. On the Modifier panel, change the parameters of the new rectangle to a length of 1.25″ and a width of 0.25″, with no corner radius. This will form the stop on the inside of the jamb.

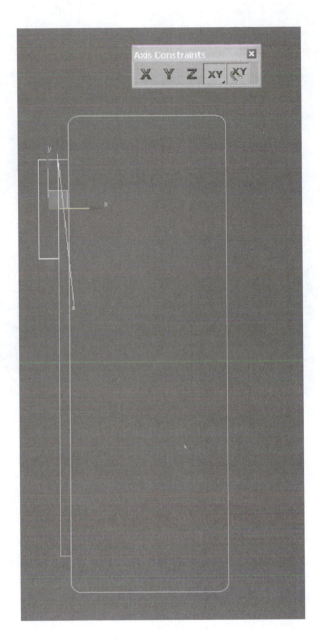

FIGURE 3.7
The second cloned
Rectangle snapped
into place.

9. Turn on the Selection Lock by hitting the spacebar. Snap on one of the right side vertices of the small rectangle, and move it on both the X and Y axes to snap onto the leftmost top vertex of the tall, slim rectangle (see Figure 3.7).

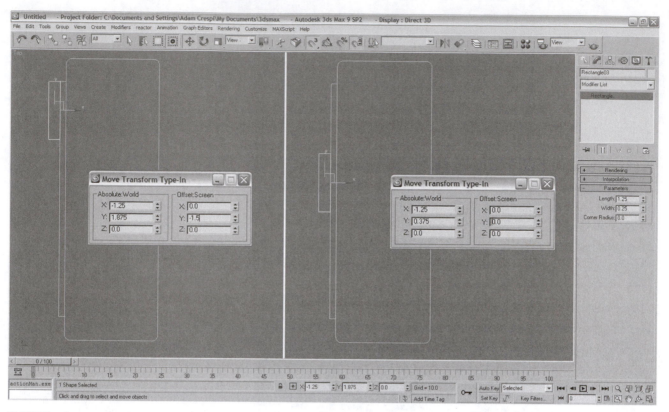

FIGURE 3.8

The doorstop Rectangle moved into place.

10. Launch the Transform dialog by either clicking the F12 button or right-clicking and choosing the dialog icon on the Transform section of the quad menu. In the Offset Y window, enter −1.5, the thickness of the door, and hit Tab or Enter (see Figure 3.8). (If your doors are different, enter that number in the Offset Y window.)

11. At this point, the shape of the casing, jamb, and stop has emerged. Now we'll join all of the rectangles together into one spline. Select one of the rectangles if you do not have one selected already. It doesn't matter which one you choose for this step. Right-click, and on the Quad menu, choose Convert to Editable Spline.

12. Right-click again and choose Attach on the Tools 2 quad menu. Click on the other two rectangles to attach them to the Editable Spline. When you have finished, right-click to stop attaching splines.

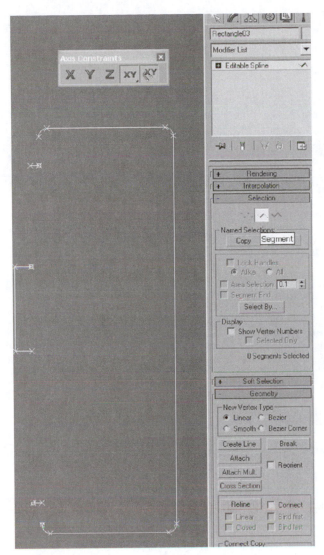

FIGURE 3.9
The Spline with deleted segments, ready for connection.

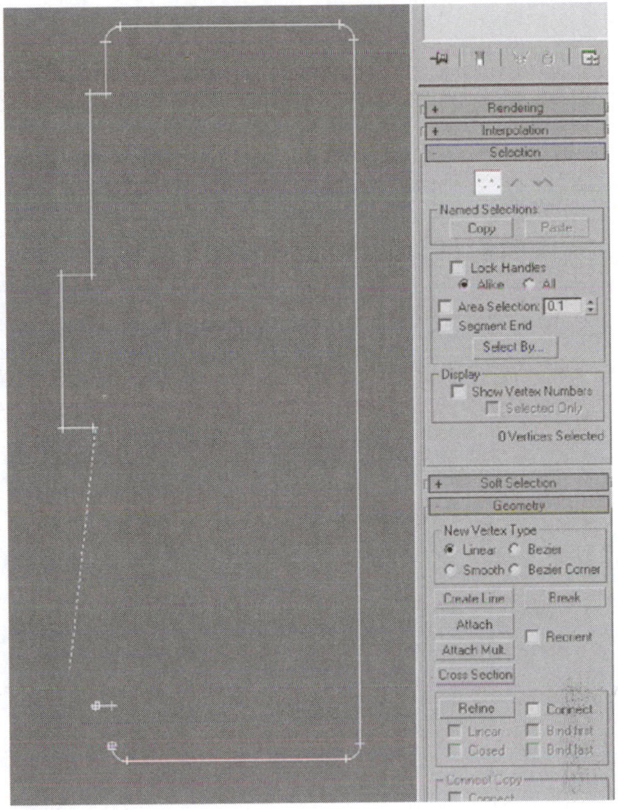

FIGURE 3.10
Connecting the open vertices.

13. Right-click and switch to Segment on the Tools 1 quad menu. Delete the overlapping segments of your splines, opening up the shapes in preparation for connecting vertices (see Figure 3.9).

14. Right-click and choose Connect on the Tools 2 quad menu. Click and drag from vertex to vertex to connect the short jamb segments to the remaining stop segments, and the casing to the jamb (see Figure 3.10).

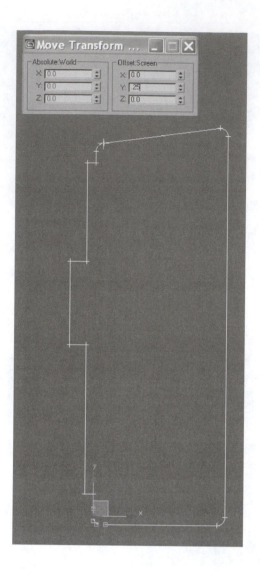

FIGURE 3.11

Angling the sides of the casing.

15. Select the top left two vertices of the casing. In the Transform dialog, enter −0.25 into the Offset Y window and hit Tab or Enter. Deselect those vertices, and select the bottom left two vertices of the casing. In the Transform dialog, enter 0.25 into the Offset Y window and hit Tab or Enter (see Figure 3.11).

16. We're almost done with the profile shape—just two more quick changes. First, while you are still in Vertex on your shape, select one of the vertices of the jamb edge, right-click, and choose Make First (see Figure 3.12). This will ensure that your door opening is the right size.

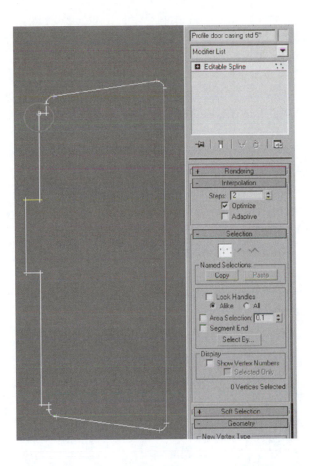

FIGURE 3.12

*Changing the First
Vertex.*

17. On the Modifier panel, in the Interpolation rollout, set the Steps to 2. This will
    still allow the curves to read as round but will save geometry and hence rendering
    power.

    Note:

    *I use a rough gauge of radius, contrasting material and viewing distance to gauge the num-
    ber of steps required in the Interpolation rollout. As an example, curves with a radius of
    0.25" or less, ranging from 0 to 90 degrees, generally have Steps set to 2. For curves with a
    radius of 0.25" to 1", I set Steps to 3, and so on. If a curved shape or object's edge is adjacent
    to a contrasting material, I'll render a quick test from a natural camera view to see if there
    are artifacts that would spoil the illusion. Examples of this include crown molding that dies
    into a wall, lampshades, and round windows and picture frames. For a smooth rendering,
    these objects may require a higher Steps setting or more segments.*

18. Right-click and choose Top Level Tools 1 quad menu. Name this object in a man-
    ner consistent with your naming conventions. I name objects that will be used as
    profiles like this one as Profile door casing std 5".

19. Press the F key to switch to the Front view. Create a rectangle of any size roughly around 0,0,0.

20. On the Modifier panel, change the parameters of the new rectangle to a length of 80″ and a width of 36″, with no corner radius.

21. In the Transform dialog, set the Absolute:World Z coordinates to 40.0. This will place the bottom of the casing at 0′0″.

22. Right-click, and on the Transform quad, choose Convert to Editable Spline. Right-click and switch to Segment on the Tools 1 quad menu. Delete the bottom segment of the shape (see Figure 3.13).

23. On the Modifier panel, drop down the Modifier list and choose Bevel Profile from the Object-Space Modifiers group.

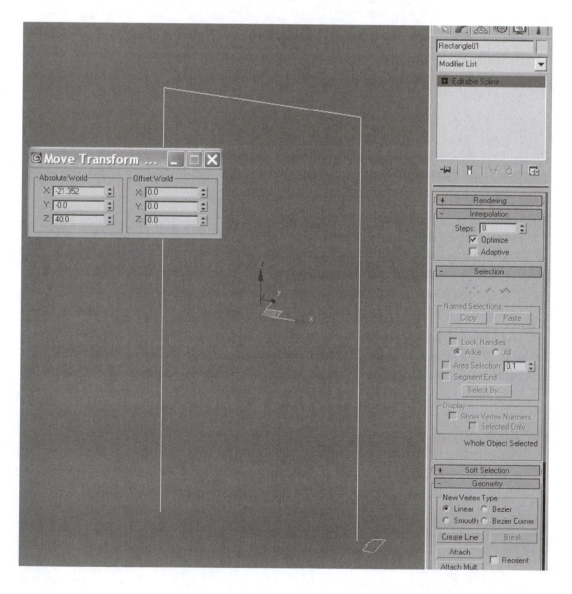

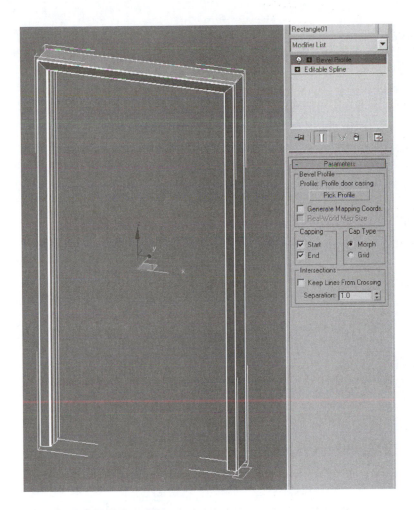

FIGURE 3.14
The door casing, with the stop on the inside.

24. In the Bevel Profile Parameters, click on the Pick Profile button, and then click on the profile of the door casing and jamb we drew. Alternatively, you can press H for Select by Name, and choose the profile object. This will generate a door casing sized for a 3068 door. Hold Alt 1 MW to arc-rotate and view your door casing. If the stop is on the inside, go to the Bonus Step or on to Exercise 2 (see Figure 3.14).

25. If your door casing is reversed, do the following: with the casing object selected, right-click and choose Profile Gizmo on the Tools 1 quad menu. Right-click again and choose Rotate on the Transform quad.

26. If your angle snap is not enabled, press A to turn it on. Click and drag on the blue Z rotation ring and rotate the Profile Gizmo by 180 degrees. Your doorstop should be on the inside of the casing. Right-click and choose Top Level Tools 1 quad menu.

27. On the Modifier panel, drop down the Modifier List and choose Normal from the Object-Space Modifiers group. In the Normal modifier's Parameters, check Flip Normals if it is not checked by default.

BONUS STEP

Create a Chamfer Box inside the casing in the Front view. Make the Chamfer Box length 80″, width 36″, height 1.5″, and a fillet radius of 0.125″. Snap the Chamfer Box inside the jamb in Front and Top views. The door should fit snugly against the stop and have a reveal from flush side when closed. If you are feeling really slick, clear the smoothing groups from the flat sides of the Chamfer Box, leaving only the fillets smoothed.

EXERCISE SUMMARY

In this exercise, we made a profile shape for a jamb, a stop, and a simple casing on both sides. We then used the Bevel Profile modifier to run the profile around a rectangle that was the size of our door.

EXERCISE 2: Building a more elaborate door casing

In this exercise, we'll build on the lessons from Exercise 1, using the same Bevel Profile technique to create a more elaborate door casing. For this profile, we'll draw the casing first and then use the jamb to clone and space it properly. The casing will be a common residential casing, often called 7-11 casing, with a straight outer field, rounded edges, and a deep reveal and concave inner section.

1. We'll start this casing with a rectangle, defining the overall size of the casing and giving us vertices to snap to during construction. In the Top view, draw a rectangle that has a length of 0.75″ and a width of 2.5″, with no corner radius. We want to make sure, just like in the real world, that our casing is deep enough to catch the baseboard without showing cut baseboard ends. This casing will accommodate a 0.5″ baseboard and provide a multitude of visual-enhancing shadow lines.

2. Clone this rectangle as a copy, and change the length and width to 0.75″, with a corner radius of 0.125″. Snap this rectangle on the X axis to the right side of the construction rectangle.

3. We're going to create several arcs and join them into the remainder of this casing. As a rule, I build objects like this casing in sequence, working from known reference to close in on the unknown, namely, the concave center section. Start with an Arc drawn in the vicinity of the construction rectangle. Change the parameters of the Arc to a radius of 0.25″, from 90 to 180 degrees.

4. Snap this Arc onto the lower right corner of the construction rectangle, then use the Transform dialog to move it up by 0.25″ in the Offset Y window.

FIGURE 3.15

The Arcs snapped to the template Rectangles.

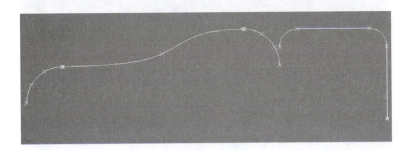

FIGURE 3.16

The attached splines of the door casing.

5. Mirror this Arc on the X axis as a copy, using the Mirror tool found on the Main Toolbar at the top of the screen.

6. Snap the top of this Arc on the X and Y axes to the top left vertex of the small rectangle you created. Change your Axis Constraints to restrict to X, and snap the bottom vertex of this Arc to the leftmost vertices of the rectangle (see Figure 3.15).

7. For the connecting concave section, we'll manipulate the Bezier handles on a Line to form the desired curve. Press Ctrl + RMB and choose Line from the Primitives quad menu. Snap the line onto one of the opposing Arc's top vertices, and click and drag a line in the space between them. Place one vertex roughly in the middle of the space, and then snap the ending vertex to the other Arc.

8. At this point, you have all of the elements of your casing—they just need to be stitched together. Delete the construction rectangle, as we don't need it any longer. Next, select the Line you just drew, right-click, and choose Attach. Attach all of the other shapes for this casing to it.

9. Right-click and pick Segment, and delete the bottom round corners and bottom segment of the small rectangle, as well as the left side (see Figure 3.16).

10. Right-click and choose Connect, and connect between the top left corner of the remains of the Rectangle and the adjacent arc. Right-click to exit the Connect tool.

11. Select all of the coincident vertices, and right-click and choose Weld Vertices on the Tools 2 quad menu. There should only be one First Vertex box on the shape, as it should be composed of one spline. If there is more than one, select those vertices and weld them.

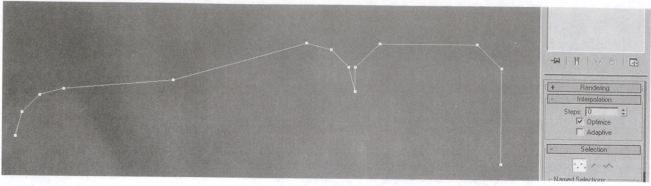

FIGURE 3.17

The door casing profile with Steps reduced to 0.

12. At this point, you may want to adjust the handles on the middle vertex of the concave section to match the image shown above in Figure 3.16.

13. On the Modifier panel, in the Interpolation rollout, set the Steps to 0 (see Figure 3.17). For this profile, we will divide some of the segments to simulate roundness, rather than use steps. The Arcs we drew are small enough to warrant only 2 steps, or 3 sections over 90 degrees, which they have by default. Hence, we don't want to add unnecessary geometry to the final model by adding additional steps.

FIGURE 3.18

The middle curve of the casing before and after division.

14. Right-click and pick Segment on the Tools 1 quad menu. Select the now flat corners of what was the small rectangle, as well as the two segments of the concave section. Scroll the Modifier panel up until you see the Divide button. In the window next to it, enter 2, and then hit Divide (see Figure 3.18). Alternatively, Divide is available on the Tools 1 quad menu.

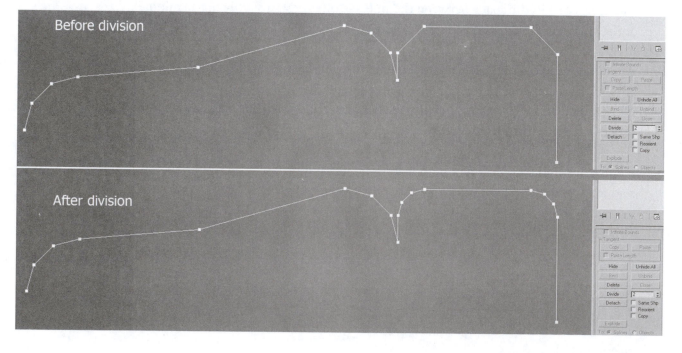

15. The casing should be complete and ready for mirroring at this point, and yes, it is longer on one side than the other. Right-click and choose Top Level on the Tools 1 quad menu. Then mirror the casing on the Y axis as a copy.

16. Constrain movement to the Y axis, and snap the mirrored casing to its twin on the lower right vertex.

17. Using the Transform dialog, move the mirrored casing down by entering −5.0 in the Offset Y window. The casing is now spaced properly for the 2 × 4 wall we talked about earlier.

18. Draw a Rectangle by snapping between the leftmost vertices of both casings. The rectangle will have a width of 0′0″ initially. Change the width to 0.125″ and the length to 5.0″ in the Modifier panel. This will form the doorjamb.

19. Constrain movement to the X axis, and snap the right side vertices of this new rectangle to the leftmost vertices of the casings.

20. Select either of your casing profiles, and attach the other casing and the new Rectangle to it.

21. Right-click and pick Segment on the Tools 1 quad menu. Delete the right side segment of the new rectangle (see Figure 3.19).

22. Right-click and choose Connect on the Tools 1 quad menu. Connect the casings to the jamb.

23. In the same manner as previous steps, create a new Rectangle that is snapped to the corners of the jamb. On the Modifier panel, change the parameters of the new rectangle to a length of 1.25″ and a width of 0.25″, with no corner radius. This will form the stop on the inside of the jamb.

24. Turn on the Selection Lock by hitting the spacebar. Snap on the top right side vertex of the small rectangle, and move it on both the X and Y axes to snap onto the leftmost top vertex of the jamb.

25. Launch the Transform dialog by either clicking the F12 button or right-clicking and choosing the dialog icon on the Transform section of the quad menu. In the Offset Y window, enter −1.5, the thickness of the door, and hit Tab or Enter. (If your doors are different, enter that number in the Offset Y window.)

FIGURE 3.19
The casing and doorjamb ready to connect.

26. Right-click and pick Segment on the Tools 1 quad menu. Delete the right side segment of the new rectangle and the long segment of the jamb.

27. Right-click and choose Connect on the Tools 1 quad menu. Connect the stop to the jamb.

28. Verify that the Steps setting in the Interpolation rollout is still set to 0.

29. Right-click and choose Top Level Tools 1 quad menu (see Figure 3.20). Name this object in a manner consistent with your naming conventions. I name objects that will be used as profiles like this one as: Profile door casing 7/11 5″.

30. Press the F key to switch to the Front view. Create a rectangle of any size roughly around 0,0,0.

31. On the Modifier panel, change the parameters of the new rectangle to a length of 80″ and a width of 36″, with no corner radius.

32. In the Transform dialog, set the Absolute:World Z coordinates to 0.0. This will place the bottom of the casing at 0′0″.

33. Right-click and on the Transform quad, choose Convert to Editable Spline. Right-click and switch to Segment on the Tools 1 quad menu. Delete the bottom segment of the shape.

34. On the Modifier panel, drop down the Modifier List and choose Bevel Profile from the Object-Space Modifiers group.

35. In the Bevel Profile Parameters, click on the Pick Profile button, and then click on the profile of the door casing and jamb we drew. Alternatively, you can press H for Select by Name, and choose the profile object. This will generate a door casing sized for a 3068 door. Hold Alt + MW to arc-rotate and view your door casing.

36. You will need to move the Profile Gizmo so it sits in the right place on the path. Right-click and choose Profile Gizmo on the Tools 1 quad menu. In the Transform dialog, try moving the Profile Gizmo by 2.625″ in the Offset X window. The casing should get larger, and be sized for a 3068 door. If this did not work, press Ctrl + Z to undo, and try the move in a negative direction.

37. Note: If your door casing is in the right direction, but shading on the back faces you, skip to step 39. If your door casing is reversed, do the following: with the casing object selected, right-click and choose Profile Gizmo on the Tools 1 quad menu. Right-click again and choose Rotate on the Transform quad.

38. If your angle snap is not enabled, press A to turn it on. Click and drag on the blue Z rotation ring and rotate the Profile Gizmo by 180 degrees. Your doorstop should be on the inside of the casing. Right-click and choose Top Level Tools 1 quad menu.

39. On the Modifier panel, drop down the Modifier List and choose Normal from the Object-Space Modifiers group. In the Normal modifier's Parameters, check Flip Normals if it is not checked by default.

40. Save your file as *Door library.max* (see Figure 3.21).

EXERCISE SUMMARY

In this exercise, we constructed a more elaborate casing for a doorframe, forming detail and curves from several Shape Primitives. We used the Bevel Profile modifier again, generating the jamb, stop, and casing in one operation.

FIGURE 3.20
The casing with the stop.

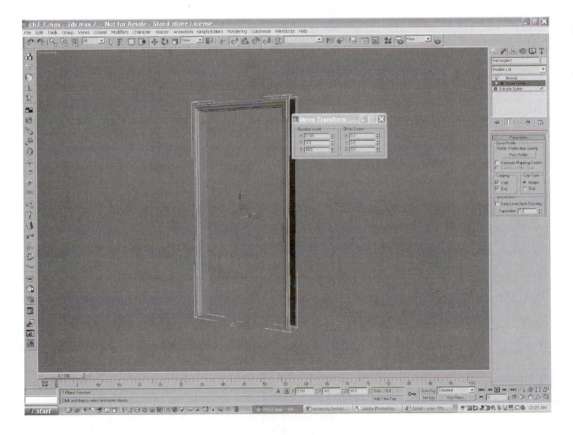

FIGURE 3.21
The completed door casing.

EXERCISE 3:   Building a window

In this exercise, we're going to construct a simple fixed window using Editable Splines, the Bevel Profile modifier, and some simple Editable Poly editing. We'll build on the skills of the previous exercises, generating profile objects that can be reused in many situations. We'll also strive for accuracy with respect to manufacturers' specifications and dimensions. We're going to be drawing a picture or fixed window first, as these are the simplest.

1.   Start 3ds Max, or choose File > Reset from the top menu.

2.   Press T to switch to Top view.

3.   We're going to be modeling a vinyl window, and since it is a fixed window, we can model the jamb and frame all at once. Start by drawing a Rectangle that has a length of 1.25″ and a width of 4″, with no corner radius (see Figure 3.22). This will form the jamb and sill, to which we will add the frame and glass.

4.   Convert this Rectangle to an editable spline. Right-click and choose Segment from the Tools 1 quad menu. Select the top segment of this spline, right-click, and choose divide. This will insert a vertex into the top segment, allowing us to form the sloped sill.

5.   Rather than create rounded corners from the start, we're going to add radii in only a few places. I am also assuming that this window will be surrounded inside and out by trim in some fashion, hence radii would not be seen in some areas. Right-click and choose Vertex from the Tools 1 quad menu. Select all of the vertices by windowing around them. Right-click again and choose Corner from the Tools 1

FIGURE 3.22
Forming the jamb and sill.

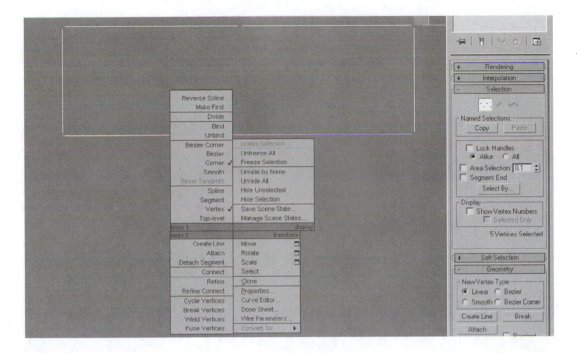

FIGURE 3.23
Adding radii to the jamb.

quad menu (see Figure 3.23). This will remove any influence the vertices have on their adjoining segments, enabling us to add 90-degree corners.

6. Select the vertex in the upper left corner. Using the Transform dialog, move it down by entering −0.25 in the Offset Y window.

7. Select the top left and right corner vertices. On the Modifier panel, enter a value of 0.125″ in the window next to Fillet, then hit Enter (see Figure 3.24).

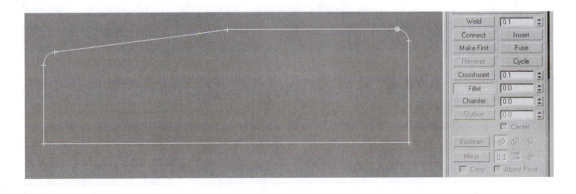

FIGURE 3.24
The vertices after applying the Fillet of 0.125″.

FIGURE 3.25

*The jamb profile
and the start of the
window frame.*

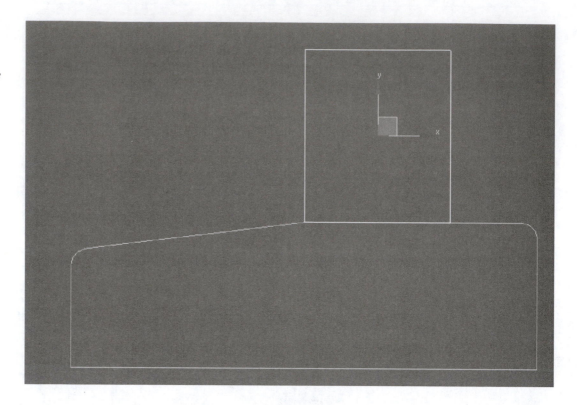

8. Create a new Rectangle roughly on top of the jamb shape, with a length of 1.5″ and a width of 1.25″, with no corner radius. Snap the lower left vertex of this new Rectangle to the top center vertex of the jamb (see Figure 3.25). This will form the window frame.

9. Create another new Rectangle by snapping to the top vertices of the window frame rectangle. Change the length to 0.375″, and the width to 1″. This will form the stop on both sides of the glass, as well as the rubber gasket (see Figure 3.26).

10. Constrain movement to the Y axis, and snap the bottom vertices of this new rectangle to the top vertices of the frame.

11. Convert this Rectangle to an editable spline. Right-click and choose Segment from the Tools 1 quad menu. Select the top segment of this Rectangle. On the Modifier panel, set the number of divisions next to the Divide button to 2, and hit Enter. The new middle segment will later become the rubber gasket (see Figure 3.27).

12. Right-click and choose Attach from the Tools 2 quad menu. Attach the other shapes to this one.

13. Delete any overlapping segments, right-click and choose Connect from the Tools 2 quad menu. Connect any open vertices together.

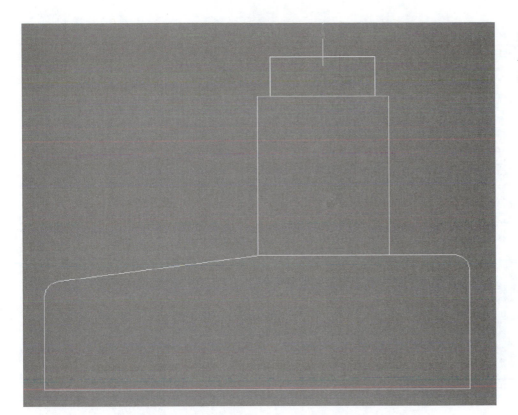

FIGURE 3.26

*A new Rectangle that will
be the glass stop.*

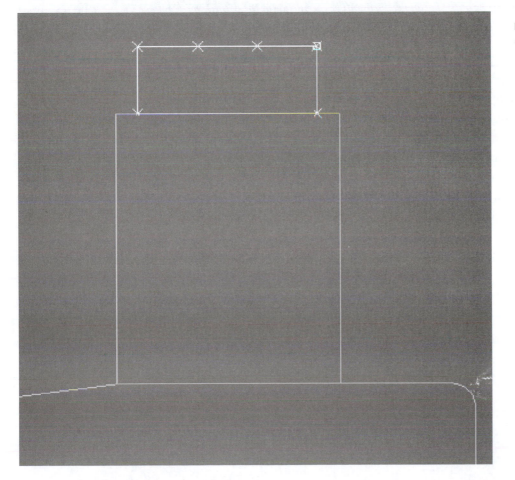

FIGURE 3.27

The divided glass stop.

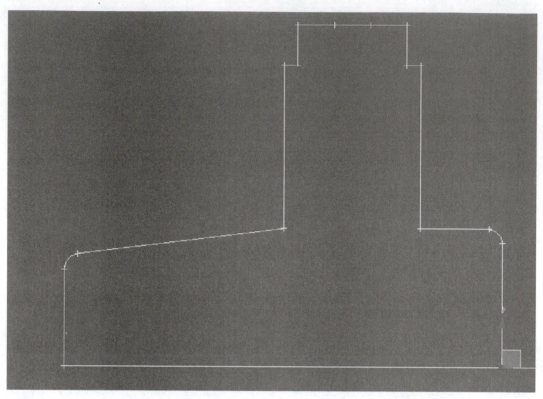

FIGURE 3.28

Changing one of the bottom (which will be the outside of the frame) vertices to be the First Vertex. When this shape is placed on a path or spline, the path or spline will pass through the First Vertex.

14. Right-click to exit the Connect tool, and then drag a Selection window around the coincident vertices at the top center of the jamb. Right-click and choose Weld Vertices from the Tools 2 quad menu. At this point, there should only be one First Vertex marker on this shape.

15. Select one of the bottom vertices, right-click, and choose Make First on the Tools 1 quad menu (see Figure 3.28).

16. Set the number of Steps in the Interpolation rollout on the Modifier panel to 2. Right-click and choose Top Level from the Tools 1 quad menu. Name this object per your naming conventions. My name for this object would be Profile MG Vinyl Picture, which tells me that it is a profile shape, from my Milgard Windows library, made for vinyl windows, and that it is suitable for fixed or picture windows.

17. Change to the Front view by pressing F. Create a Rectangle with a length of 72″ and a width of 30″, with no corner radius. This Rectangle should be sized to the overall dimensions of the window.

18. Apply a Bevel Profile modifier to this new Rectangle from the Modifier List. Select the profile object we just drew as your Profile Gizmo. The window frame should be on the inside of the Bevel Profile object (see Figure 3.29).

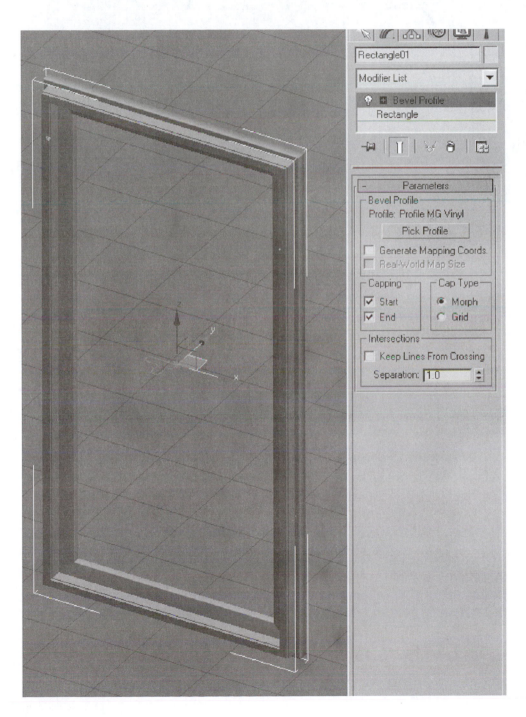

FIGURE 3.29
The profile is around the frame but in the wrong orientation.

FIGURE 3.30
The Profile Gizmo rotated to the correct orientation.

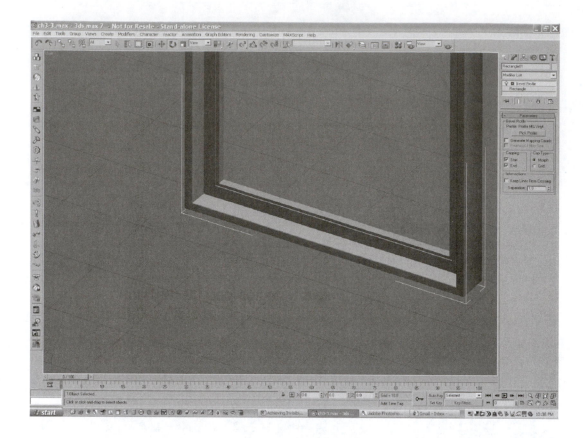

19. If your angle snap is not enabled, press A to turn it on. Right-click and choose Profile Gizmo from the Tools 1 quad menu. Click and drag on the blue Z rotation ring and rotate the Profile Gizmo by 90 or 180 degrees, until the frame is on the inside of the jamb (see Figure 3.30).

20. Name this window per your naming conventions. My name for this object might be Window frame vinyl 2660 fixed01.

21. Right-click and choose Convert to > Convert to Editable Poly on the Transform quad menu. We're going to clear most of the smoothing on this window frame, so what is flat looks flat, and what is round looks round.

22. Right-click and choose Polygon on the Tools 1 quad menu, or click on the Polygon button on the Modifier panel. This object is no longer a parametric object, but a highly flexible combined object and toolset called the Editable Poly.

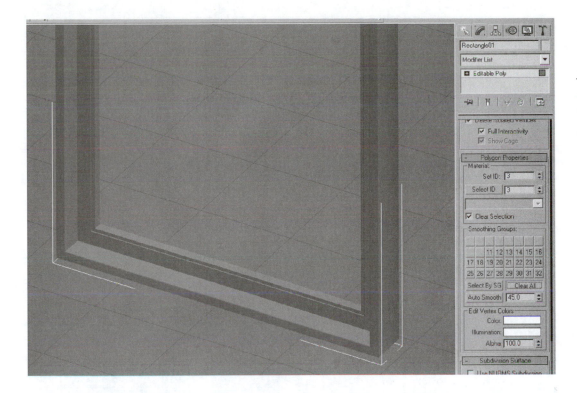

23. Polygons are the smallest unit of the Editable Poly that will hold a surface and simulate roundness. However, most of this window frame should not be round, only the two corners we added fillets to. Select all of the polygons in your object by windowing around them. On the Modifier panel, scroll the menu up until you see the Polygon Properties section. In the Smoothing Groups area, click on Clear All (see Figure 3.31).

Note:
I make a point of clearing smoothing off all flat faces during modeling, rather than having to go back and fix possibly many objects. Many modifiers smooth polygons by default, causing things like this window frame to look bubbly or warped in a shaded view or rendering. Smoothing groups applied to flat objects, such as doors or walls, can also cause those polygons to flash or shimmer in an animation. Nothing is more painful than re-rendering an animation, especially under a tight deadline, so model carefully and preempt problems like this before they start.

FIGURE 3.32
*Reassigning the
Smoothing Groups
to preserve the
corners.*

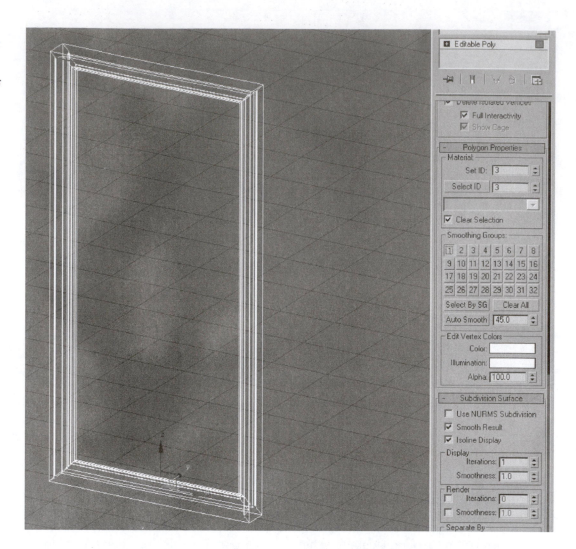

24. Select the horizontal curved corners of the window frame, and click on the Smoothing Groups button 1 (see Figure 3.32). This will assign smoothing to only those polygons, leaving the adjacent flat faces looking flat.

25. Select the vertical curved corners of the window frame and click on the Smoothing Groups button 2. Again, this will constrain smoothing to just those areas. In addition, by having two different smoothing groups on horizontal and vertical areas, the mitered corners will stay crisp. If those areas were all in one group, they might lose distinction between horizontal and vertical, and shade oddly.

26. Press L for Left view, and zoom in around the sill of your window. We need to add a little more slope to the sill than the profile shape provided.

27. Right-click and choose Vertex from the Tools 1 quad menu. Drag a Selection window around the upper vertices of the sill on the outside of the window. Using your Transform dialog, move them down by −0.25″ by entering that value in the Offset Y window.

28. In a Front view, create a Rectangle that is snapped to the inside vertices of the stop. This will form the one side of the window glass. Right-click and select Convert to > Convert to Editable Poly on the Transform quad menu. Shapes or splines can be converted straight to Editable Poly objects for use as single-sided objects.

29. Name this object per your naming conventions. My name for this object would be Glass outer01, denoting that it will have a glass material applied that is suitable for exterior renderings. You may want to check for and clear Smoothing Groups from this object as we did previously.

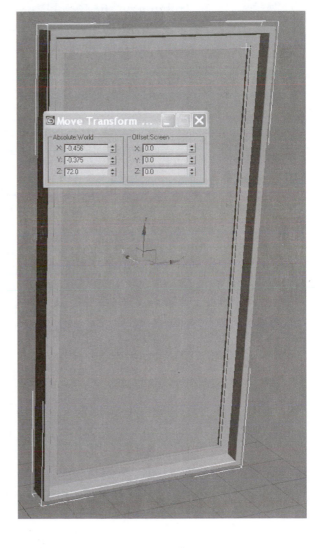

FIGURE 3.33
The window frame with glass.

30. Press T to switch to Top view.

31. With this new glass object selected, press the spacebar for the Selection Lock, and constrain movement to the Y axis. Snap the glass to the bottom edge of the stop, and then use the Transform dialog to move the glass into the gasket area by entering 0.375 in the Offset Y window (see Figure 3.33). This should leave a thin strip of the gasket polygon showing outside of the window.

32. Mirror this object into the inside of the window by clicking on the Mirror button on the Main Toolbar. Constrain the mirror to the Y axis, and enter an offset value of 0.25″, the thickness of the glass. Clone this new object as an Instance, so that if this glass is adjusted, both pieces will change.

33. Name this object per your naming conventions. My name for this object would be Glass inner01, denoting that it will have a glass material applied that is suitable for interior renderings.

34. Save your file.

EXERCISE SUMMARY

Windows add detail, life, and character to a building, not to mention letting in the all-important sunbeams for sexy renderings. Therefore, it is important to take the time to model window details correctly. In this exercise, we used the Bevel Profile modifier again to generate the jamb, frame, and stop of the window all at once. We added a new tool, Fillet, to our spline-modeling arsenal, allowing us to selectively add radii to shapes. Finally, we explored a tiny bit of the Editable Poly tool, clearing and reapplying smoothing from polygons so that flat surfaces look flat.

EXERCISE 4: Building a double-hung window

In this exercise, we'll construct a more complex double-hung window, with jamb, track, frame, stop, and glass elements. We'll use spline modeling techniques again, relying on the Bevel Profile modifier. I prefer to build objects such as this window the way they are constructed in the real world, from separate elements. Often, I see my students modeling objects like this window from a box, or extruding edges of a hole in a wall. While it is possible to build this way, I believe that the precision afforded my way, combined with reusable profile shapes, leads to a more successful rendering.

For this exercise, we'll work in the same file as before, although you may work in a clean application if you wish.

1. Hide all of the objects in your scene by right-clicking and choosing Hide Selection and then Hide Unselected from the Display quad menu.

2. We'll start by drawing the profile shape for the jamb and sash. In a Top view, create a Rectangle that has a length of 1.25″ and a width of 5″, with no corner radius.

3. Convert this Rectangle to an editable spline, and then right-click and choose Segment from the Tools 1 quad menu.

4. Divide the top segment of the rectangle, with one division.

5. Right-click and choose Vertex from the Tools 1 quad menu. Select all of the vertices and change them to Corner vertices by right-clicking and choosing Corner from the Tools 1 quad menu.

6. Add a 0.125″ fillet to the top left and right corners of the jamb by selecting those vertices and inputting 0.125 in the window next to Fillet on the Modifier panel.

7. Select the top left vertices, and move them down by entering −0.25 in the Offset Y window on the Transform dialog.

8. As you may have noticed, adding the fillet to the top corner vertices restored Bezier handles to them. Moving the top left corner vertices down introduced a curve into the top of the sill. We can correct this easily by right-clicking and choosing Segment on the Tools 1 quad menu, and then selecting the curved segment. Right-click again and choose Line from the Tools 1 quad menu (see Figure 3.34). It should return to being straight.

9. Select the top center vertex, and move it to the left by entering −1.375 in the Offset X window in the Transform dialog. This X movement will allow us to add three track guides at 0.25″ wide, plus an upper and lower window at 1.5″ wide each.

10. Create a new Rectangle near the top of the jamb shape. Resize this Rectangle to a length of 0.5″ and a width of 0.25″, with no corner radius.

11. Snap the lower left vertex of the new Rectangle onto the top center point of the jamb shape, where the slope begins.

12. Clone this small Rectangle in place by pressing Ctrl + V, or right-clicking and choosing Clone from the Transform quad menu. Make this clone a copy.

13. Move this new Rectangle to the right by using the Transform dialog and entering 1.75 in the Offset X window. Remember, by default, objects in 3ds Max think that

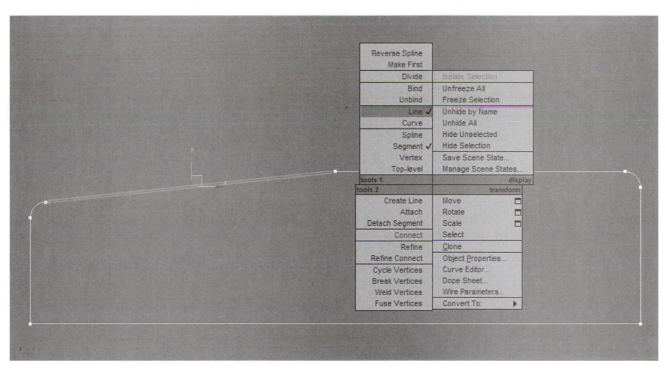

FIGURE 3.34
Changing the sloped section of the sill back to a straight segment.

FIGURE 3.35

*The new
Rectangles will
form the window
tracks.*

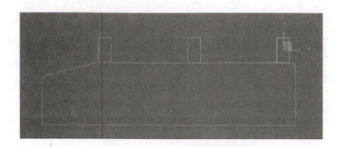

their pivot is in the center. The 1.75″ comes from the width of the window frame (1.5″) plus two times half of 0.25″, the width of the track.

14. Repeat steps 12 and 13 to form the inside track as well, for a total of three small rectangles (see Figure 3.35).

15. Select the jamb shape, right-click, and choose Attach from the Tools 2 quad menu. Attach the three small rectangles to the jamb.

16. Right-click and choose Segment from the Tools 1 quad menu. Delete any overlapping segments.

17. Right-click and choose Connect from the Tools 2 quad menu. Click and drag to connect the open vertices.

18. Select and weld any other coincident vertices.

19. Set the number of Steps in the Interpolation rollout on the Modifier panel to 2.

20. Name this object per your naming conventions. My name for this object would be Profile MG jamb vinyl dh, denoting that this is a Milgard window, or whatever manufacturer's specifications you are following, that it is the jamb and sill, made for vinyl, and that it is suitable for a double-hung window. (Single-hung windows would not have the outside track.)

21. In the Front view, draw a new Rectangle. Change the length to 72″ and the width to 36″, with no corner radius.

22. Apply a Bevel Profile modifier to this new Rectangle from the Modifier List. Select the profile object we just drew as your Profile Gizmo. The window frame should be on the inside of the Bevel Profile object.

23. If your angle snap is not enabled, press A to turn it on. Right-click and choose Profile Gizmo from the Tools 1 quad menu. Click and drag on the blue Z rotation ring and rotate the Profile Gizmo by 90 or 180 degrees, until the tracks are on the inside of the jamb.

24. Once again, we need to clear most of the smoothing, so what is flat looks flat, and what is round looks round. To do this, refer to steps 21–27 in Exercise 3.

25. Name this object per your naming conventions. My name for this object would be jamb 3060 dh01, denoting a vinyl window jamb for a double-hung window that is 3′0″ wide and 6′0″ tall, and that this is the first one.

Note:

I am a naming fanatic. Everything, including everything, is named in my scenes, as accurately as possible. I assume when I create objects that many clones will be made, all of which may need further modification or selection. I also assume that this model may sit for periods of time while I wait for client feedback, and hence I will lose immediate familiarity with it. Alternatively, this model may be passed off to someone else in a production environment, someone who needs to become acquainted easily with the organization.

Naming is also crucial for lighting. It is much easier to choose a wall object called Wall Living Fireplace, and exclude it from a light, than to search through Line01 to Line54 for the right object. In addition, when merging objects from a library like we are creating, it is far better to look through a list of windows named by type and size than several hundred Rectangles.

26. We'll create the window frames in the same manner as the jamb, by defining a profile object first and then using the Bevel Profile modifier. Start in a Top view by creating a Rectangle with a length of 1.75″, a width of 1.5″, and no corner radius.

27. Clone this Rectangle as a copy, and change the length to 0.5″ and a width of 1″ to form the stop.

28. Constrain movement to the Y axis only, and snap the bottom of the small Rectangle to the top of the larger one.

29. Convert either Rectangle to an editable spline, and attach the other one to it.

30. Right-click and choose Segment from the Tools 1 quad menu. Delete any overlapping segments.

31. Right-click and choose Connect from the Tools 2 quad menu. Click and drag to connect the open vertices.

32. Right-click and choose Segment from the Tools 1 quad menu. Select the top segment of the stop and divide it, setting the number of divisions to 2.

33. Right-click and choose Vertex from the Tools 1 quad menu. Select either of the bottom vertices of the frame profile, and choose Make First from the Tools 1 quad menu.

34. Name this object per your naming conventions. My name for this object would be Profile MG frame vinyl, denoting a Milgard window frame profile suitable for use in a variety of vinyl windows.

35. In a Front view, draw a new Rectangle, snapping to the vertices at the inside of the tracks.

36. On the Modifier panel, in the parameters for this new Rectangle, enter /2 in the Length field after the length. Press Enter or Tab, and the original value will be divided by 2. Add 0.875 to that number, and enter the result in the Length field. We just divided the overall height in half, and then added length to overlap the top and bottom window frames by the depth of the frame.

37. Apply a Bevel Profile modifier to this Rectangle, and choose the profile shape we just drew as the Profile Gizmo.

38. If your angle snap is not enabled, press A to turn it on. Right-click and choose Profile Gizmo from the Tools 1 quad menu. Click and drag on the blue Z rotation ring and rotate the Profile Gizmo by 90 or 180 degrees, until the stop is on the inside of the frame, and the frame sits in the tracks on the jamb.

39. Name this object per your naming conventions. My name for this object would be Window frame dh01, denoting a moving frame that is part of a double-hung window assembly.

40. Move this frame up to snap to the top outside track of the jamb.

41. Mirror this frame on the Y axis in a Front view as an Instance. Move the instance down to snap to the bottom inside track of the jamb.

42. Save your file.

EXERCISE SUMMARY

In this exercise, we looked at modeling several parts of a building component using splines and sampled a little more poly editing. You can apply the techniques we used to almost any shape of window and generate many different sizes easily for your library. Precision modeling like this will prove its worth many times over in crisply fitting objects, accurate shadows, and a reduction of light leaks in renderings—and hopefully fewer headaches for you.

BONUS STEPS

1.   Add glass to the window frames as per the previous exercises.

2.   Clear smoothing groups from the window frames.

SECTION D: CONCLUSION

Spline modeling is a powerful method for accurately modeling objects. In conjunction with the Bevel Profile modifier, many of the real-world building materials that are made with linear manufacturing processes or milling, such as window frames, door casings, baseboards, and crown molding, are easily constructed in 3D space. Careful attention to perceivable detail in commonly seen items such as these will reinforce clients' appreciation of your work and allow the subtle aspects of your design to shine.

CHAPTER 4 Ceiling and Wall Construction

SECTION A: MODELING EFFICIENCY AND ELEGANCE

Most walls are flat. Granted, there are curved or curvy walls in many places, but most walls tend to be flat as they are easier and cheaper to build. Even walls that are curved tend to be curved only in one direction. Compound curves tend to be in the domain of fabrics, inflatable structures, furniture, and rock star architect-designed blobjects. Undoubtedly, you will be faced with a compound curve to model at some point, but the majority of visualization work will include straight walls, structures, and windows. Thus, the focus of this chapter is on spline-based modeling techniques for easy, efficient, and elegant construction of walls that light subtly, are precisely aligned, and use the minimum of polygons to get the job done.

One of the main advantages to spline modeling for walls, floors, ceilings, and such is single-sided modeling. No matter how fast computers are, we as visualization artists can always find a way to use up all of the available processing power and then ask for more. All of the fancy global illumination tricks we use take a lot of processing power, as do reflections, refractions, blurs, translucency, skin, and so on. Hence, we need to keep a very careful watch on the amount of geometry we are applying said bells and whistles to. There is no need to "spend" unnecessary geometry. Single-sided modeling allows us to make only what we need to see, exactly, and from the start cut out the excess. Additionally—and this is highly useful as a design concept development tool—by default with a single-sided model, each side of a wall can easily have a different material without resorting to complex material assignments. This flexibility allows a designer to change wall colors or coverings as needed while still maintaining organized, easy to select and read materials.

The basic working method of the spline-based wall system is to model the detailed objects first, such as doors and windows, and then snap the walls around them. Alternatively, if the doors and windows are not yet constructed, their openings can be placed as part of the wall precisely, ready for snapping later. The goal is to construct a watertight model. Not that we are going to perform fluid simulations inside the walls, or convert conference rooms into aquariums; rather, the mark of a professional is that all of the walls, ceilings, floors, doors, and windows are snapped and perfectly formed. Thus, we could fill the space in between each side of the walls with water and it would not leak into the rooms. Careful construction of walls, floors, and ceilings will yield far easier and realistic lighting with far less headaches and time spent combating and fixing lighting anomalies or leaks.

SECTION B: CEILINGS

EXERCISE 1: Drawing a flat ceiling

In this exercise, we will construct a flat ceiling as a way to explore snapping, drawing tools, and working methods of splines. Additionally, starting with the ceiling allows the walls to be snapped to a precise ceiling height when they are constructed.

1. Open the base scene file for this exercise, *C2–E1 base.max,* located in the Scenes folder on the CD, by either choosing File > Open from the File menu or pressing Ctrl + O. This scene has a sample floor plan in it, a group of objects named Dwgs–Floor Plan 01 (see Figure 4.1).

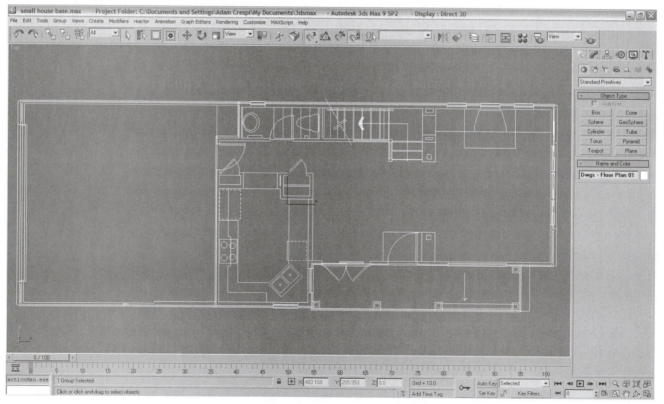

FIGURE 4.1

The imported CAD drawing.

2. Select the Dwgs–Floor Plan 01 object and right-click, then choose Object Properties from the quad menu. In the Object Properties dialog, uncheck Show Frozen in Gray in the Display section (see Figure 4.2). This will allow you to freeze the object so it cannot be accidentally moved or misaligned, but still show all of the layers in their various colors for easy identification.

3. Freeze this group by clicking on it to select, then right-clicking to bring up the quad menu. Choose Freeze Selection from the Display quad on the upper right (see Figure 4.3). As a working method, I will group, place, and orient any imported drawings, and then freeze their groups. If a reference object such as this floor plan were to be accidentally moved, the mistake could affect hours of modeling and require further hours of reconstruction and Frankenstein-esque model squishing.

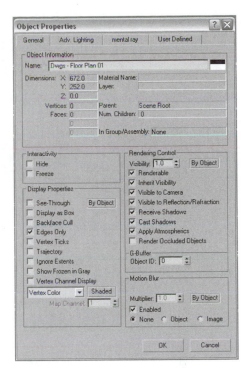

FIGURE 4.2

The Object Properties dialog.

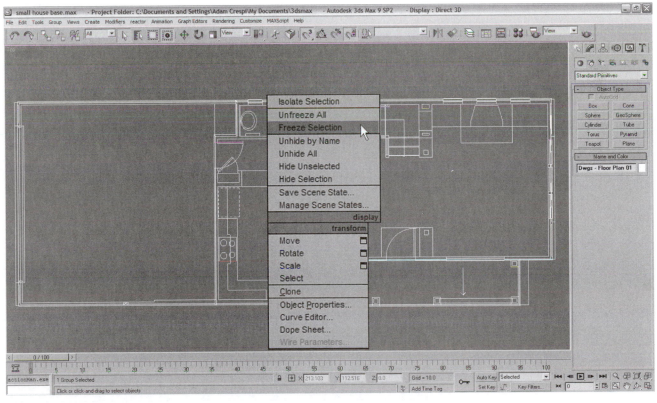

FIGURE 4.3

Freezing the selected grouped drawings.

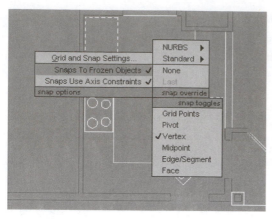

FIGURE 4.4

*Configuring the
Snap Overrides.*

4. If you haven't already done so in previous work or tutorials, check to see that your Snap settings are set to allow snapping to frozen objects. Hold Shift and right-click to bring up the Snap quad. Under the Snap Toggles section, check Vertex and uncheck Grid Points. Under the Snap Options section, check both Snaps Use Axis Constraints and Snaps To Frozen Objects (see Figure 4.4).

5. Now that everything is set up, we can start drawing. Hold Ctrl and right-click anywhere in the viewport to bring up the Modeling quad. Choose Line from the Primitives section (see Figure 4.5). When drawing a ceiling such as this one, start your line by snapping onto any corner vertex on the inside of the walls. Click without dragging from corner to corner, following the contours of the plan (see Figures 4.6 and 4.7). The line can span doorways, as the doors will be contained in wall polygons. Be careful to watch for soffits, dropped ceilings, coffers, and multistory openings. When the line is connected back to its beginning, a dialog will pop up asking whether to close the spline or not; click Yes (see Figure 4.8).

FIGURE 4.5

Starting the Line.

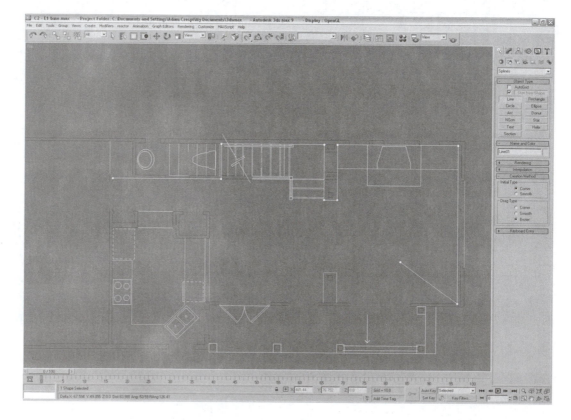

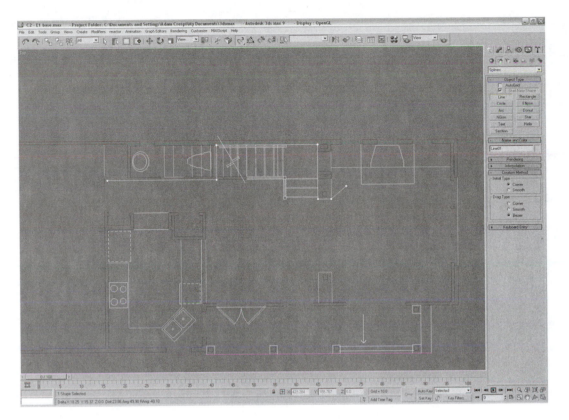

FIGURE 4.6
Snapping the Line to the vertices of the drawing.

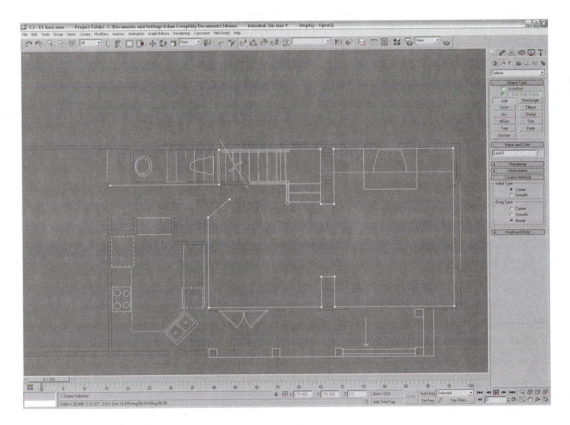

FIGURE 4.7
Continuing to follow the contours of the plan.

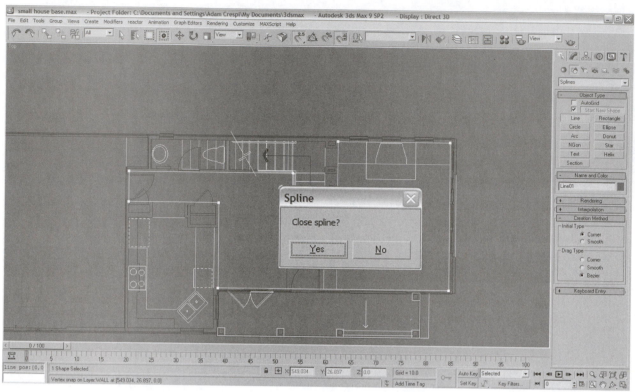

FIGURE 4.8

The Line is connected back to its beginning.

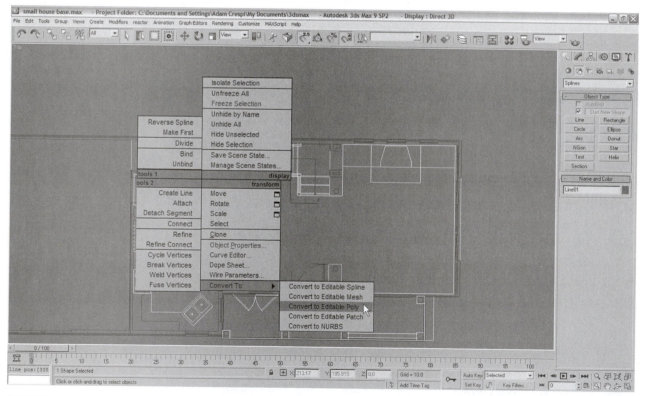

FIGURE 4.9

Converting the Line to an Editable Poly.

6. With the shape complete, it's time to move it into the right place and convert it into a surface that will render. Right-click and choose Convert to Editable Poly from the Transform section (see Figure 4.9).

7. In the Name Field above the Modifier Stack, rename the object Ceiling living/dining. It is always a good idea to name objects as they are created versus trying to sort out a mess later.

   Note:
   I name my walls, floors, ceilings, and such by a general category first, with the room name following, and a floor number if needed. Floor numbers are not usually necessary for residences but are quite handy for apartment buildings or multistory offices. The ceiling we just made was named Ceiling living/dining *to signify that it is a ceiling that spans the living and dining rooms. The kitchen ceiling, for example, would be named* Ceiling kitchen, *the master bedroom ceiling* Ceiling MBed, *and so on. Floors follow the naming conventions of the ceilings, being named Floor and the room title. Walls start with either* Wall *(for a single wall) or* Walls *(for multiple linked walls), and then the name of the room they are in. If a wall is an interior wall adjacent to another room, I will often name that wall for the two rooms, with the first name denoting the room the wall is in. As an example, the wall between the master bedroom and master bathroom would be named* Wall MBed/Mbath *on the bedroom side, and* Wall Mbath/Mbed *on the bathroom side.*

8. Pull up the Transform Type In dialog by pressing F12 or choosing Tools > Transform Type In from the File menu. As this object was created with 2.5D Snap, it resides on the XY plane, with a Z location of 0. Enter 9'1" or 109 into the Absolute:World Z field, as the ceiling height in this room is 9'1" above finish floor height (see Figure 4.10).

9. Go to the Polygon or Element sub-object by pressing 4 or 5 or right-clicking and choosing Polygon or Element from the quad menu. Either sub-object will work; if there is more than one ceiling element, be sure to select them all. Click on the ceiling to select the polygon or element (see Figure 4.11).

10. Right-click and choose Flip Normals from the Tools 2 quad (see Figure 4.12). This will flip the surface normal of the ceiling so that it faces down into the rooms.

11. On the Command panel, scroll down until you see the Polygon Properties rollout. Press the Clear All button in the Smoothing Groups section to clear any smoothing groups from the polygons (see Figure 4.13). This will avoid lighting issues later, such as bubbly looking polygons, flashing polygons, or oddly shaded polygons. Remember, if it is round, make it round; if it is flat, make it flat.

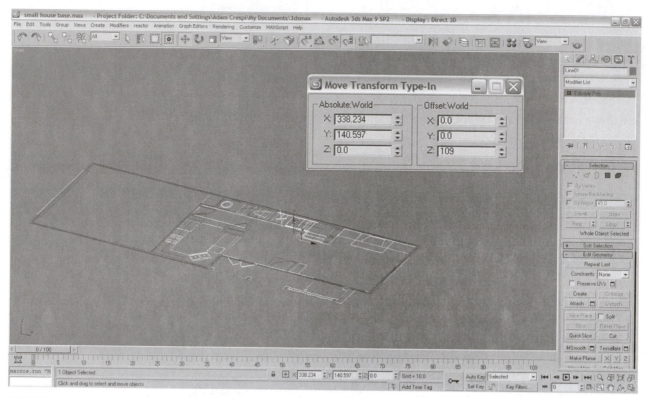

FIGURE 4.10

Moving the ceiling up to the correct height.

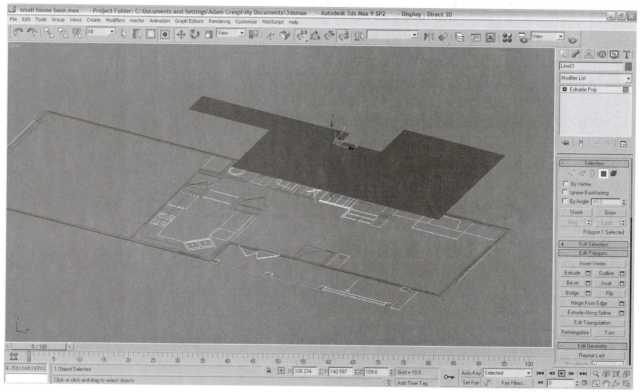

FIGURE 4.11

Selecting the polygons of the ceiling prior to flipping the surface normals.

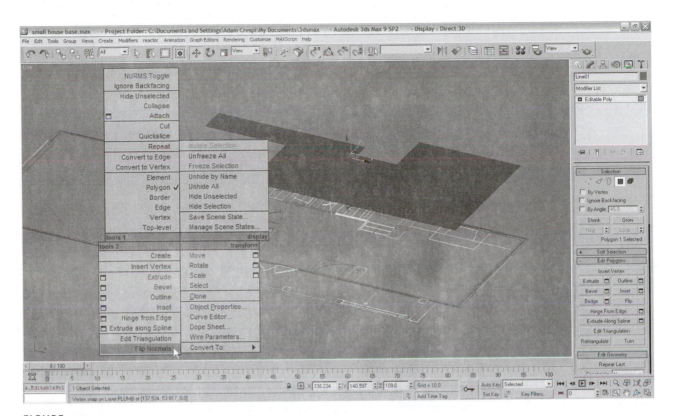

FIGURE 4.12

Flipping the surface normals.

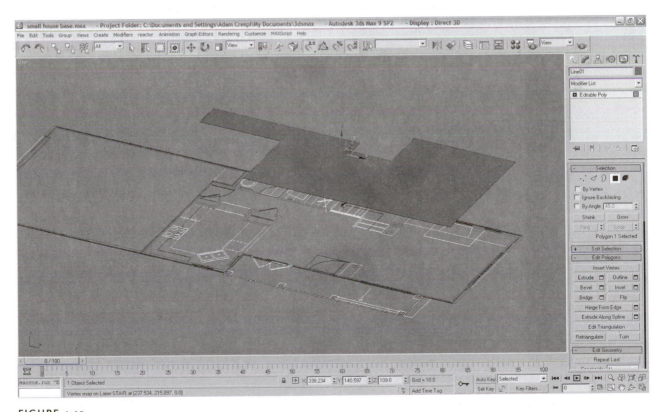

FIGURE 4.13

The flipped surface normals, shown in dark red when selected.

12. Click anywhere in the viewport to deselect the polygon, then either right-click and choose Top Level on the quad menu or press 6. The ceiling is now complete and ready for walls, surface-mounted light fixtures, and material application.

SECTION C: SPLINE-BASED WALLS

EXERCISE 2: Constructing a wall using splines

The spline is a highly versatile tool for forming architectural objects. So far, you have seen how they can be used to form ceilings, profiles, window frames, and so forth. This tutorial builds on the objects made in previous chapters for the retail store. The windows we made will be placed on the plan, and we will form the walls around them. In building architecture in 3D, it is always better to construct the detailed objects such as windows and doors, and then shape the bigger wall surfaces around them, using the plans as a template when possible. Additionally, remember that we are striving for technical elegance in our models. Walls should be constructed as surfaces facing away from each other, with bridging polygons as needed, rather than as extruded solids. This gives us the opportunity to easily shape window and door openings and apply different materials on each side of the wall without resorting to Multi/Sub-Object materials that may be hard to keep track of.

This tutorial will focus on the construction of the outer surface of the long south elevation of the store, with its arched windows and service door. If you have not completed the tutorials from Chapter 3 concerning creating windows and doors, you may want to do them after this chapter. The provided 3ds Max file for this exercise includes all of the development from the previous chapters if you are working out of sequence.

1. Open the *retail renovation ceiling finished.max* file from the Chapter 3 Assets folder. At this point, the file should have the merged and organized plans, the windows and doors modeled and placed, the ceiling and can lights modeled and placed, and be ready for casework and walls.

2. Switch to the Right view. Press the Layer Manager button on the main toolbar, or choose Tools > Layer Manager from the top menu. Hide the INT Ceilings and INT light fixtures layers, leaving only the imported AutoCAD drawings visible.

3. The first step in making the outside wall is actually to construct the brick arches and sills above and below the windows, as well as the arched wood insets above the windows. Press Ctrl + RMB and choose Box from the Modeling quad. Snap a box to the upper left and right corners of the first window group, with any length or height.

4. On the Modifier panel, change the Length to 12, the Height to 12, and the Width Segments to 16. We are going to apply a Bend Modifier to this Box above the mapping coordinates, so that the brick texture we apply will bend with the arch. Rather than trying to paint an arched map on an unwrapped mesh, this method will yield evenly arched bricks that can be tailored to match the spring points.

5. Apply a UVW Map modifier to the Box, and check Real-World Mapping on the Parameters. For this exercise, a sample material has been provided so that you can see the bricks on the arch.

6. Press M to start the Material Editor. This scene includes the sample brick materials for the arches, the soldier courses, the front and side walls, and the stone.

7. The top left sample sphere in the Material Editor has the *stack bond stretcher* material for the arches. With the Box selected, either drag the material onto it or press the Assign to Selection button. If your viewport is in Smooth mode, you should see the brick map on the arch.

8. From the Modifier List, apply a Bend Modifier to the arch.

9. Right-click and choose Center from the quad menu. On the Transform Type In dialog, move the Center down on the Offset Y by −6, so that the Center is aligned with the bottom of the arch.

10. Set Bend Angle to 45, and Axis to X. Sometimes, the Bend Modifier will not seem to bend in the right direction no matter what axis you try. In these cases, the Direction parameter provides an easy way out. Change the direction to 90 and the bend should go the right way.

11. The height of the arch should now be correct, but the arch is not wide enough; we have lost a little width in bending the box. On the Modifier panel, drop down to the Box under the UVW Map and Bend modifiers. Change the width of the Box to 49.25, and it should come very close to the sides of the window. (Where did that 49.25 number come from? Trial and error, of course. I added an inch to the width, saw that it wasn't enough, and increased it again by 0.125 increments until I found the right number. Depending on the arch, you may end up with some odd width measurements for the box. Make it fit correctly and don't worry about the number. It will look right in the rendering.)

12. Before we construct the wall, let's get the look of the brick correct on the arch. Go to the Modifier panel, click on the UVW Map modifier in the Stack for the arch. Right-click in the viewport and choose Gizmo from the quad menu, and then switch to Rotate.

13. Rotate the Mapping Gizmo by 90 degrees on one or two axes so that the bricks appear to wrap around the arch. Which axes you use depends on the view you are in; for example, from a Right view, a rotation of 90 degrees will work, but in a User view it may require a rotation on X and Z.

14. Switch to Move, and move the Mapping Gizmo to produce one full and one half brick on both the front and back and the bottom. Move the Gizmo so that a half brick on the front wraps around to a full brick on the bottom, and so forth. Right-click and choose Top Level when you are finished.

15. Name this arch Brick Arch01.

16. In a Top view, align the outside of the arch with the building plan.

17. Switch back to the Right view and create another box that is snapped to the window sill on the drawing. This will be the brick sill below the wood window sill. Make the height of this Box 13, with 2 Height Segments.

18. In the Top view, move the box to align with the inside wall and protrude from the outside wall by 1″.

19. Switch to the Front view, and convert this box to an Editable Poly.

20. Switch to Vertex, and move the middle vertices to snap to the outer edge of the wood window sill.

21. Select the upper right vertices of the brick sill in the Front view, and move them down on the Y axis by 1″. This will add the slope to the sill we expect to see, and more importantly, change subtly the way the light bounces off the sill and into the window.

22. Clear any Smoothing Groups from this object by switching to Polygon, selecting all of the polygons, and pressing Clear All in the Polygon Properties rollout on the Modifier panel. Right-click and choose Top Level when you are done.

23. Map this object in the same manner as the arch, with the arch, using the *stack bond brick* material loaded with the scene. Land the grout joint that crosses the bricks under the window sill so it is hidden. Name this object Brick Window Sill01.

24. The last piece to create for these windows is the arched wood trim below the brick arch and above the window. In a Right view, right-click and choose Create Line from the quad menu. Snap a line to every vertex of the brick arch and back to the start point.

25. Add an Extrude Modifier to the line, with an amount of 5. This will add another shadow line to the window, as it is recessed slightly from the window frame.

26. In the Front view, center this piece on the window frame, so that the window frame sticks out from it by ¼″ on both sides. Name this object Ext Trim Window Arch01.

27. Select the brick arch and sill and the window arch trim, and clone them as instances on the other windows on this wall. Save your file.

28. The first step to making the wall is to create the cutouts for the windows. In the Right view, press Ctrl + RMB and choose Line from the quad menu. Draw a line that is snapped around the window sill, the window, and the top of the arch, making sure to place a vertex on each segment of the arch. (In this design, because the arches are flush with the wall, we need to scribe the wall around the arch. If the arch is proud from the wall, the line can span from the outermost points on the arch.) When asked to close the spline, click Yes.

29. Copy this line to the other windows as copies.

30. Using the building elevation as a template, draw Lines and Rectangles around each window, snapping to the vertices at the top and bottom of the wall. These Lines and Rectangles should scribe over the stone facing that wraps around from the front, over the door, and form a base for the soldier courses at the building parapet. As we will see with the can lights in Chapter 5, at a certain point, 3ds Max cannot close a Polygon properly when it has too many holes. By dividing the wall into pieces, each window will be in its own polygon, and hence close properly.

31. With one of the Lines selected, right-click and choose Attach from the quad menu. Arc-rotate into a User view by holding Alt + MW and clicking and dragging on the view. Spin until you can see the window cutouts and the wall outlines clearly, right-click to stop arc-rotating, and then click on each window cutout to attach it to the wall outline. It does not matter which line you attach to, only that all of the pieces are attached and in the same plane.

32. Right-click and choose Convert to Editable Poly from the quad menu. With the viewport in Smooth or Smooth + Edged Faces, the wall should be a solid with holes in the shape of the windows and a notch for the door. If this is not the case, try the following remedies: (a) Make sure all of the parts are attached to one Line. (b) After all of the parts are attached, go to Vertex, select all of the vertices around the windows, and Weld them. (c) Make sure that all of the spline objects are in one plane by checking in a Top or Front view.

33. Name this object Brick Wall Side01.

34. In the Front or Top view, move and snap this wall onto the outside line of the building plan.

35. Press 4 or right-click and choose Polygon from the quad menu. Select the polygons of the wall, hold Shift, and clone them to the inside line of the building plans. This will create the inside face of the wall. When the Clone dialog pops up, clone the new polygons as an Element.

36. With the new polygons selected, right-click and choose Flip Normals from the quad menu. As the wall was drawn in the Right view, the polygons face that way when the splines are converted. By flipping the surface normals, the polygons face into the building.

37. In the Top view, select the vertices at the front of the building on the inside wall surface. Move them to the inside corner of the retail space. Do this with the rearmost vertices as well.

38. In the Front view, select the top vertices of the inside polygons, and move them down to meet the ceiling. This will provide a clean intersection for lighting later, rather than forcing the program to decide where polygons meet.

39. In a User view, switch to Edge by pressing 2 or right-clicking and choosing Edge from the quad menu. Select pairs of edges along the window sides, and on the Modifier panel, choose Bridge. This will create the visible thickness on the wall, placing polygons only where they need to be. Because we have constructed the arch and sill, the only brick that will show the wall thickness is on the sides of the windows.

Note:

There is no one right way to work, as you have probably surmised by now. How you get the job done is up to you; I am merely trying to provide alternative methods so you may discover what suits you best. I personally switch between views and shading modes quite often. F3 will toggle between Smooth and Wireframe views, and F4 toggles Edged Faces in Smooth mode. Perhaps the biggest piece of advice I can offer is to not constrain yourself to one view or one shading mode; spin around the scene using the Arc-rotate tool so you can see everything clearly. Switch between Smooth and Wireframe often as well. I cringe when I see students working in some oblique squished view, or on a postage stamp–sized viewport, with most of the screen going unused. Maximize your view, use your hotkeys to switch between views, and customize the heck out of your interface. Remember the old adage "When all you have is a hammer, every problem looks like a nail." The tool should be transparent to the design, not a major shaping force of it.

40. Map this wall in the same manner as the arch, using the *Brick running w/stretchers* material that came with the scene. Apply a UVW Map modifier to the wall, and check Use Real-World Mapping Coordinates in the Parameters.

41. Right-click and choose Gizmo from the quad menu. Rotate the Gizmo so that bricks flow around the outer wall, across the polygons at the windows, and onto the inside wall. Right-click and choose Top Level when you are done.

42. Repeat these steps to build the remaining walls.

BONUS EXERCISE: Finishing the building

Build the rest of the exterior and interior walls using the methods from this chapter. Vary the façade material by using the light tan bricks provided with the scene as accents. Additionally, draw the floors as splines, and then add UVW Map modifiers straight on them, without converting to an Editable Poly. This way they can be reshaped as needed.

SECTION D: CONCLUSION

Excessive geometry and undefined intersections are the bane of rendering engines; our models should be lean and elegant, no matter what the design. Splines allow precise formation of walls, floors, ceilings, and trim, letting us add polygons only where they need to be. Keep your models as spare and elegant as they can be. You will have more than enough opportunities to spend precious processing power on other things than walls, so model them well . . . and quickly.

CHAPTER 5

Developing More Library Objects and External References

SECTION A: BUILDING A RECESSED CAN LIGHT

Can lights, or recessed lighting in trade parlance, are interesting creatures in a rendering. The light they supposedly provide is actually from 3ds Max light sources placed in the scene. In most renderings, they flatten into ellipses of metal or plastic with perhaps a bright center, confined to the outer reaches of the camera frame by the need to focus on things at eye level. However, the light they provide is a showpiece and talking point in any design; one need only peruse the real estate section of any Sunday newspaper to find ads extolling recessed lighting as architectural salvation. The good news for the visualization professional is that can lights are easy to model and take advantage of one of the strengths of computer-aided design: the ability to clone objects exactly.

In this tutorial, we will build generic can lights suitable for most residential and commercial applications. In doing so, we'll set up the beginning of a light fixture library that can be externally referenced into a 3ds Max scene. By doing this, the model can be easily changed if or when specified light fixtures are chosen.

EXERCISE 1: Building a can light

---

1. We will first build a six-inch diameter can light. We'll use a technique based on splines combined with the Lathe modifier. Start 3ds Max or choose File > Reset from the top menu. Save this file as *recessed light library.max* in your Scenes folder or in the directory where you keep your building product libraries.

2. Switch to the Front view by pressing F. We'll build this light so that it is facing down from the ceiling, with its pivot point at ceiling height.

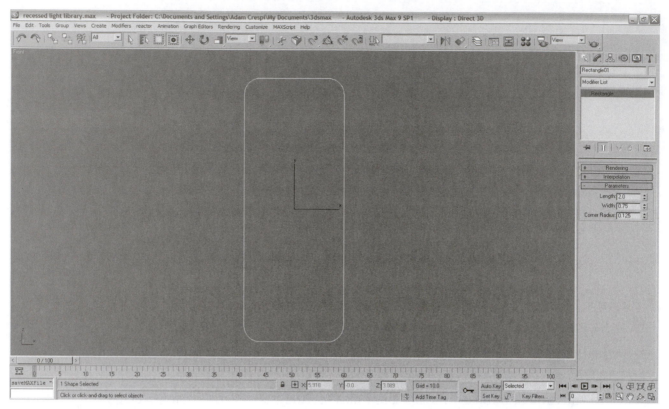

FIGURE 5.1

The starting

Rectangle.

3. Press Ctrl + RMB and choose Rectangle from the Modeling quad. Draw a small Rectangle in the view around 0,0, then click on the Modifier tab on the Command panel. Change the length of the Rectangle to 2.75 and the width to 0.75, with a corner radius of 0.125 (see Figure 5.1). This will form the trim ring and housing.

4. Right-click and choose Convert to Editable Spline from the Transform section of the quad menu.

5. In the Modifier panel for the spline, open the Interpolation rollout. Set the number of Steps to 0, so that the corners have flat chamfers instead of radii (see Figure 5.2). Can lights, due to their placement on the ceiling at the periphery of the view, do not need a huge amount of detail. As long as these fixtures have a few edges to catch the light, they'll look just fine. Additionally, depth of field blur may affect them more because they are at the edge of the frame.

6. Press 2 or right-click and choose Segment. Delete the segments shown selected in the picture, to produce a J shape (see Figure 5.3).

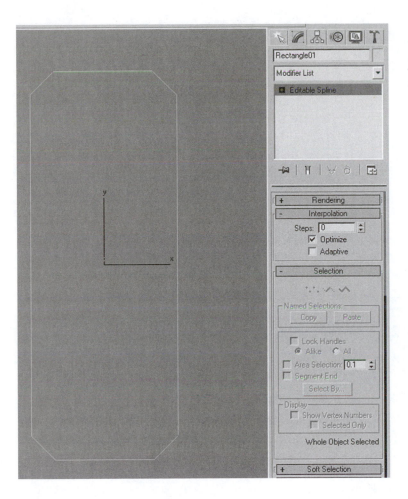

FIGURE 5.2
Setting the Interpolation for the shape.

FIGURE 5.3
The shape with segments deleted.

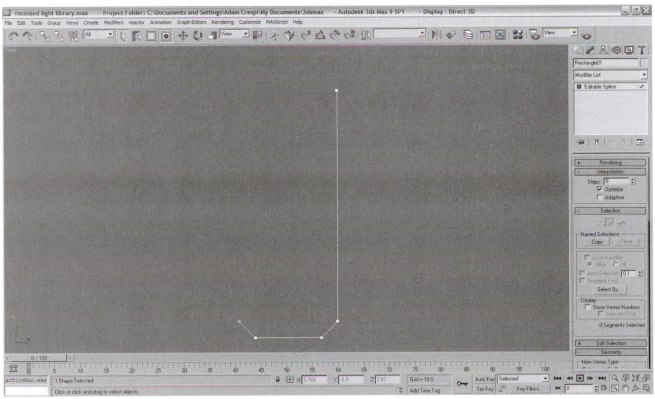

FIGURE 5.4

Setting the First Vertex for correct lathing.

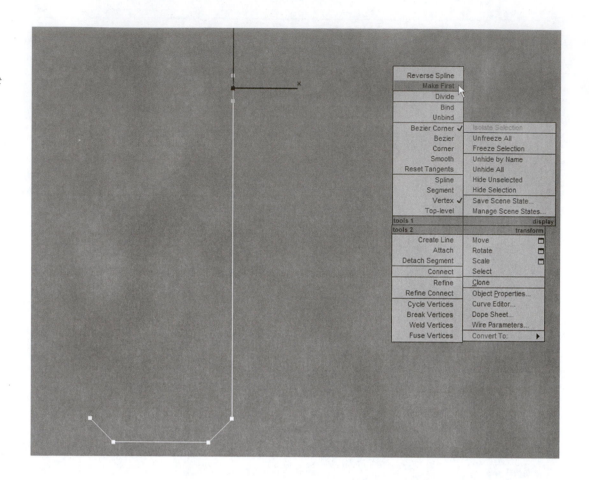

7.   Press 1 or right-click and choose Vertex. If the top vertex of the J does not have a box around it, continue with this step. If it does, go to step 8. Select the top vertex of the J, right-click, and choose Make First from the quad menu (see Figure 5.4). This will set the First Vertex of the shape to that vertex. (Note that in 3ds Max 9, First Vertices are shown in yellow, while others are shown in white.) We did this so that when we lathe this shape, it revolves around this point.

8.   On the Modifier panel, drop down the Modifier List and choose Lathe from the Object Space modifiers (see Figure 5.5).

9.   In the Lathe Parameters, press the Min button. This will set the Lathe axis to align with the long leg of the J.

10. Press 1 or right-click and choose Axis from the quad menu (see Figure 5.6). Because of the way we set this light up, changing this light fixture to be a 4″ or 6″ can will be easy.

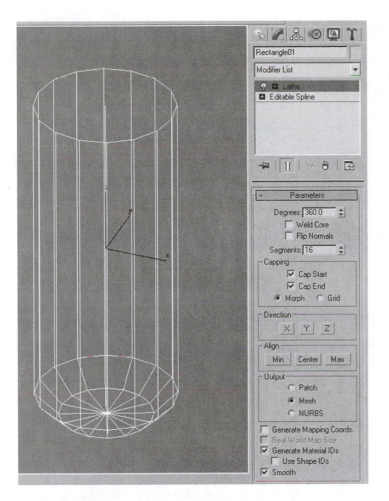

FIGURE 5.5

The Lathe modifier applied to the shape.

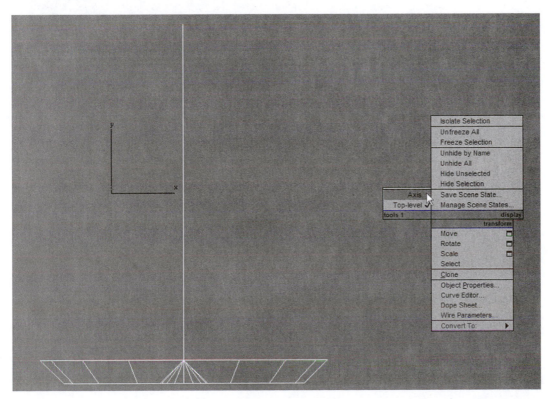

FIGURE 5.6

Selecting the Axis of the Lathe modifier.

Section A: Building a Recessed Can Light

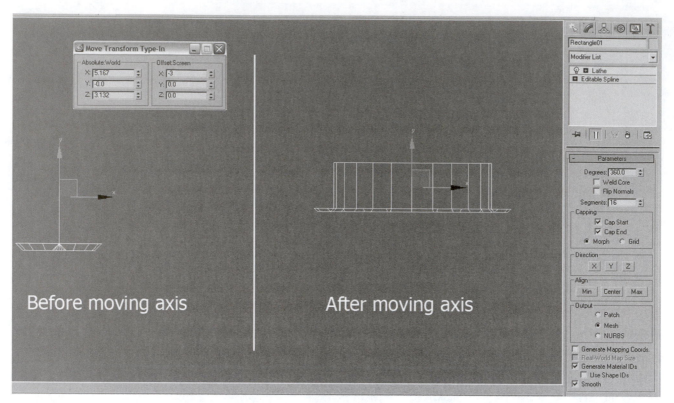

FIGURE 5.7

Moving the Lathe axis.

11. Press F12 or right-click and choose the dialog box next to Move on the quad menu to pull up the Transform Type In dialog. Enter −3 in the Offset X field (see Figure 5.7). This will open up the light to be 6″ across inside the trim ring.

12. Name this object Can Housing 6″-01. In the Lathe Parameters, change the number of segments to 24 (see Figure 5.8). This increases the number of segments around the housing to 24. Although can lights are at the edge of the frame, there is always a chance that one will be close to the camera. Additionally, can lights are usually made of a different material than the ceiling, and read as such. Hence, they need to look smooth in a rendering; by setting the segments to 24, the facets become small enough to be obscured by the anti-aliasing in the rendering and hence disappear.

13. Go to the Pivot tab on the Command panel, and click on the Pivot button if it is not already highlighted. Click the Affect Pivot Only button, and then click the Center to Object button (see Figure 5.9). This will center the pivot point on the housing.

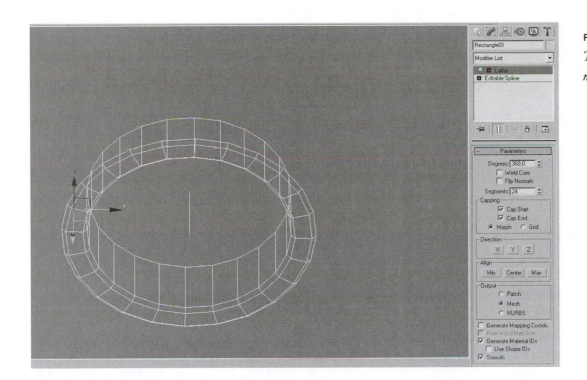

FIGURE 5.8
The can light with more segments.

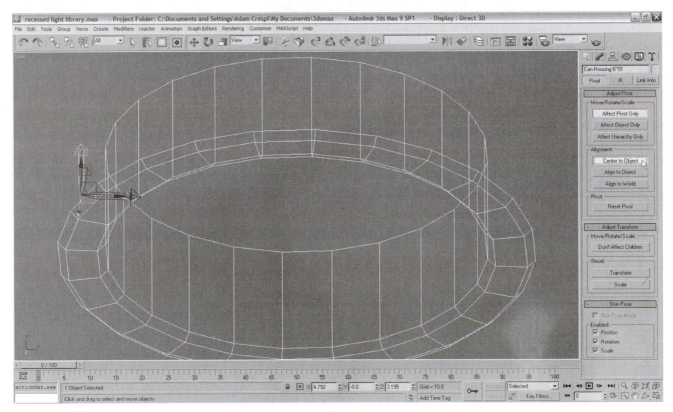

FIGURE 5.9
Moving the Pivot.

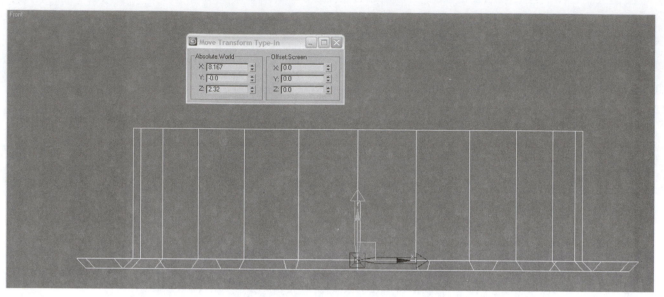

FIGURE 5.10

The pivot in the correct position at the top of the trim ring, shown in a Front view to highlight the pivot at the edge of the trim ring.

14. Press F12 to pull up the Transform Type In dialog if it is not up already. Enter −1.1875 in the Offset Y field (see Figure 5.10). This will place the pivot at the level of the ceiling, with the trim ring below it. (Where did that number come from? The original Rectangle was 2.75 in length. We removed the top segments, which took off 0.125, leaving a length of 2.625. Centering the pivot placed it 1.3125 in from either end. Subtracting 0.125, the radius of the corner, from that number, yields 1.1875, the distance from the centered pivot to the ceiling line.)

15. Click on the Affect Pivot Only button again to work on the whole object. Press B to change to the Bottom view. The housing is built, and it's on to the bulb.

16. On the Command panel, go to the Creation tab and choose Geosphere. Geospheres, as the name suggests, are geodesic in nature, with triangular divisions, an equator, and no latitude or longitude lines. While not the best choice for slicing into exact pie slices, they have a lower polygon count than regular spheres and are ideal for applications needing a whole sphere or hemisphere—like the visible part of this light bulb. Change the Creation Method to Diameter, and snap a Geosphere inside the housing (see Figure 5.11).

17. On the Modifier panel, in the Parameters for the Geosphere, check Hemisphere, and set the Geodesic Base Type to Tetra, with 4 segments. The different Geodesic Base Types triangulate the Geosphere in different ways; Tetra is the simplest. By setting the Segments to 4, every other segment of the housing lines up with a vertex of the Geosphere.

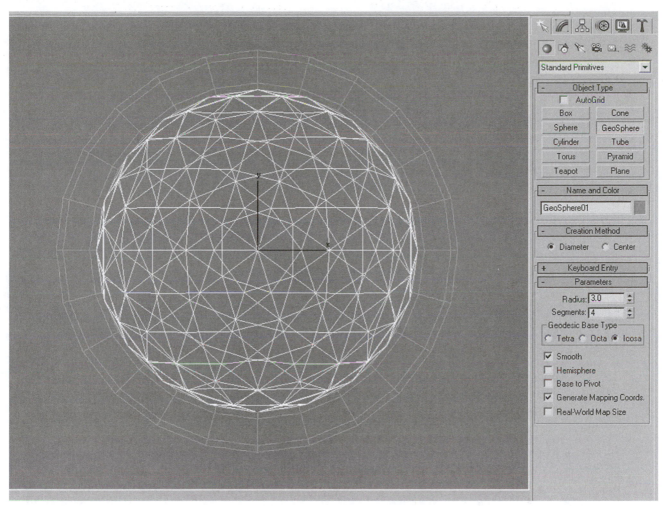

FIGURE 5.11
*Creating the
Geosphere for
the bulb.*

Note:

When dealing with radial objects such as light bulbs, it is generally good practice to keep the number of segments the same for aligned objects. However, as we will probably never look up into a can light, we can reduce the segments of the bulb. Making every other segment align is a way to minimize any odd triangular artifacts between the housing and the bulb should we see a can light at just the right angle. As long as there is a regular alignment of segments in something that we expect to be radially smooth, we'll make up the difference in our minds. If the artifacts are irregular or oddly spaced, the rendering is called into question because we do not expect that in a commonplace item such as a can light.

18. In a Front or Left view, snap the top of the bulb up to the top of the housing. Choose Non-Uniform Scale by flying out the Scale button on the Main Toolbar, and then scale the bulb down on the Y axis only by 60% or so (see Figure 5.12). This will flatten the bulb and recess it inside the housing. Name the Geosphere Bulb 6″-01.

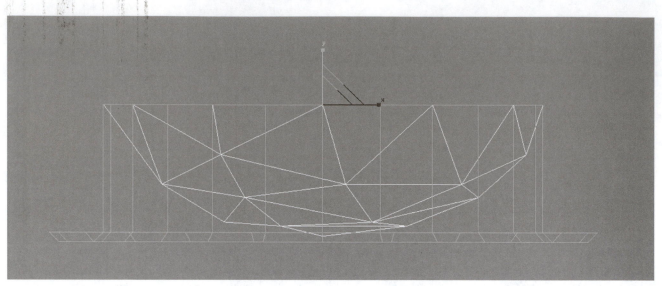

FIGURE 5.12

The bulb in proper position after scaling.

19. Press B to switch back to the Bottom view. Hold Ctrl + RMB, choose Rectangle from the Modeling quad, and snap a Rectangle from the top of the housing to the bottom. This Rectangle should have a length of 7.5 and a width of 0, rendering it invisible for the moment.

    Note:
    I'll often use this technique to center objects or align them quickly. By creating the Rectangle snapped perfectly onto the housing, when the parameters of the Rectangle are changed, it will be centered on the housing. The trick is to spot the parts of the objects that are tangent to or at the bounding box corners and snap objects to them when creating. Look for opportunities to minimize switching between tools; this will allow a more uninterrupted thought process.

20. Go to the Modifier panel and change the length and width of the Rectangle both to 36. This will form the section of ceiling around this can light, isolating this particular ceiling hole from interfering with other ceiling pieces (see Figure 5.13).

21. Still in the Bottom view, choose N-Gon on the Creation panel under the Shapes button. Change the Creation Method to Edge from the default of Center, and snap an N-Gon precisely onto the outermost points of the housing (see Figure 5.14).

22. Change the number of sides of the N-Gon to 12, so that every other point on the N-Gon lines up with a point on the housing. This will form the cutout in the ceiling for the can light.

23. Right-click and choose Convert to Editable Spline from the quad menu. The N-Gon is now no longer a parametric object.

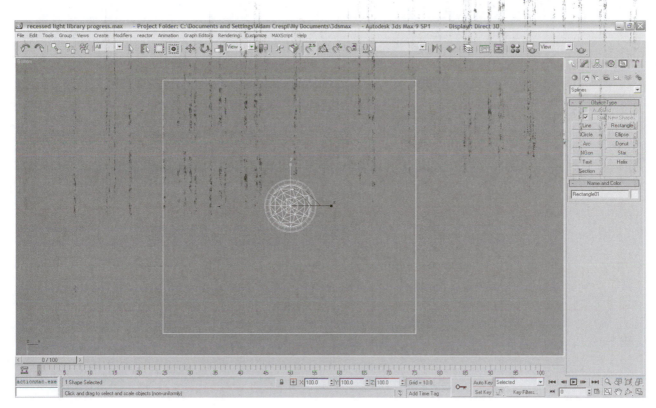

FIGURE 5.13

The Rectangle that will form the ceiling section.

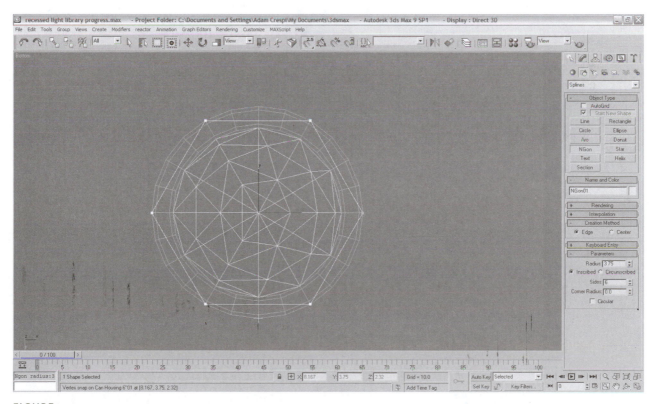

FIGURE 5.14

Creating an N-Gon around the housing to form the ceiling void.

24. Right-click again and choose Attach from the quad menu. Click on the Rectangle to attach it to the N-Gon. Right-click to stop attaching objects.

25. On the Modifier panel, go to the Interpolation rollout and set the number of Steps to 0. This will delete any divisions or Steps from the segments of the spline, making sure that everything is linear.

26. Right-click and choose Convert to Editable Poly from the quad menu. The ceiling section is almost complete.

27. Press 4 or right-click and choose Polygon from the quad menu. Select the polygon, scroll down on the Modifier panel to the Polygon Properties rollout, and clear any Smoothing Groups from the ceiling panel. Remember, make round things round, flat things flat, and don't muddy the difference. Press 6 or right-click and choose Top Level from the quad menu when you are done (see Figure 5.15).

28. Rename this object TEMP Ceiling Section01. As the name suggests, this is a temporary object, as once the ceiling is placed and assembled we will attach all of the sections together.

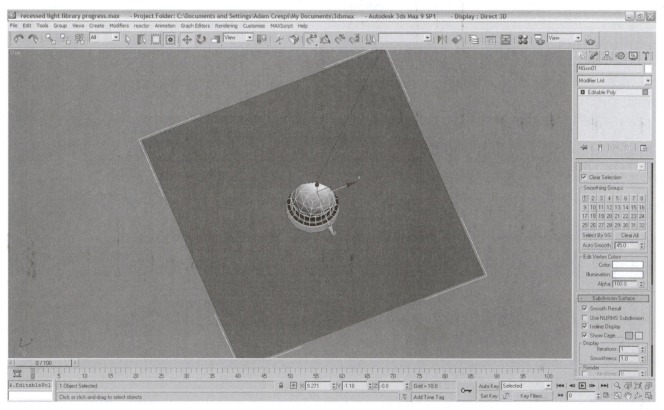

FIGURE 5.15
Clearing the Smoothing Groups from the ceiling panel.

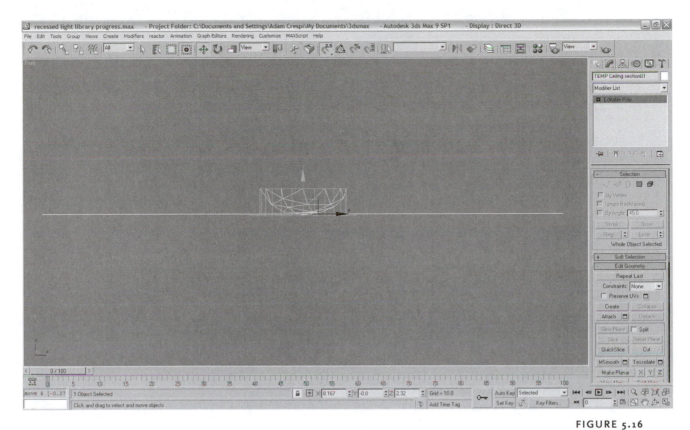

FIGURE 5.16
The ceiling panel in the correct position.

29. Press F to switch to the Front view. Constrain the movement to the Y axis and snap the ceiling panel to the top of the trim ring of the can light (see Figure 5.16).

30. Select the housing and the bulb objects, but not the ceiling panel, and choose Group > Group from the top menu. Name this group *Can light 6″-01*.

31. Select the ceiling polygon and the can light group and shift-clone both objects next to the original as copies.

32. Rename the second can light group *Can light 4″-01*. This will be a generic 4″ diameter can light.

33. Select the *Can light 4″-01* group if it is not selected already, and then choose Group > Open from the top menu (see Figure 5.17). Groups are very useful for organizing fixtures such as these, furniture, or any assemblage of parts that is considered a unified whole in practical use and reference. Grouping objects also cuts down on scene clutter, as it is very easy to suddenly have several thousand objects in a scene.

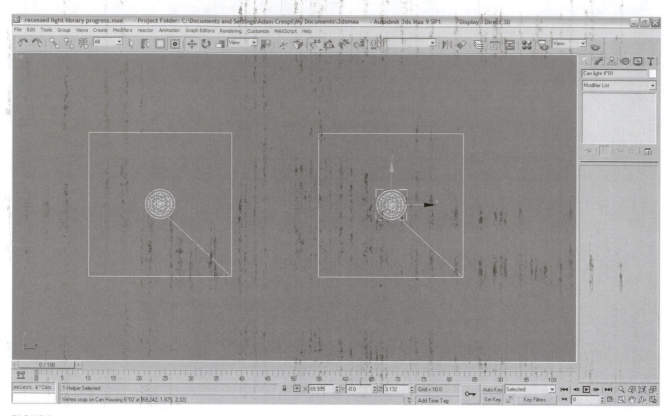

FIGURE 5.17

The cloned can light group, opened for editing.

34. Select the housing object, right-click and choose Axis from the quad menu. Press F12 for the Transform Type In dialog, and move the Lathe axis by 1″ in the Offset: World X window (see Figure 5.18). This will reduce the housing from a 6″ diameter to a 4″ diameter. Right-click and choose Top Level from the quad menu.

35. Select the bulb object, and change its diameter to 4″ as well. Align it with the housing as done previously (see Figure 5.19).

36. Select the ceiling polygon object, and choose Vertex from the quad menu. Select all of the vertices around the opening in the center.

37. Making sure the Transform Coordinates are set to the Selection Center, scale the vertices down on the X and Y axes by 73% (see Figure 5.20). This will reduce the size of the opening in the ceiling to fit the housing. Right-click and choose Top Level from the Quad menu when you are finished.

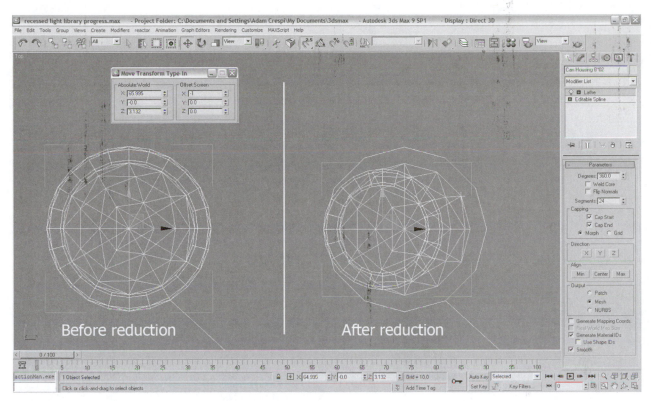

FIGURE 5.18

Reducing the diameter of the housing.

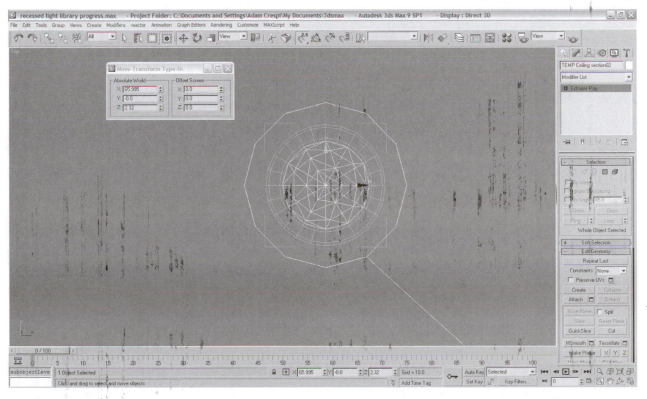

FIGURE 5.19

The bulb reduced in size and centered in the housing.

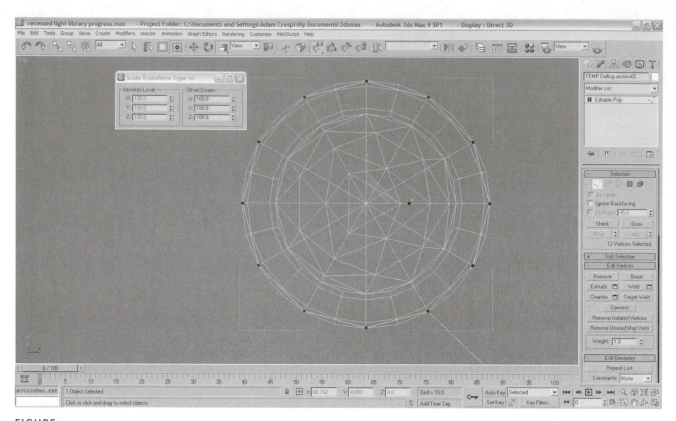

FIGURE 5.20

The opening in the ceiling panel scaled to fit the can housing.

SECTION B: EXTERNAL REFERENCING

EXERCISE 2:   Inserting and cloning can lights

The method we will use to insert and clone the can lights into the retail store is by externally referencing them into the scene. This way, the light fixture can be updated once in one file, and the changes will ripple through any file referencing that fixture. When we copy the can light around, we'll copy the ceiling polygon with it, and then bind all of the ceiling polygons into the scene at once.

1.   Open the *retail renovation.max* file in the Chapter 4 Assets folder, or the *retail renovation.max* file you worked on in Chapter 3.

2.   Choose File > XRef Objects from the top menu. When the XRef Objects dialog pops up, click on the Create XRef From File button, and browse to your building libraries folder. Select the *recessed light library.max* file (see Figure 5.21).

3.   Pick the can light groups and TEMP ceiling objects to import.

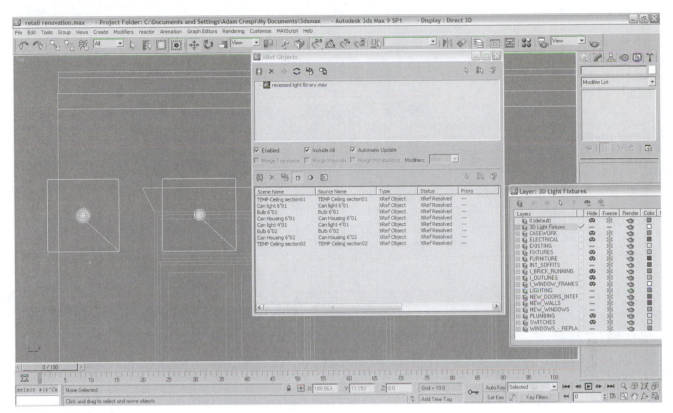

FIGURE 5.21

Inserting the XRef can light.

4. Select the can light group and ceiling polygon, and press the spacebar for the Selection Lock. Snap the center of the can light bulb to the center of each of the 6″ can light symbols on the plan, or use the crossbars of the CAD symbol to align the clones. Clone the can lights and ceiling panels as instances (see Figure 5.22). If the can light symbols are separate objects, you can use the Clone and Align tool in the Tools menu.

5. Repeat the XRef insertion and placement with the 4″ can light from the recessed lighting library.

6. When you have cloned all of the can lights and ceiling panels, select and hide all of the can lights, leaving the ceiling panels visible (see Figure 5.23).

7. Select one of the ceiling polygons, right-click, and choose Convert to Editable Poly from the Quad menu. Right-click again and select the dialog box next to Attach. In the Attach dialog, select all of the ceiling panels to attach, so that they all become one object.

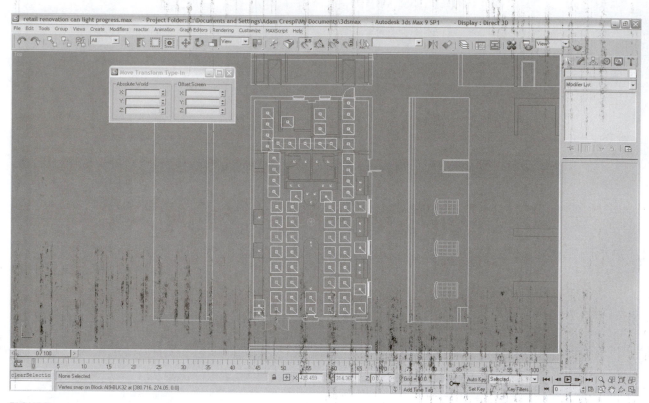

FIGURE 5.22

The can lights cloned in the store.

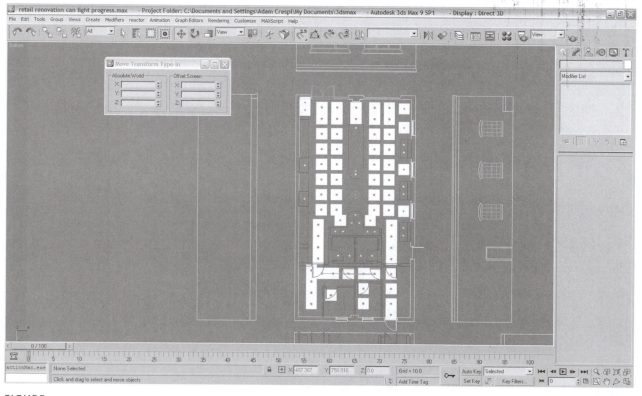

FIGURE 5.23

The ceiling panels in place.

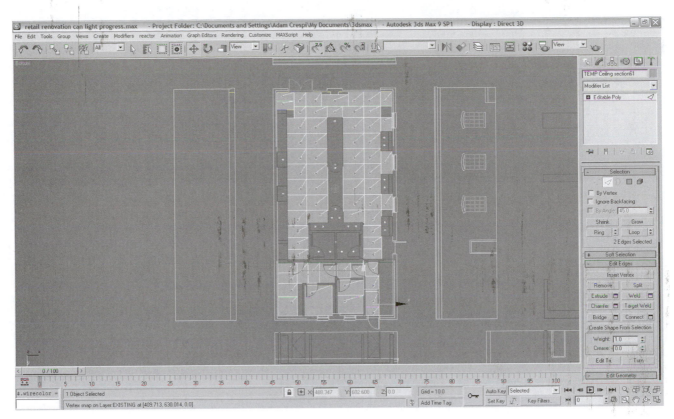

FIGURE 5.24

The panels attached and snapped to each other, as well as to adjacent walls.

8. Snap any adjacent panel edges to other panels or close walls to remove any gaps between panels or eliminate overlaps (see Figure 5.24).

9. In the Bottom view, press Ctrl + RMB and choose Rectangle from the Modeling quad. Snap Rectangles between the can lights' ceiling polygons and any of the wall or soffit drawing lines (see Figure 5.25). You should end up with a ceiling that is composed of an irregular pattern of rectangles punctuated by can light holes. The reason for doing this, rather than drawing a line around the ceiling perimeter and attaching N-gons to become can light holes, is that after a certain number of holes, the ceiling simply will not close. The triangles in the ceiling poly will become so long and thin that they do not light properly, producing all manner of odd artifacts in what should be a smooth ceiling. We have now isolated each hole in its own polygon and then filled in the gaps.

10. Go to the Layer Manager by clicking on the button on the Main Toolbar or choosing Tools > Layer Manager from the top menu. Select all of the TEMP ceiling polygons, right-click, within the Layer Manager, and choose Create New Layer (add selection).

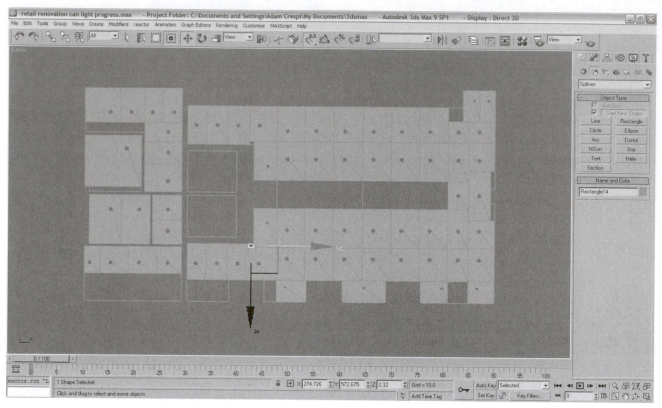

FIGURE 5.25

The additional Rectangles placed into the ceiling.

11. At the moment, the layers in the scene are only those that imported from AutoCAD. When the new layer is created, rename it Ceilings. Add the rectangles you created for the ceiling to this layer as well. Hide all of the other layers by clicking on the Show/Hide toggle (see Figure 5.26).

12. Select all of the ceiling parts, right-click, and choose Convert to Editable Poly from the quad menu.

13. Press F to switch to Front view, and check to see that all of the polygons are on the same plane, most likely 0,0. If they are not, move them up or down as needed to a consistent level. At this point, the ceiling is ready to attach into one object and weld together.

14. Select any one of the objects, right-click, and select the dialog box next to Attach on the quad menu. Highlight all of the other objects and choose Attach. Name this object Int Ceiling main retail (see Figure 5.27).

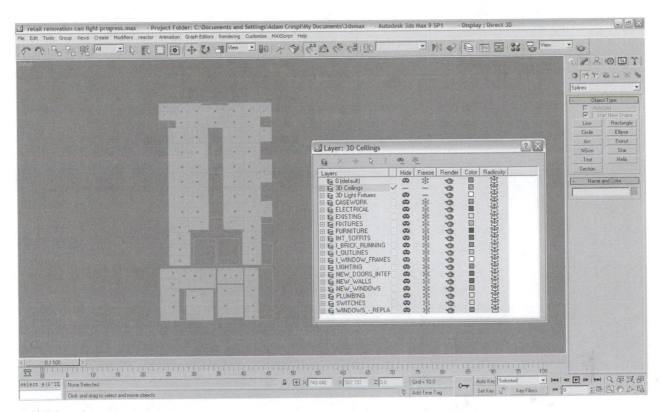

FIGURE 5.26

The new Ceilings layer.

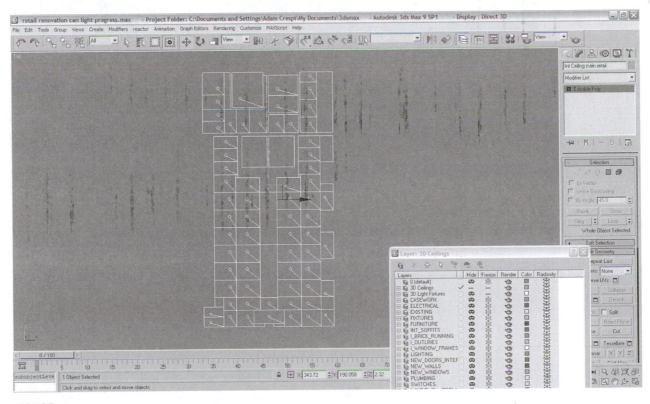

FIGURE 5.27

The ceiling pieces attached together and renamed.

FIGURE 5.28

Welding the ceiling
vertices.

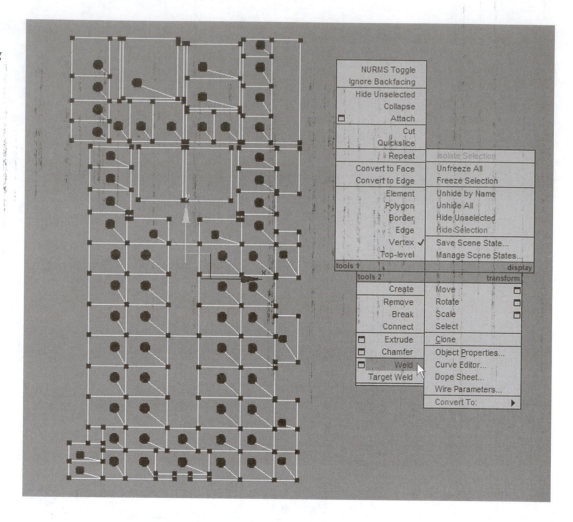

15. Press 1 or right-click and choose Vertex from the quad menu. Select all of the vertices, right-click, and choose Weld (see Figure 5.28). This will weld all of the polygons into one element.

16. Press 4 or right-click and choose Polygon from the quad menu. Select all of the polygons, and scroll down on the Modifier panel until you see the Polygon Properties rollout. Click Clear All in the Smoothing Groups section to clear any inadvertent smoothing of the ceiling that might cause a bubbly look. Right-click and choose Top Level when you are done (see Figure 5.29).

17. Unhide the can light groups and select everything in the view. On the Transform Type In dialog, move the ceiling and can lights up to 120 inches above the floor at 0'0". The ceiling is complete and ready for material application (see Figure 5.30).

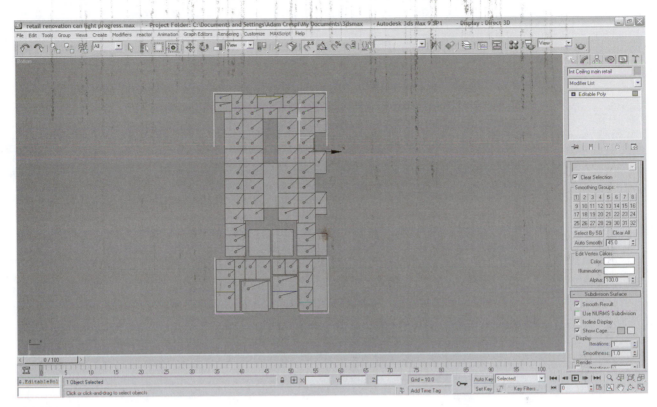

FIGURE 5.29

Clearing the Smoothing Groups from the ceiling.

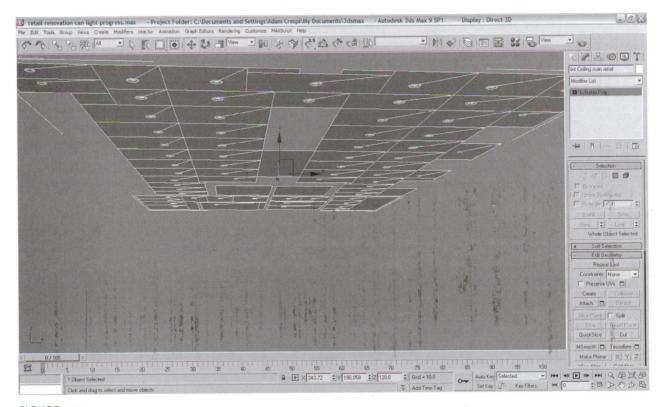

FIGURE 5.30

The completed ceiling shown with can lights turned on.

SECTION C: CONCLUSION

The unfortunate part of being a visualization professional is that there are no warehouses of library objects ready for you to use, unlike all of the things you'd specify for a real building. Thus, you are both the designer and fabricator, of, well, everything. With this in mind, and also realizing that a well-developed library is one of your greatest assets, take the time to do it right. Build the things you will use time and again, such as the can lights from this chapter, so that they are ready to use in a project with no alteration. However, do not make every library object perfect from any view, whether three inches or thirty feet. Rather, make them as perfect as they need to be for the typical conditions in which you will show them. Library objects should be terrific-looking and invisible, fading into the background as the commodities they are, and letting the viewer see the design first and foremost.

CHAPTER **6**   Common Building Materials

SECTION A: SIDING

This first exercise concerns the construction of horizontal lap siding commonly found in residential, office, and commercial applications. Siding is really about a series of horizontal shadow lines across a façade in either a uniform or evenly patterned spacing. When we look at siding, we expect to see the thin shadow at the bottom of each board and a saw-toothed edge in any shadow crossing the siding. We also expect to see the trim associated with siding, such as corner boards, water tables, window surrounds, and so forth. Where siding meets any of these elements, it produces a saw-toothed pattern along any perpendicular surface. In the following tutorial, we will construct a prototypical horizontal siding with a 6″ exposure; every horizontal shadow line will be 6″ above or below the next.

EXERCISE 1:   Simple lap siding

---

1. Open *Siding base.max* from the Assets folder for this chapter. The scene contains an example structure with several typical locations and conditions for the application of siding (see Figure 6.1).

2. First, we will apply siding to the front wall surrounding the ganged windows. The first step in doing this is to create a piece of siding that we can clone and cut. Press L to switch to the Left view.

3. Press Ctrl + RMB and choose Rectangle from the Modeling quad. Draw a Rectangle, and then switch to the Modifier panel and change the length to 6.0 and the width to 0.75, with a corner radius of 0 (see Figure 6.2).

4. Set the Steps in the Interpolation rollout to 2.

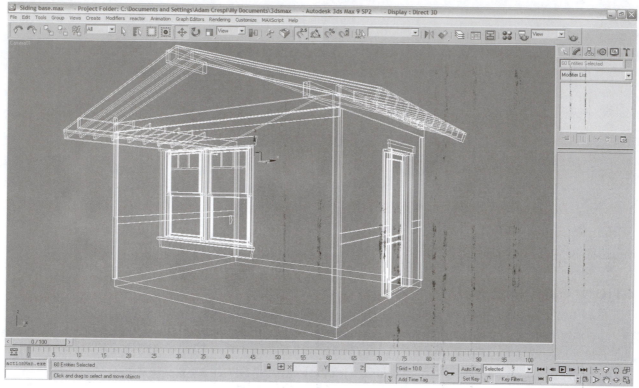

FIGURE 6.1

The example structure ready for siding application.

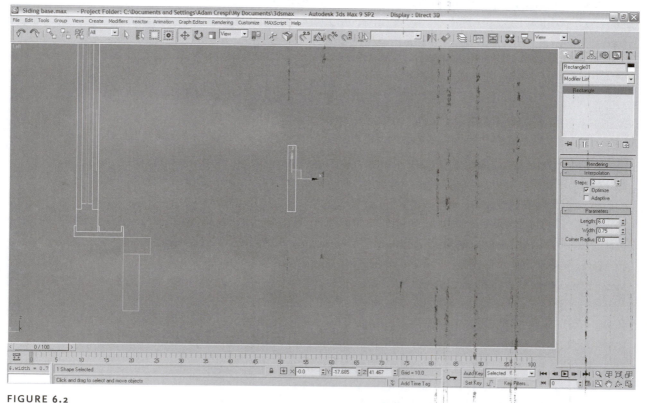

FIGURE 6.2

The Rectangle that will form the first siding plank.

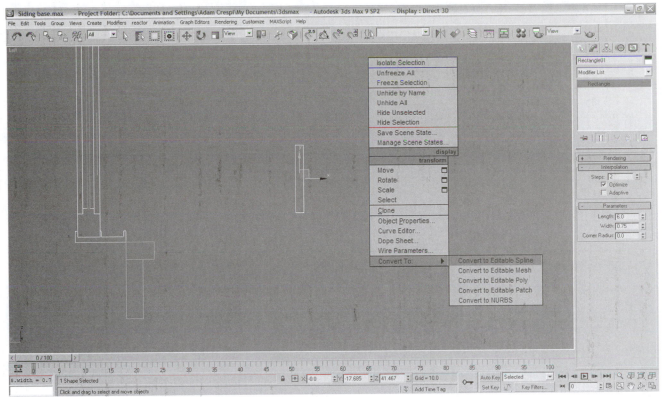

FIGURE 6.3

Converting to an
Editable Spline.

5. For this tutorial, we will make a simple lap siding ¾″ thick. (Most siding as sold is not quite this thick; however, in 3D sometimes it helps to beef up the thickness of items like siding to make sure that the shadow lines stay crisp and visible. Additionally, the extra shadow depth will prevent the shadow from becoming faint or blurred due to the anti-aliasing in the rendering process.) Right-click and choose Convert to Editable Spline from the quad menu (see Figure 6.3).

6. Press 2 or right-click and choose Segment from the quad menu or Modifier panel. Delete the left and top segments as shown to leave a backward L shape (see Figure 6.4).

7. Press 1 or right-click and choose Vertex from the quad menu or Modifier panel. Select all of the vertices, right-click, and choose Corner from the quad menu to change the interpolation type to Corner (see Figure 6.5). This will remove any influence the vertices have on their adjoining segments. (Rectangles by default are created with vertices set to Bezier Corner, with the handle length unequal between shorter and longer sides. Hence, if a fillet is applied, it will have an uneven radius. Changing the interpolation to Corner will cause any fillet to have an even radius from short to long side.)

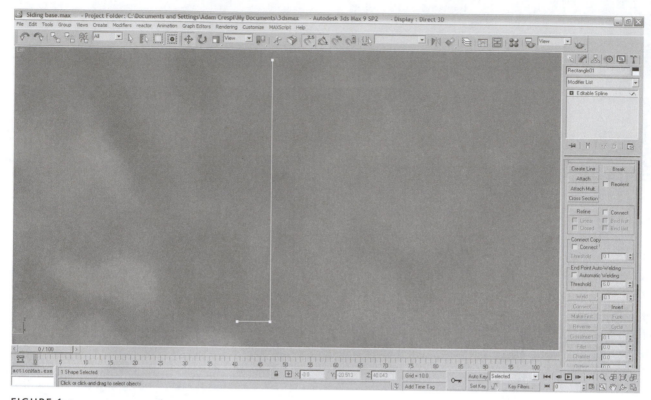

FIGURE 6.4

The spline with segments deleted.

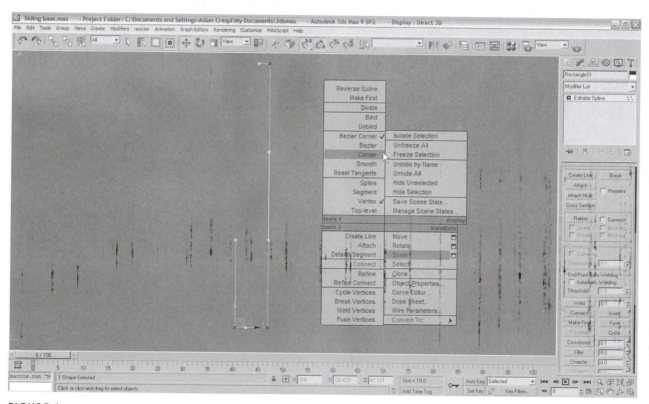

FIGURE 6.5

Changing the vertices to Corner prior to applying the Fillet.

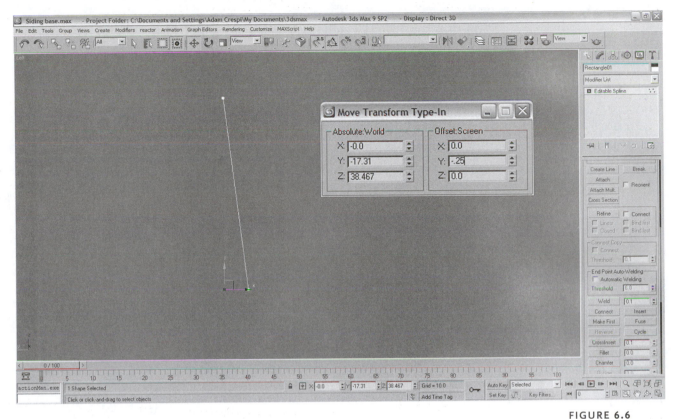

FIGURE 6.6

The vertices moved into the correct position.

8. Press F12 to pull up the Transform Type In dialog. Select the corner vertex and enter 0.2 in the Offset Y field.

9. Select the top vertex and move it only on the X axis to snap directly above the left vertex. The siding profile should resemble a check mark standing upright (see Figure 6.6).

10. Select the corner vertex, and scroll down on the Modifier panel until you see Fillet. Enter 0.25 in the field next to the button and press Tab or Enter to apply the value (see Figure 6.7). The siding profile is now complete, with a softly rounded bottom edge, a sloped face, and a minimum of geometry.

11. Pull down the Modifier List and choose Extrude from the Object-Space Modifiers.

12. Set the Amount to 120 and press Tab or Enter (see Figure 6.8). This is the proto-typical plank we will copy along the façade. Name this object Siding Plank01.

13. Press F to switch back to the Front view. By creating the siding in the Left view, it is facing toward the front, ready to install on the front of the building.

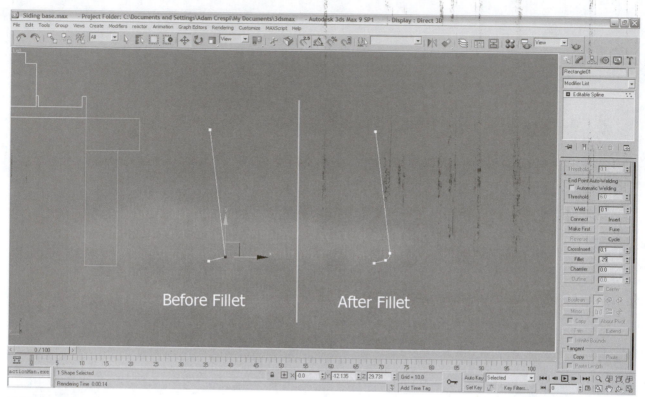

FIGURE 6.7

Applying the Fillet to the corner vertex.

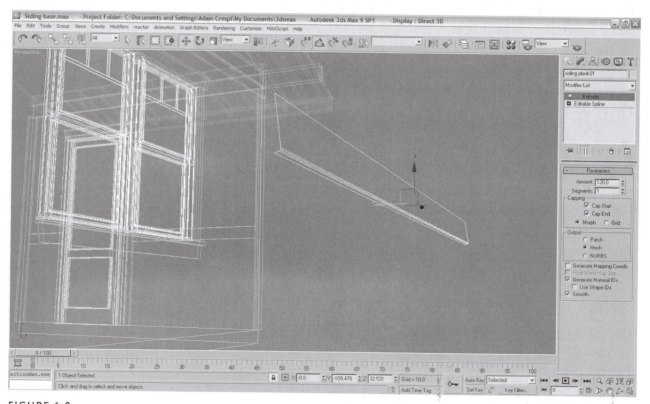

FIGURE 6.8

The prototypical siding plank extruded to 120 inches.

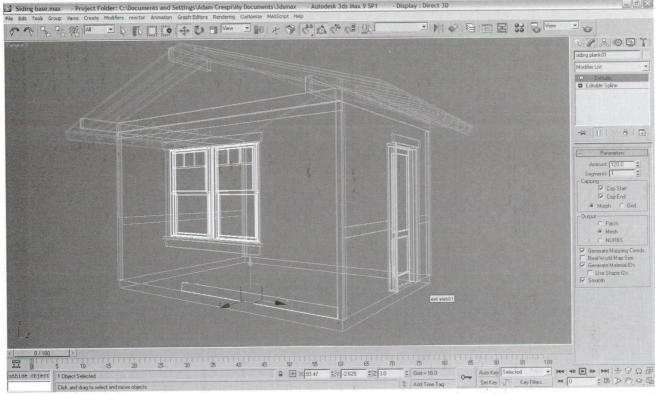

FIGURE 6.9

The siding plank in position on the building.

14. Move and snap the lower right corner of the siding plank to the lower right corner of the building, inside the corner board and snapped to the top of the slab. Notice that the pivot point of the siding is on the right edge, centered on the original spline. By creating the siding in the Left view and snapping the siding to the right corner board, we can adjust the Amount parameter of the Extrude modifier to lengthen or shorten it to fit (see Figure 6.9).

15. Set the Amount parameter to 187 so that the siding cleanly snaps between corner boards.

16. At this stage, depending on where in the Left view you created the siding, you may need to switch back to the Left view and snap the siding plank to the wall. It should align with the inner edge of the corner board, or the slab (see Figure 6.10).

17. In the Front view, make sure the siding is selected, press the spacebar for the Selection Lock, hold Shift, and move and snap the siding on top of itself to make the next plank (see Figure 6.11). Clone this plank as an instance when you move it, making four copies.

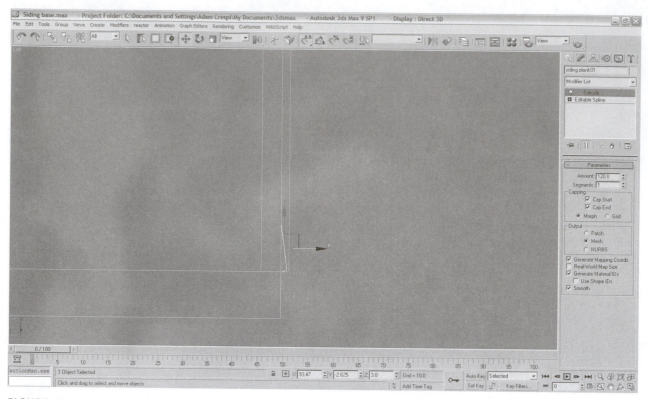

FIGURE 6.10

The siding plank in position on the building in the Left view.

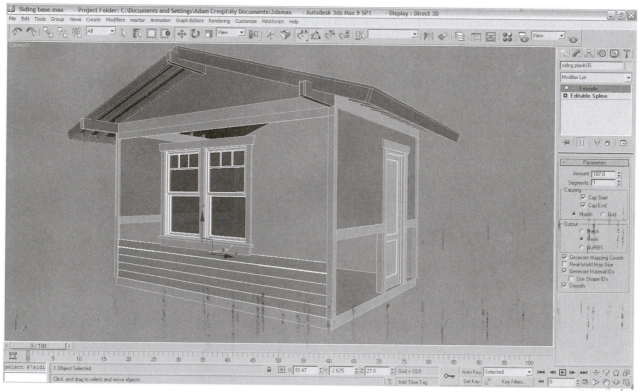

FIGURE 6.11

The plank cloned on the façade.

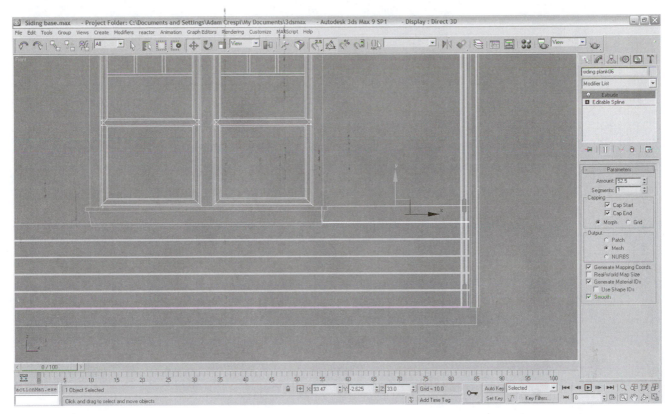

FIGURE 6.12

Shortening the plank next to the window sill trim.

18. The lower portion of the wall is sheathed and light-tight. Move and clone the siding up again, but this time clone it as a copy. This will be the first siding plank next to the windows.

19. Set the Amount of the Extrude modifier to 52.5, so the siding just intersects the window sill trim (see Figure 6.12).

20. Clone the plank up again as a copy, and set the amount to 52, so this plank neatly fits between the window trim (see Figure 6.13).

21. Clone this plank up again as an instance, making 9 copies. This will bring the siding to the bottom of the window header trim (see Figure 6.14).

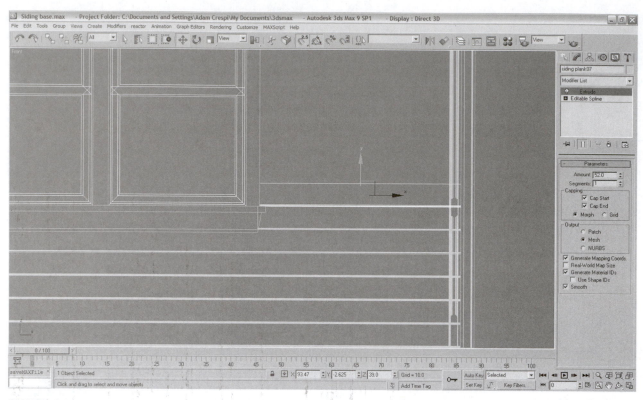

FIGURE 6.13

The plank cloned again and sized to fit snugly up to the window trim.

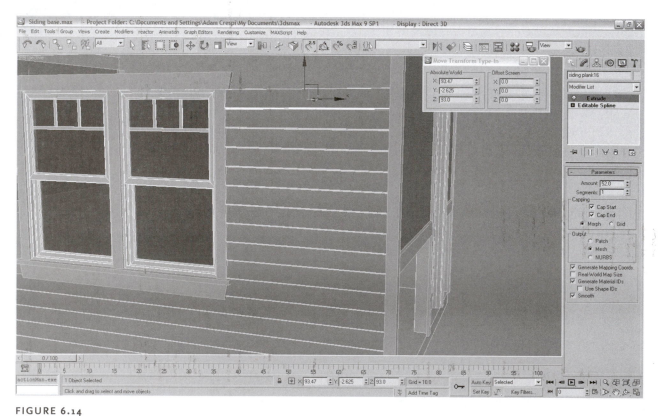

FIGURE 6.14

Planks cloned up the wall next to the window.

FIGURE 6.15
*The planks
mirrored across
the window.*

22. Select all of the siding next to the window, and click on the Mirror button on the Main Toolbar. Mirror the siding on the X axis as an instance, and snap it to the opposite corner board as needed (see Figure 6.15). (Occasionally, you may actually encounter an asymmetric façade needing siding. If this happens, mirror the siding as a copy. The new copies will still instance each other, but will not change the originals.)

23. Clone one of the top planks up again as a copy, and change the Amount back to 187 so the plank goes across the façade. Set the Segments of the Extrude modifier to 3 (see Figure 6.16). This will be the siding that is cut around the window trim.

24. Right-click and choose Convert to Editable Poly.

25. Press 4 or right-click and choose Polygon from the quad menu. Select all of the polygons of the middle section except for the siding face, and press Delete (see Figure 6.17).

FIGURE 6.16

The new plank across the top of the window.

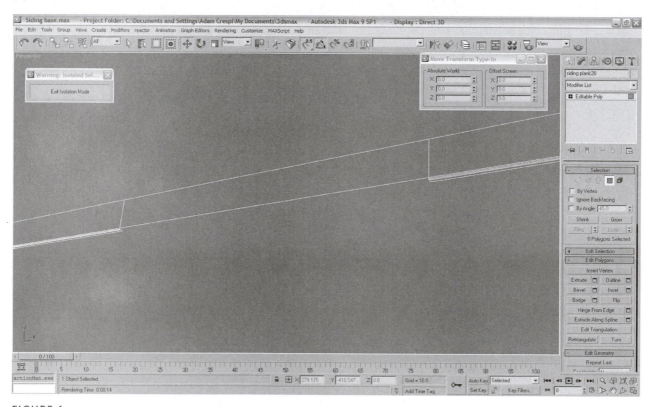

FIGURE 6.17

Trimming the plank at the top of the window.

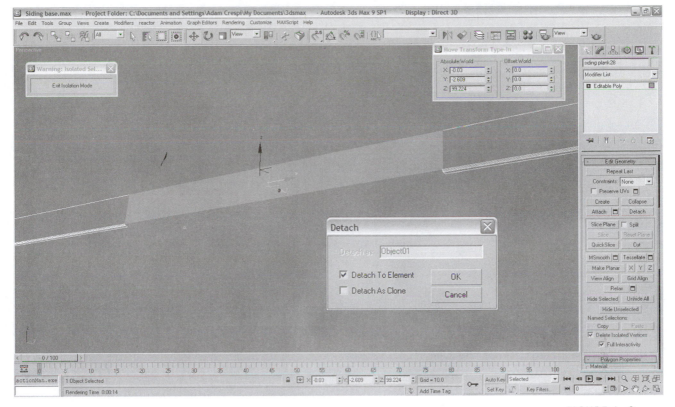

FIGURE 6.18

Detaching the middle section of the plank.

26. Select the remaining polygon of the middle section and press Detach on the Modifier panel. When the Detach dialog pops up, choose Detach as Element (see Figure 6.18).

27. Press 2 or right-click and choose Edge from the quad menu. Select the bottom edge of the middle polygon and snap it up to the top of the window trim.

28. Switch to the Left or Right view, and align the bottom edge with the sloping edge of the other siding panels (see Figure 6.19).

29. Select the middle sets of vertices of this plank and snap them to the lower left and right vertices of the window header trim (see Figure 6.20).

30. Select one of the full-length siding planks from the bottom and move, snap, and clone it to fill in the gap at the top. The siding for this section of wall is complete.

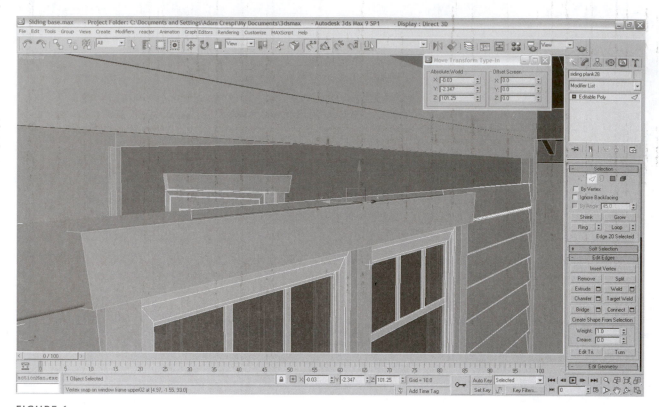

FIGURE 6.19

Aligning the bottom edge of the siding.

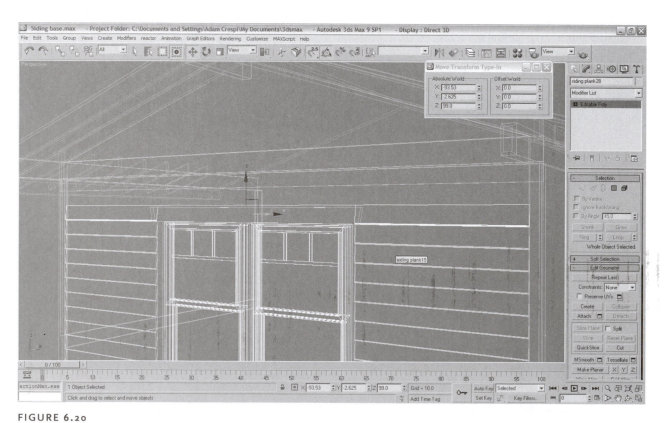

FIGURE 6.20

The finished trimmed plank above the window.

SECTION B: SHINGLES

Wood or cement-based shingles are a common exterior and occasionally interior cladding material in many regions, either on a whole structure or as an accent. Like clapboard siding, shingles create horizontal shadow lines along the elevation. Depending on the design of the elevations, they can either be woven at the corners, known as married in trade parlance, or capped by corner boards. For the visualization professional, what really matters is the shadow line along the bottom of each row of shingles, and the shading along the exposed face of each shingle.

In this tutorial, we will construct a portion of a residential elevation with shingles on both a wall section and a gable accent. We will look at shingles with evenly and unevenly trimmed ends and see how the light plays on each. For demonstrating the construction and rendering of shingles, we have provided a test model constructed and lit in the Assets folder for this chapter. However, the exercise can still be performed from scratch or on another model if you wish.

Note:

This tutorial assumes that you have Snap set to Vertex only, with Snaps Use Axis Constraints and Snaps To Frozen Objects both checked on the Snap Configuration menu. To access the Snap Configuration menu, right-click on the Snap button on the Main Toolbar. On the Snaps tab, make sure Vertex is checked and all of the other options are not checked. On the Options tab, make sure Snaps Use Axis Constraints and Snaps To Frozen Objects are both checked. Alternatively, press Shift + RMB to access the Snap quad and check the appropriate settings. Make sure that Snap is on by pressing S. Snaps are active when the button for that particular snap is depressed on the Main Toolbar.

EXERCISE 2:   Creating and applying shingles

---

1.   Open *Shingle base.max* from the Chapter 6 Assets folder. The structure is based on typical residential production housing design, with a mix of siding and shingles in a Craftsman-style elevation (see Figure 6.21). We will make shingles for three main areas: the wall surrounding the windows, the gable accent, and the front door surround. These elements will give us the opportunity to explore applying shingles in typical places.

2.   The first step is to create a backing polygon for the shingles for each portion of the elevation they will be applied to. Press F to switch to Front view, and zoom in on the triangular section of wall below the roof gable (see Figure 6.22).

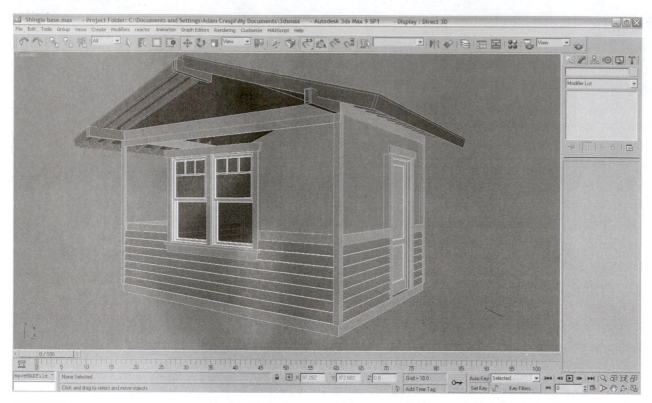

FIGURE 6.21

The base model ready for shingle application.

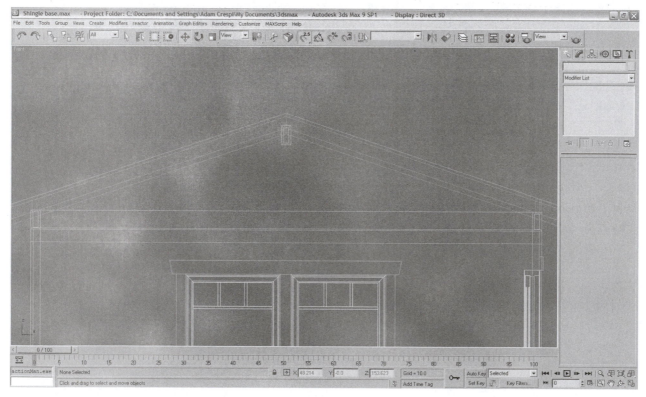

FIGURE 6.22

Creating the backing polygon for the shingles.

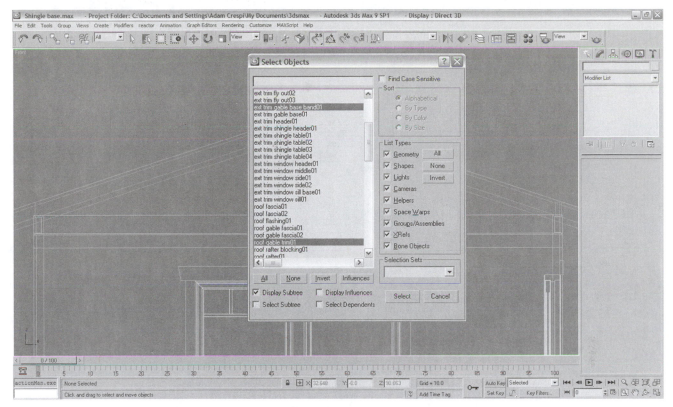

FIGURE 6.23

Selecting objects by name.

3. As you can see, there are several overlapping pieces of wood at the gable. Press H to Select Objects by Name, and then click on the objects ext trim gable base band01 and roof gable trim01. Press the Select button to close the dialog (see Figure 6.23).

4. Right-click and choose Hide Unselected from the quad menu. This will hide all of the other objects, leaving a much clearer view of what we need to draw. Alternatively, you can right-click and choose Isolate Selection from the quad menu to isolate just those pieces (see Figure 6.24).

5. Press Ctrl + RMB and choose Line from the Modeling quad. Snap a line inside the two trim boards, returning to the first vertex. When the Close Spline dialog appears, choose Yes to close the spline (see Figure 6.25). This will form the backing object for the shingles we will be making. As we are going to build each shingle, there is a chance that small gaps will appear between them. This backing object will seal the exterior against light leaks and shadow artifacts.

6. With the line selected, right-click and choose Convert to Editable Poly from the quad menu. Name this object shingle backing gable01.

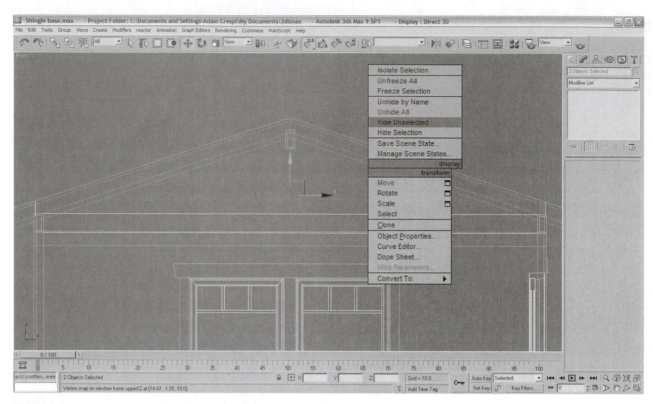

FIGURE 6.24

Hiding everything else or isolating objects.

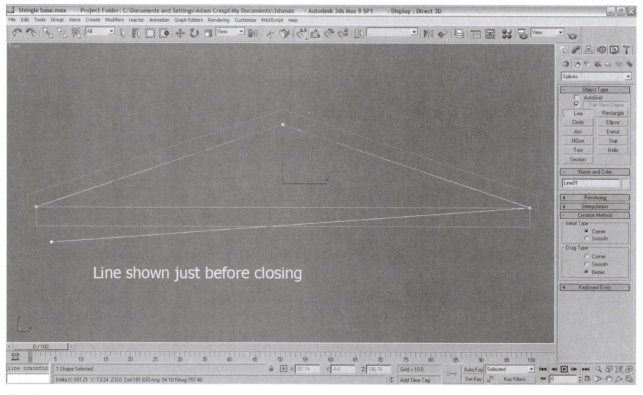

Line shown just before closing

FIGURE 6.25

Drawing the backing polygon.

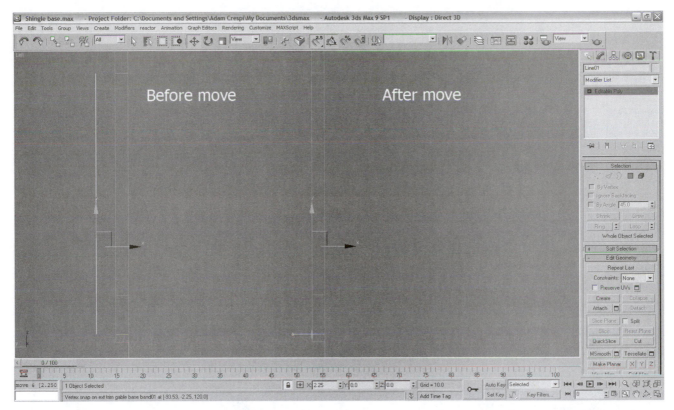

FIGURE 6.26
Positioning the
backing polygon.

7. Press L for Left view and move the shingle backing object to the left side of the trim boards. Make sure to snap the vertices together when doing this to avoid light leaks (see Figure 6.26).

8. Following steps 3 through 7, create another shingle backing object between ext trim shingle table01 and ext trim shingle header01 on the left side of the structure.

9. Press F to switch back to Front view. Press Ctrl + RMB and choose Box from the Modeling quad. Create a box that has a length of 8, a width of 6, and a height of 0.5. Additionally, check Real-World Map Size on the Modifier panel (see Figure 6.27). (Yes, most shingles are ¼″ thick or so; in 3D, though, sometimes a little extra thickness sharpens the shadow lines and makes it fade less due to anti-aliasing.) Name this box Shingle01. This will be the first shingle, which we will copy and change to make various sizes.

10. Press W for Move or right-click and choose Move from the quad menu. Hold Shift, and drag the shingle to the right on the X axis to clone it as a copy, with the number of copies set to 8 (see Figure 6.28). These nine shingles will form the modules for the field of shingles, allowing us to assemble an area of shingles that can be copied across a wall. The following table represents the sizes of the shingles we need to make for our modules.

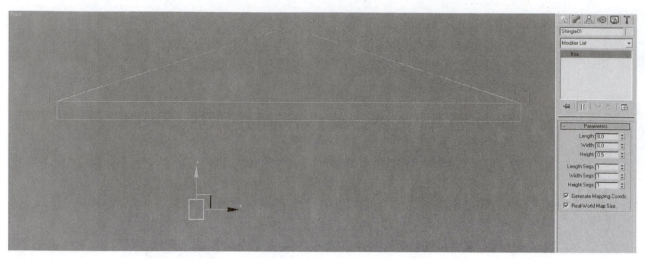

FIGURE 6.27

The first shingle.

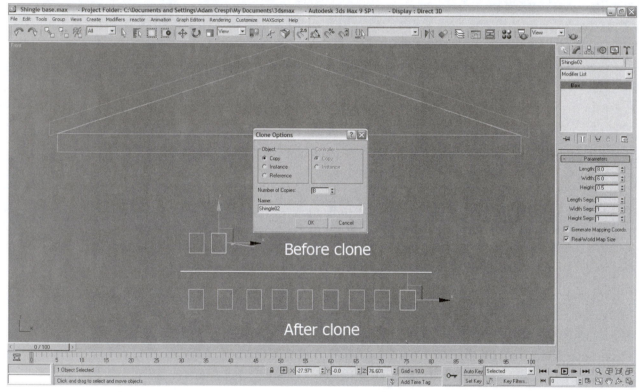

FIGURE 6.28

The cloned shingles ready for resizing.

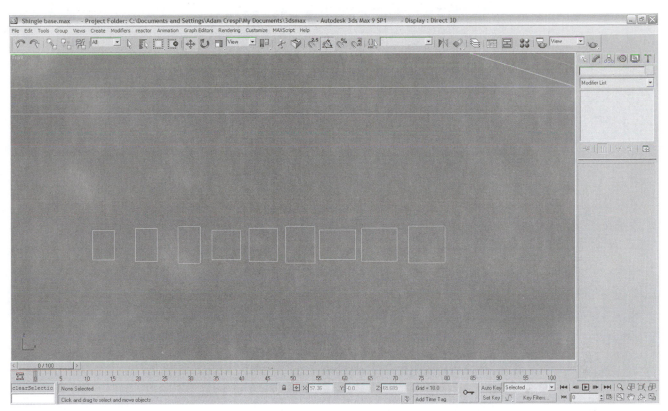

FIGURE 6.29

The shingles set to the various sizes.

Calculating Shingle Sizes: Length (across) × Width (down)

	8	9	10
6	6 × 8	6 × 9	6 × 10
8	8 × 8	8 × 9	8 × 10
10	10 × 8	10 × 9	10 × 10

11. Go to the Parameters for each shingle and change its length and width to correspond to one of the sizes listed. You should have nine different sizes when you finish (see Figure 6.29).

12. Still in the Front view, draw a Plane with a length of 48 and a width of 72, and 6 length segments (see Figure 6.30). This will be our module of shingles to copy along the wall. For this model, the shingles will have an 8″ exposure, with a staggered bottom edge on each course. Freeze this Plane once you create it.

13. Move and snap the first shingle to the top left corner of the Plane. Snap the others next to it, making sure that each shingle is longer or shorter than the one next to it.

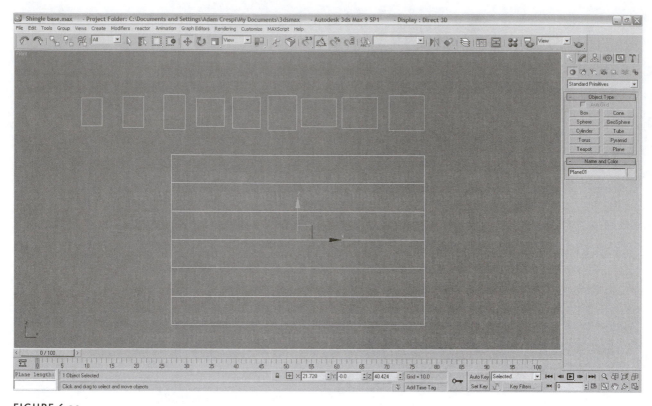

FIGURE 6.30

Creating a Plane to use for measuring a panel of shingles.

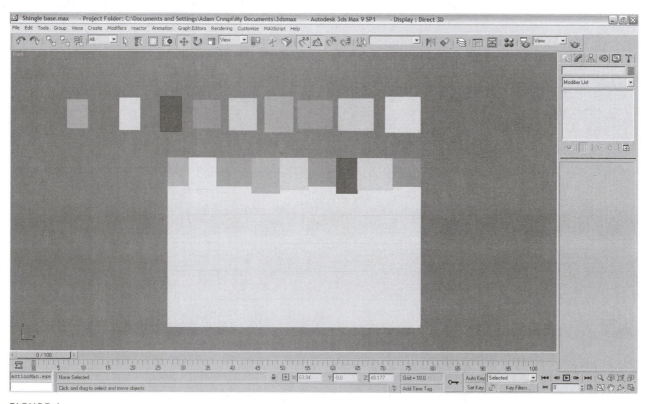

FIGURE 6.31

The first shingle course.

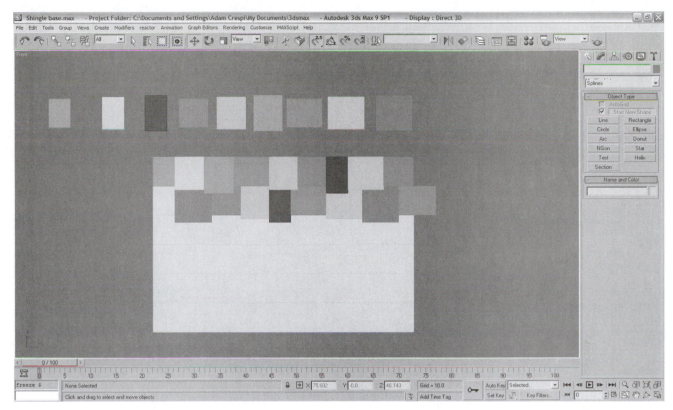

FIGURE 6.32
*Constructing the
second shingle
course, making
sure to offset the
starting shingle.*

Note:

*When constructing a base module that should look random, such as this area of shingles,
I often color each flavor of object differently. As an example, all of the 6″ wide shingles
might be orange, all of the 8″ wide shingles yellow, and the 10″ wide shingles green. That
way I can look at the overall arrangement of colors rather than the staggered edges for
randomness.*

14. Once the first course is complete (you may need to clone a few shingles to finish;
    be sure to clone them as instances), select one of the 10″ wide shingles and move
    and snap its top left corner to the second course line on the Plane (see Figure 6.31).

15. Press F12 for the Transform Type In dialog, and move that shingle by −6 in the
    Offset X field (see Figure 6.32). This will create an offset second course, so that there
    is less chance of seeing a repeat in the pattern due to a consistent vertical joint.

16. Clone the shingles from the first course down to the second course one at a time
    as instances, randomizing the placement of long and short, narrow and wide shin-
    gles. Make sure that there is a gap at the end that is 4″ wide to accommodate the
    overhanging shingle the course started with.

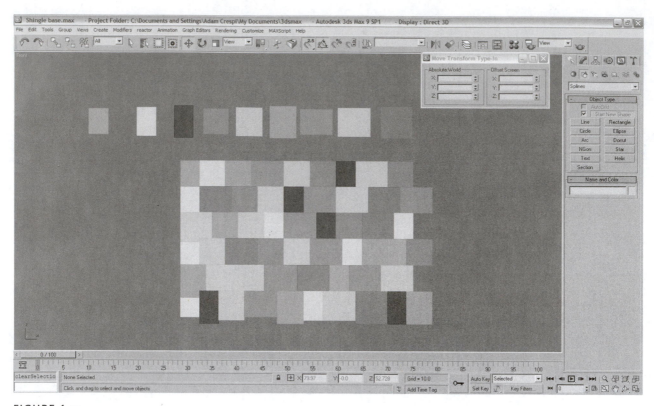

FIGURE 6.33

The remaining shingle courses in place.

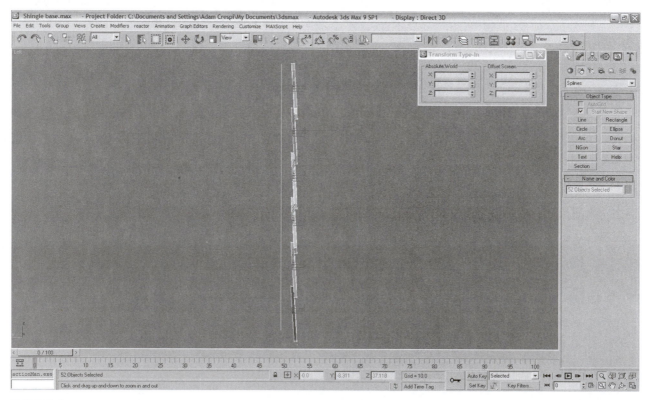

FIGURE 6.34

Rotating the shingles once they are placed so that each course laps the one below.

17. Repeat steps 14 through 16 to clone shingles for the remaining courses. Offset the fourth and sixth course like the second; leave the third and fifth courses aligned with the Plane (see Figure 6.33). Note that overlaps are not visible in shaded view.

18. When the courses are all complete, select all of the shingles of the top course, and press L for Left view. Right-click and choose Rotate from the quad menu. In the Transform Type In, enter 3.5 in the Offset Z window (see Figure 6.34).

19. Snap the top left corner of the first shingle course to the Plane.

20. Repeat the rotation and move described in steps 18 and 19 with each course of shingles.

21. Unfreeze the Plane by right-clicking and choosing Unfreeze All from the quad menu. Select and delete this Plane object.

22. At this point, we have a repeatable module of shingles that can be copied along a façade and will nicely mimic most staggered edge shingles, either fiber cement or actual wood. However, they are lacking some crucial details, such as the vertical space between the shingles, as well as a wood grain texture and some sort of color. Press L to return to the Left view, and select all of the shingles in the module.

23. Rotate the selected module by 90 degrees so it faces to the left.

24. Hold Shift and snap the bottom left corner of the bottom left corner shingle to the bottom left corner of the shingle backing02 panel on the left side of the building. Make sure that you clone the shingles module as an instance, and keep the original module off to the side. When these shingles are cloned and placed, make sure that the module rests on the trim perfectly at the bottom of one of the 8″ tall shingles, with any 9″ or 10″ shingles overhanging the top of the trim. Shingles such as these are installed from the bottom up (see Figure 6.35).

    Note:
    When creating a modular installation such as this, I usually keep the original module separate and clone it as needed on the structure. This way, I can build up my building products library as I go, ready for the next project.

25. Clone the module across and up the wall, up to the header trim and over to the corner board (see Figure 6.36). Overlap the trim for now—we'll trim the shingles in the next steps.

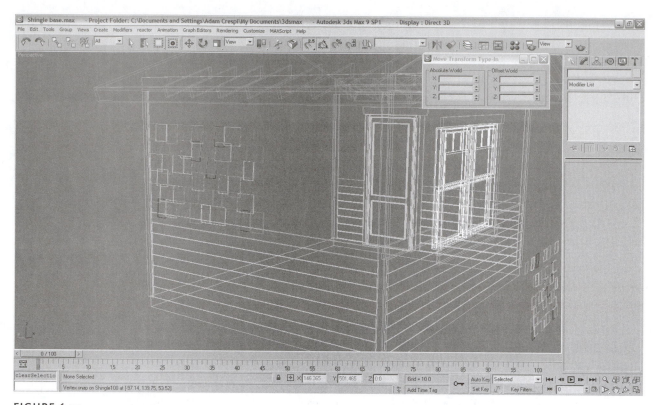

FIGURE 6.35

The shingle module placed on the wall.

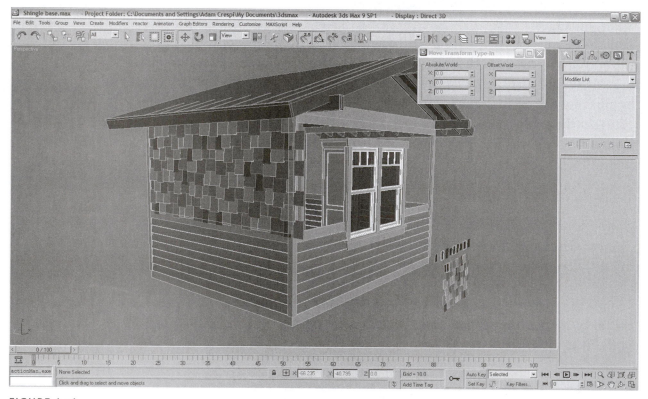

FIGURE 6.36

The module cloned along the wall.

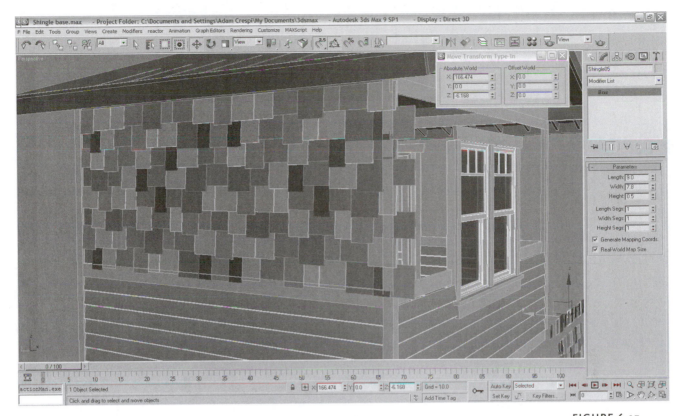

FIGURE 6.37

Reducing the size of each shingle to define the vertical joints.

26. Select one instance of each size of shingle and change the width to be 0.2 less than it is (see Figure 6.37). For example, shingles that are 10 inches wide should now be 9.8, those that are 8 should be 7.8, and so on. This will add the vertical shadow line between each shingle so that they read as an assembly versus one monolithic piece. (Why not just start at this size? Ease of math, that's why. It is much easier to copy and create a module based on even measurements such as inches than to worry about 0.2″ spaces on each side.)

27. Select one of the shingles that overlaps the corner board, and click on the Make Unique button on the Modifier panel. Change the width of the shingle to meet the corner board as needed (see Figure 6.38). Repeat this step with any other shingles that overlap the trim.

28. This section of shingled wall is now complete and ready for material application. Select the original shingle module and go to File > Save Selected, and save the shingles as *Shingle library.max* or whatever you wish to call your shingle library (see Figure 6.39). (Alternatively, if you already have a library file going, save the shingles as a temporary file and then merge them into the library file.)

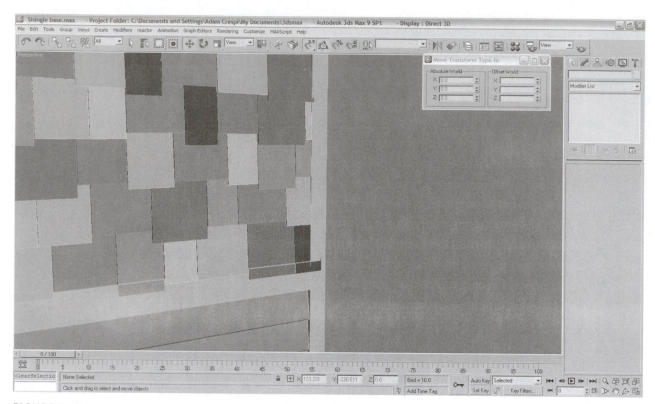

FIGURE 6.38

Trimming the shingles at the corner board.

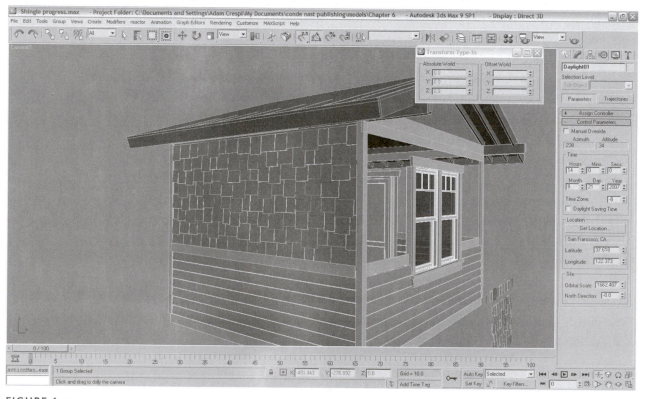

FIGURE 6.39

The completed section of shingled wall.

CHAPTER 6 : COMMON BUILDING MATERIALS

SECTION C: CONCLUSION

The shingles at this point are ready for material application and rendering. Depending on how close the camera will be to the shingles, you may want to apply a simple solid color to them or a material with a diffuse and bump map. How you finish them also depends on whether the shingles are real wood or fiber cement, textured or smooth, and so forth. By modeling them as actual geometry, the shingles will light and render properly, with all of the little shadows and detail that we expect to see. If the camera is more than about eight feet away, most of the surface texture will blend together anyhow; the richness of the geometry allows a simple material to shine.

CHAPTER 7 Materials in Mental Ray

SECTION A: CREATING MATERIALS IN 3DS MAX

A material, as we use the term in 3ds Max, is the method of shading, texture, and other properties assigned to geometry in a scene. As objects do not have a default material assigned, we need to generate and apply materials so that they render correctly. Creating materials in 3ds Max, or any 3D program for that matter, is really about pronouncing the characteristics of the material as discrete parts. These parts are then combined into a whole material, which is then assigned to an object or objects in the scene. Although most programs ship with some decent templates that will generate many common materials, in my mind they are just that, decent but by no means exceptional. Also, some materials that come with programs bear little resemblance to anything found in the real world, at least to lay eyes. We do not, for example, walk into a room and remark on the lovely blue in an Oren-Nayar Blinn shader with moderate diffuse roughness painted on the walls.

Thus, we are faced with the potentially staggering problem of creating a material library from scratch. This is not as much of a crisis as it may seem on the surface, but rather an opportunity. Think of library creation as an extended tutorial series. By creating a personal or proprietary library of materials, you will be able to offer your clients a look that no other artist can offer, and in the process, finely hone your material creation skills. Many of my clients become repeat customers for exactly this reason: they know that my library is something that no one else has and that I will custom-create materials and texture maps for them. The other comfort to be taken in the face of creating a material library from scratch is that it does not need to be created all at once.

As this book is written assuming that you will be using the mental ray rendering engine, most of this chapter will be dedicated to making materials look exceptional using it. The ideas and lessons can be applied to any other rendering engine, such as Brazil or V-Ray as needed; most things that we will do will have equivalent processes and names in those engines.

EXERCISE 1:   Basic paint colors

This tutorial explores the new Arch & Design material that debuted in 3ds Max 9. This new material is designed expressly for creating realistic architectural materials for use with mental ray. It includes many templates for establishing a base version of a material, such as a matte or pearl finish, or masonry with a very soft reflection. The shaders are also good for non-architectural surfaces, as they can be set to react in a very physically true manner. We will use the Arch & Design material to create a variety of solid paint colors for use in renderings and establish a naming convention and library system.

1.   Start 3ds Max or choose File > Reset from the top menu to begin with a clean scene.

2.   Press F10 or choose Rendering > Render from the top menu to pull up the Render Scene dialog. Scroll down to the bottom of the Common tab, and open the Assign Renderer rollout. Choose mental ray for the production renderer; the Material Editor is locked to the production renderer by default (see Figure 7.1).

FIGURE 7.1

Changing the production renderer to mental ray.

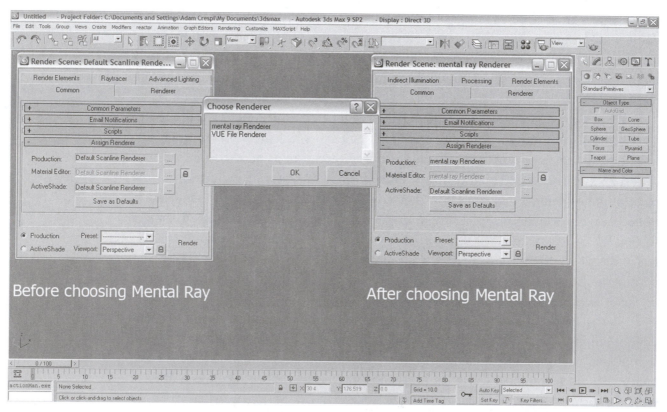

Note:

Most of the time, the Production Renderer and Material Editor use the same rendering engine and hence can be left locked. Occasionally, a plug-in rendering engine will use a different renderer for the Material Editor, such as Brazil, which uses the Scanline Renderer. In general, unless expressly instructed to do otherwise, keep the Production Renderer and the Material Editor locked so that the sample spheres in the Material Editor share the properties and material types available to the rendering engine.

3. Press M or click on the Material Editor button on the Main Toolbar to bring up the Material Editor.

4. Six, fifteen, or twenty-four sample spheres may be displayed at the top of the Material Editor. (To change the number of spheres shown, right-click on any sample sphere and choose 2 × 3, 3 × 5, or 6 × 4 from the pop-up dialog.) If the top left sample sphere is not highlighted with a white border, click on it to make it active. Active materials are shown highlighted with a white border, while materials assigned to objects in the scene have white triangles in their corners.

5. When creating materials, first figure out the type of material to use, and then decide on the shader. Different materials have different capabilities, such as Standard, which is a single-layer material, Shellac, which has a base and gloss coat, and Blend, which blends two materials according to a percentage or a mask; the 3ds Max Help has an excellent glossary of all types. With the mental ray renderer enabled, additional materials are available, such as mental ray, DGS, SSS Fast Skin, Glass, and the new Arch & Design. For this tutorial, we are going to jump to the Arch & Design material, so click on the button in the Material Editor labeled Standard. A Material/Map Browser will pop up allowing you to choose the material type (see Figure 7.2).

6. Standard 3ds Max materials are shown in the Material/Map Browser with a blue sphere, while mental ray materials are shown with a yellow one. Additionally, standard 3ds Max maps are shown with green parallelograms, while mental ray shaders are shown in yellow. In the Material/Map Browser, double-click on Arch & Design, or select Arch & Design, and click on the OK button at the bottom.

7. You may have noticed that the properties of the material changed when you selected the new material type. Materials in 3ds Max are designed by using the parameters, rollouts, and dialogs below the sample spheres. The Arch & Design material was made expressly for use in architectural renderings, and in general for realistic building materials. (Yes, you can use them on cars, robots, swords, and so forth. Don't panic.) In this exercise, we'll make a few paint colors from the Frazee library. The first thing to do when creating a new material is to name it by describing it in as many discrete ways as possible. In the name field, change the

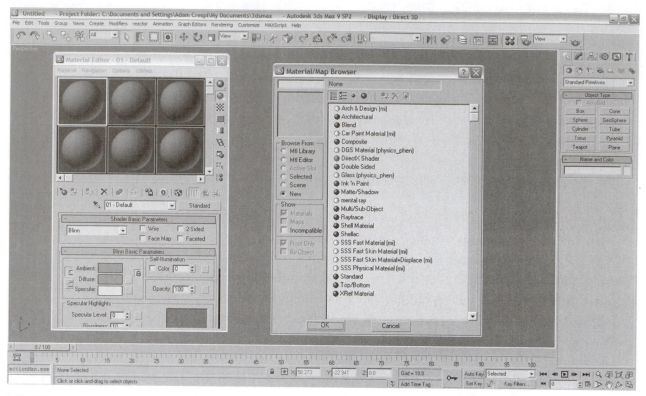

FIGURE 7.2

The Material/Map Browser with the Arch & Design material highlighted.

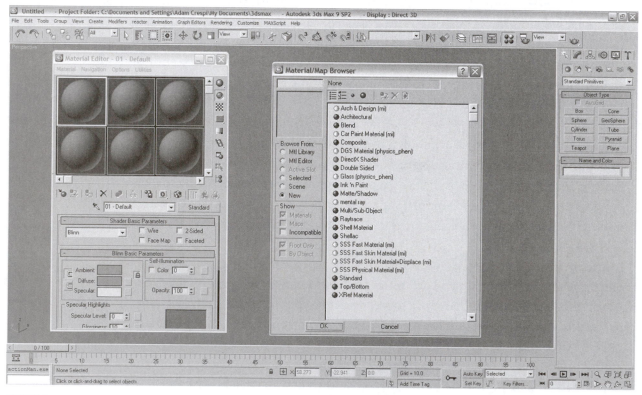

FIGURE 7.3

The renamed Arch & Design material in the Material Editor.

name from 01 - Default to FZ8215 Tattersall Brown (f). Here's what this name means: the two-letter abbreviation FZ stands for the manufacturer, Frazee Paint and Wallcovering; 8215 Tattersall Brown is the Frazee name and number; and (f) stands for flat (see Figure 7.3). Once the color is made, you can simply change the shininess and reflection to create this paint in flat, eggshell, semi-gloss, and gloss. Thus, for every one paint color created, four sheen levels can be added to your library.

8. Now comes the tricky part: how to get the exact color match to the paint. My studio has a color-calibrated professional graphics monitor, special overhead fluorescent lights that accurately simulate even daylight (no, not the cheap daylight fluorescents from a home renovation store—these go for $9 a bulb and have a color temperature closer to indirect sunshine), clean white walls and blackout shades, and an expensive (well, it was when I bought it) color-calibrated scanner. I occasionally scan a sample, but often I rely on Mark-1 eyeballs to estimate the color. How close your estimation of color is will depend on the output. I take a lot of my work to print, so I tweak the color until a sample print on my (color-calibrated, of course) printer, using my typical print stocks, matches the paint chip or sample. The best course of action, assuming you may not have all of this (outrageous, sky-high, wallet-draining—i.e., expensive) stuff, is to get the color as close as you can by eye. Try to look at your sample in even overhead light, preferably not green fluorescents or incandescent. Hold it flat, not vertical, and match the color in the diffuse slot as well as you can to the swatch. If this seems somewhat iffy, remember that you are going to apply this color to a surface that will be seen in all kinds of lighting conditions, in shade and shadow, and next to other colors, which will bounce light and color onto it. As long as it looks close in a rendering, you'll be fine (see Figure 7.4).

9. With the color matched, pull down the Appearances & Attributes menu in the Templates rollout for this material. Since this is a flat paint, choose the Matte Finish template. The sample sphere should change from a shiny material to a matte surface (see Figure 7.5).

10. The Matte Finish template uses an ideal Lambertian shader to approximate the spread of light on a rough surface. While the light spread quality is fine, the one tweak to make is to lower the roughness number from the default 0.2 to 0.15. This will let the surface be just a bit smoother and hence brighter in the Lambertian shading model (see Figure 7.6).

11. Drag the sample sphere for this material across to the next space, making a clone. Change the name from FZ8215 Tattersall Brown (f) to FZ8215 Tattersall Brown (es). This will be the eggshell version (see Figure 7.7).

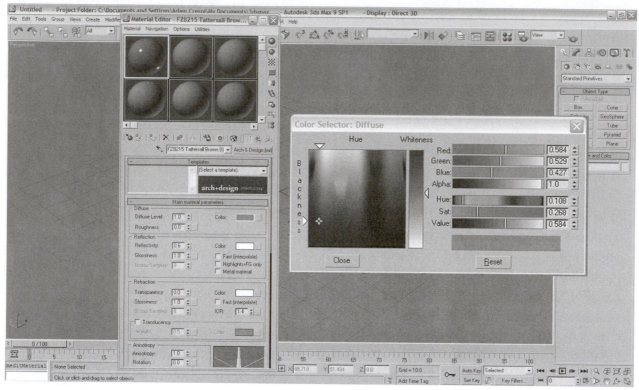

FIGURE 7.4

Matching the color.

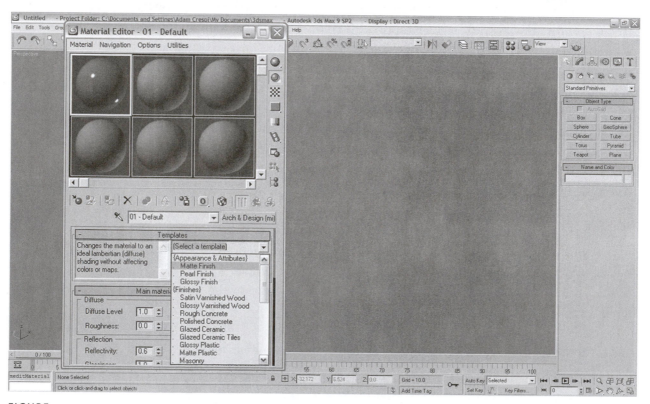

FIGURE 7.5

Changing the template of the Arch & Design material.

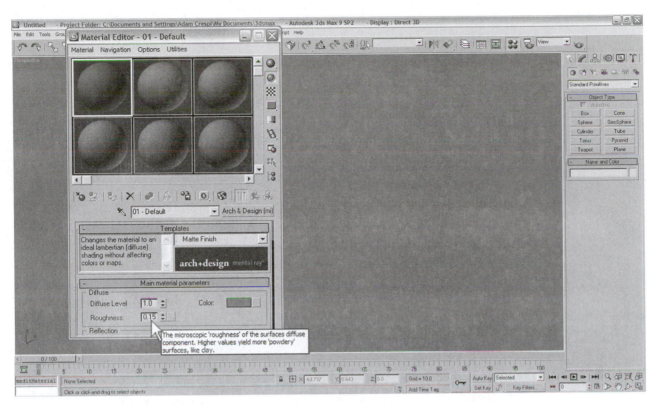

FIGURE 7.6

Adjusting the roughness of the material.

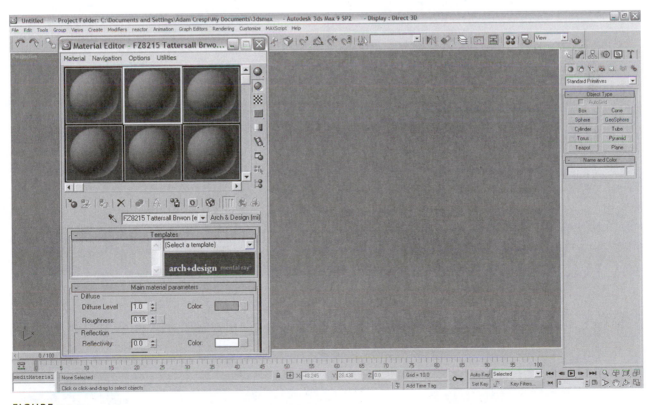

FIGURE 7.7

The cloned paint, renamed and ready for editing.

12. Leave the template at Matte Finish, but increase the reflectivity to 0.2 and the glossiness to 0.3. This will add a subtle sheen and tiny reflectivity, visible mainly as a color shift or variance when next to a contrasting material. Because the reflection is set so low, check Fast (Interpolate). This will speed up the calculation of the reflections by interpolating and enlarging a lower resolution reflection for the final rendering. This is particularly useful when reflections are very slight or blurred.

13. Scroll down to the Fast Glossy Interpolation rollout for the eggshell material. This section allows you to choose the resolution for the reflections as a fraction of the rendering size. For the eggshell, we can reduce the reflections to their lowest size, ⅕ (see Figure 7.8).

14. Make a copy of the eggshell material by dragging it to the next sample sphere. Name this material FZ8215 Tattersall Brown (sg). This will be the semi-gloss version of the paint, suitable for use on trim, doors, walls in wet areas, and so forth.

15. Change the template of this material to Pearl Finish. This will bring up the gloss and reflection, while checking Fast (Interpolate) in the Reflection section; it will also bring up the interpolated resolution to ½ (see Figure 7.9).

FIGURE 7.8

Setting the Fast Glossy Interpolation.

16. Bring up the reflectivity to 0.35 and the glossiness to 0.4 to add a little more luster to the surface.

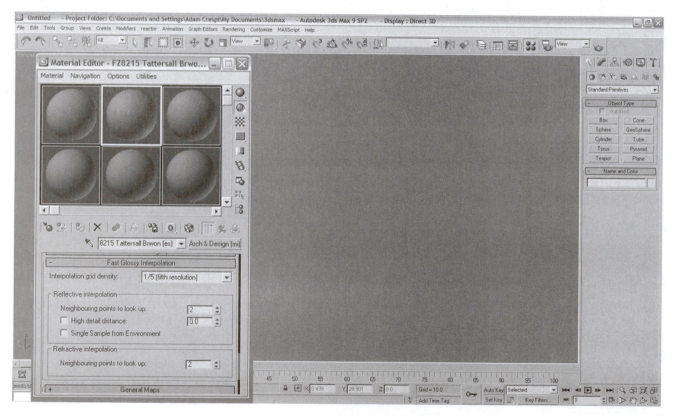

CHAPTER 7 : MATERIALS IN MENTAL RAY

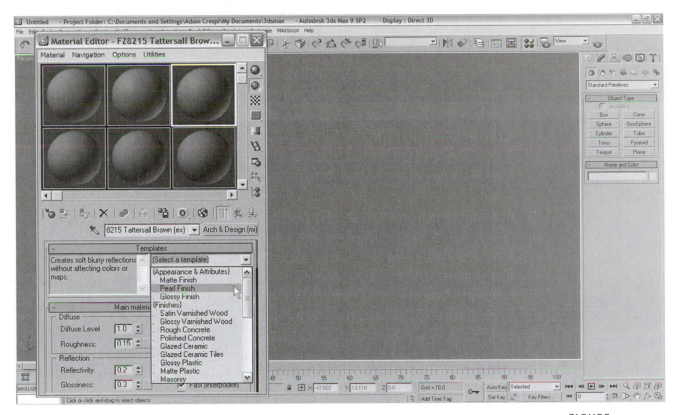

FIGURE 7.9

*Changing the
template to Pearl
Finish for the
semi-gloss paint.*

17. Clone this material to the next open slot, and name the copy FZ8215 Tattersall Brown (g). This will be the last of four sheen levels, gloss.

18. Change the template of this material to Glossy Finish. This will be a full-on glossy paint, with all the expected reflection and shine. (Use this one sparingly, as it will reflect more light around the scene. Additionally, remember one of the cardinal rules of visualizations: people like shiny objects. Their eyes will be drawn to the shiny reflective material and they may ignore more important parts of the image. See Figure 7.10.)

19. Do this step if you are creating a new material library. If you are adding these colors to an existing library, skip to step 21. Click on the Get Material button on the Material Editor. The Material/Map Browser will pop up again.

20. On the left side of the Material/Map Browser, click on the radio button for Material Library, shown as Mtl Library. This will show the materials that are loaded in the 3ds Max default material library, or possibly be blank. If the library is not blank, click on the Clear Material Library button at the top of the Material/ Map Browser.

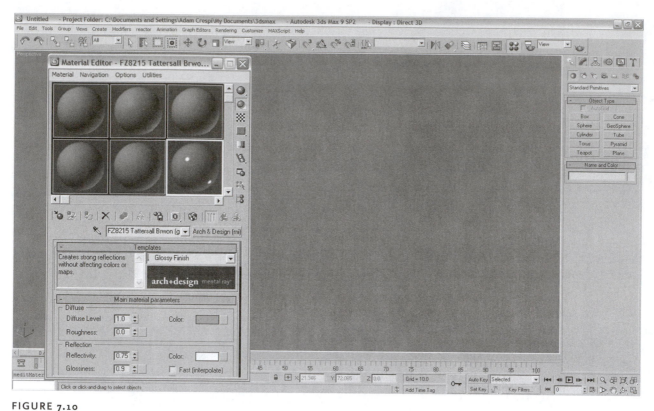

FIGURE 7.10

The final clone of the paint using the Glossy Finish template.

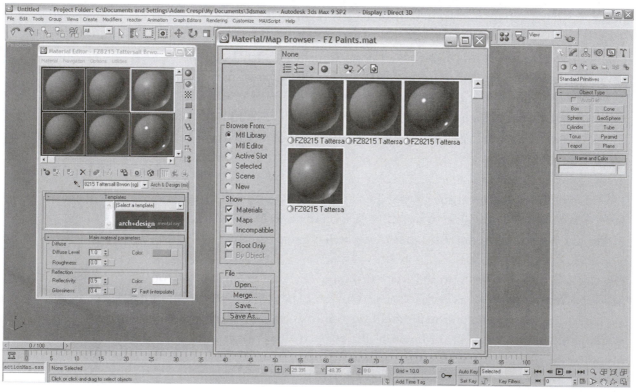

FIGURE 7.11

The materials in a new library.

21. If you are adding these materials to an existing library, choose Open . . . from the buttons on the left side of the Material/Map Browser, and open your material library. Drag the new paint colors you have just created from the Material Editor to the Material/Map Browser. When you have done this, click on the Save As . . . button if you are saving this library for the first time, or Save . . . if you are saving a library you have already made. If you are saving this library for the first time, name this library for the manufacturer, Frazee Paint (see Figure 7.11).

Note:

I name and categorize materials and products by their manufacturer, and keep them in a central location versus a project-specific one. On my server, for example, there is a drive mapped for projects, one for materials and maps, one for research and development, and one for my teaching work. In the materials and maps section, I have directories for textures, organized by type and manufacturer, and a directory where I keep my material libraries. This mapped drive also has directories for manufactured objects, such as doors, windows, and so forth, so that they can be referenced into scenes. In the material libraries directory are libraries such as Frazee, Dunn-Edwards, Sherwin Williams, and Benjamin Moore, as well as TIGER Drylac, Eagle Roofing, US Tile, Walker Zanger, and many more. Even though I am a one-person shop, I try to stay on my toes regarding organization; there are simply too many assets that go into a scene to have things haphazardly scattered or misnamed. If all of this organization sounds over the top, think of it in this light: every hour spent creating a map that has been already made and then lost is an hour less of billable time (money) in your pocket.

SECTION B: MORE COMPLEX MAPPED MATERIALS

EXERCISE 2: Masonry

Solid materials can go a long way in visualization; I have done work without any texture maps, relying instead on lighting and camerawork to create interest and drama. However, since many surfaces you are likely to use come in a wide variety of colors, patterns, and features, at some point, your scenes will need some sort of texturing. What makes a brick wall look like brick is not the overall red color, it is the pattern of brick and mortar in a recognizable coursing, combined with the shading and surface variance that bricks provide. Texture maps enhance the realism of our materials.

In this exercise, we will construct several brick materials for our rapidly expanding libraries, incorporating brick texture maps to define not only color but surface roughness, which spreads the light; add surface texture for variable shading; and even create maps that limit reflections to only glazed bricks and not their mortar. Maps are provided for your use in this exercise, but feel free to substitute your own images as needed, being mindful to stay consistent and true to the outlined function.

1. Start 3ds Max or choose File > Reset from the top menu to begin with a clean scene.

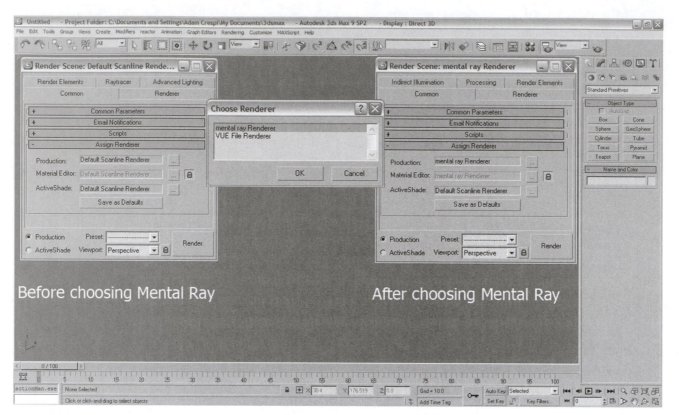

FIGURE 7.12

Changing the production renderer to mental ray.

2. Press F10 or choose Rendering > Render from the top menu to pull up the Render Scene dialog. Scroll down to the bottom of the Common tab, and open the Assign Renderer rollout. Choose mental ray for the production renderer; the Material Editor is locked to the production renderer by default (see Figure 7.12).

3. Press M to bring up the Material Editor. Click on any open sample sphere to make it the active material.

4. Click on the button marked Standard to change the material type from Standard to Arch & Design.

5. The templates provide a good jumping-off point for many materials. Change the template to Masonry in the pull-down menu. This will change the material to a preset brick, using default textures that come with 3ds Max. We'll swap in our own textures and tweak a few properties (see Figure 7.13).

6. First, click on the M button next to the Diffuse color. In 3ds Max, maps can be accessed through the Maps rollout farther down in the material's parameters, or anywhere there is a small gray button next to a color or property. When you click on this button, it will take you to the map's parameters, in this case a Bitmap (see Figure 7.14).

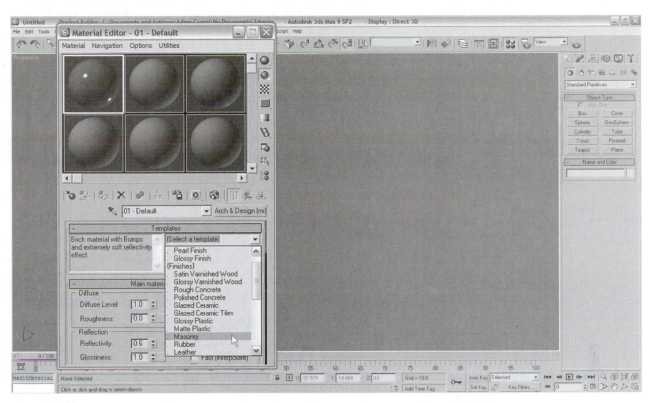

FIGURE 7.13

Selecting the Masonry template in the Arch & Design material.

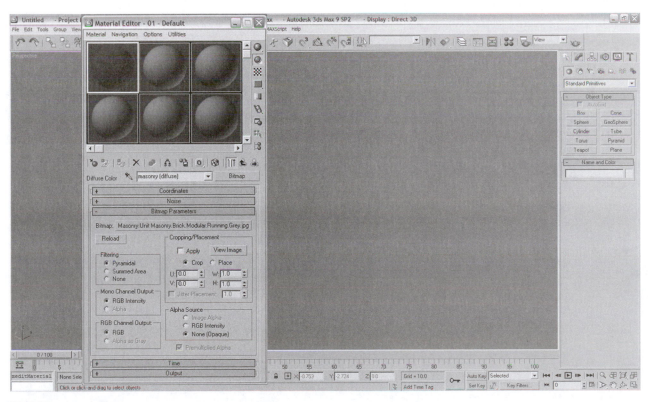

FIGURE 7.14

Accessing the Bitmap in the Diffuse slot.

7. Once you are in the Bitmap parameter section of the material, click on the bar that shows the name and path of the Bitmap. (Remember, in 3ds Max, a Bitmap is any kind of pixel-based image or video file, not just a BMP.) Browse to the Assets folder for this chapter, and go into the Maps folder. In the Maps folder, go into the Brick directory, and choose *BB Williamsburg common running stretchers-C.tga*.

8. Click on the Go To Parent button on the top row of buttons under the sample spheres, or pull down the menu in the center labeled Masonry (diffuse), and choose Default-01 or whatever the material name is. This will return you to the root of the material (see Figure 7.15).

9. Click on the M in the map square next to the Reflectivity Color to go to the Bitmap parameters section for this map. Maps can be copied as instances between slots in materials, so this map does double duty as the reflection and the bump map. Click on the map's name and path button, and browse to the same brick directory as before. Choose *BB common running stretchers-B.tga*, which is a generic bump map for Boral Bricks in a common running bond with stretcher courses.

FIGURE 7.15
Returning to the parent or root material (both methods highlighted).

Note:
Although in this case maps are instanced between slots, this may not always be a good idea. Some materials may have considerable surface detail and low reflectivity, or high reflectivity and low detail, and so on. For example, a brick may have a fairly uniform bump map

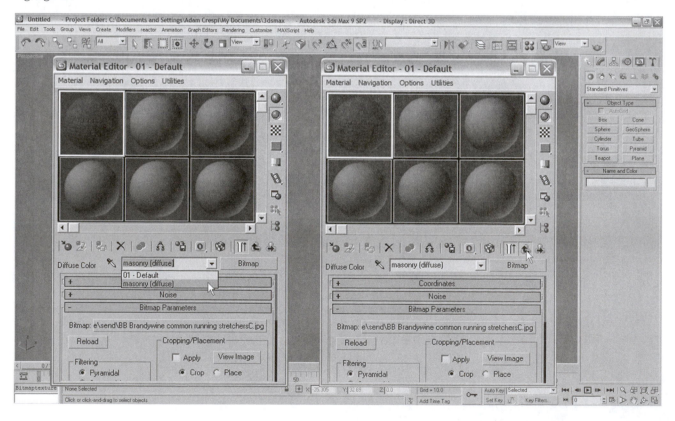

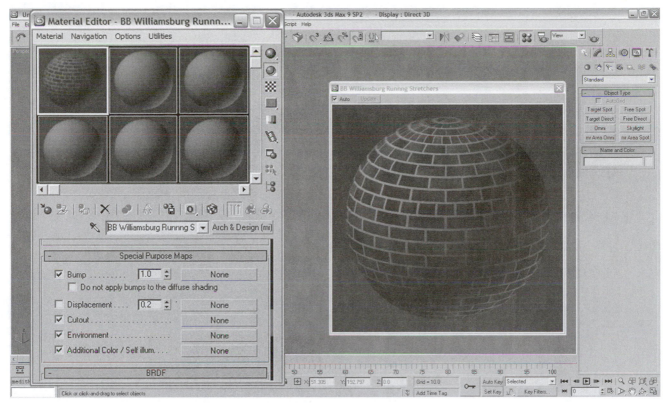

FIGURE 7.16
The brick material ready for the bump map.

that simply delineates bricks and mortar with subtle variations in the brick face. However, this brick may have streaking or spotting that is somewhat glazed; this would require two separate maps for reflection and bump.

10. Go back to the root of this material, and name it *BB Williamsburg (common running stretchers)*. See Figure 7.16.

11. Scroll down to the Special Purpose Maps rollout, and make sure that the Bump amount is set to 1.0. (It should be for materials starting from this template, but always check before wasting time on a rendering.)

12. This step is optional, if you are using Real-World Mapping Coordinates. Click on each of the maps used in this material, and in the Bitmap Parameters section, go to the Coordinates rollout. Check World Mapping Coordinates and set the size to 160″ × 72″. Real-World Mapping Coordinates ensure that when a map is used, it is always the same size in scene units, which are inches by default. If you design the map using one measurement system, and your scene uses another, be sure to convert the numbers appropriately. Additionally, make sure to check Real-World Mapping Coordinates in the UWV Map or Unwrap UWV modifier for those objects that have this material applied (see Figure 7.17).

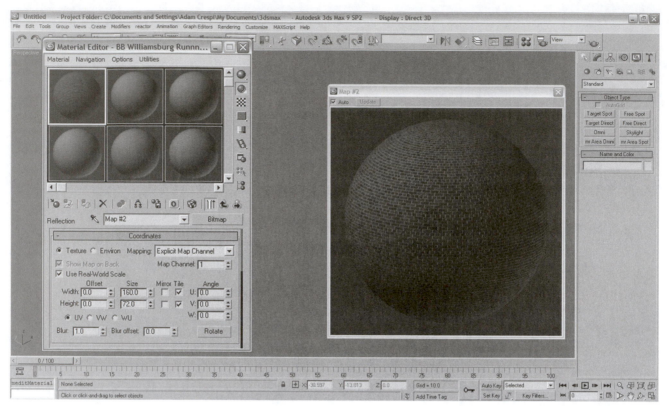

FIGURE 7.17

Specifying the Real-World Mapping Coordinates.

13. The material is now ready to be added to your library. Follow the steps in the previous tutorial for doing so.

14. As with the solid paint colors, it is a good idea to construct materials of one brick in several patterns for versatility in design. Click and drag the material sample sphere that has the *BB Williamsburg (common stretchers running)* over to an open slot to clone the material.

15. Click on the M next to the diffuse color to access the diffuse map. We can simply change the map and keep the other properties of the brick, such as reflection and glossiness, so that all of the brick in the family looks the same. Click on the bar containing the map name, and browse to the Assets folder on the CD. Select *BB Williamsburg stack-C.jpg* and click Open.

16. Go up to the root of the material, and then into the Bump slot to change that map as well. Replace the existing bump map with the *stack bond-B.jpg*.

17. Go up to the root of the material again, and rename this material to *BB Williamsburg (stack bond)*.

18. Add this material to your material library and save the file.

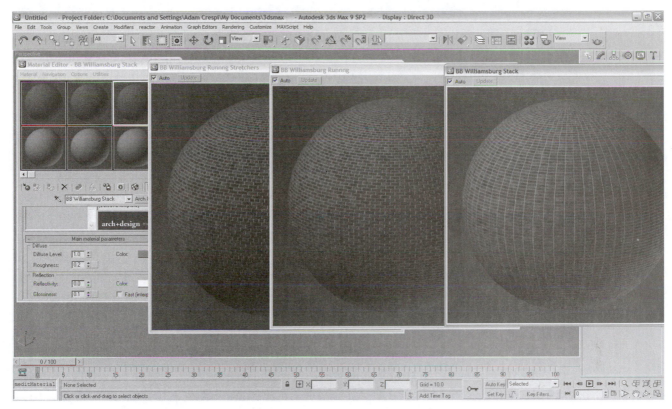

FIGURE 7.18

*The completed
brick variations.*

19. Repeat steps 14 through 18, this time using the common running maps and generating a material called *BB Williamsburg (common running)*. See Figure 7.18.

BONUS EXERCISE: Using normal maps

Normal Maps allow a model to have greater detail than can be reasonably accommodated by a rendering engine or game engine. Essentially, Normal Maps provide simulated displacement on a mesh, with the addition of direction vectors that affect lighting. Because they provide this additional reaction to lighting, they allow for dynamically changing shadows; hence, they offer a perceived level of detail not available with one channel or unidirectional bump maps. As an example, normal maps are excellent candidates for surface detail such as veins on muscular characters' arms, exposed heartwood grain, or the crenellations and crevices of stone.

In 3ds Max, using a Normal Map is fairly easy. Simply click on the Bump Map slot in any material in the Material Editor. When the Material/Map Browser pops up, choose Normal Bump from the available maps. The Normal Bump map has slots for the Normal Map, as well as an additional Bump Map. This can be thought of as layering of detail, where the Normal Map provides large-scale details, and the Bump Map adds fine detail.

Normal Maps are somewhat prone to jitter or scintillation if their detail is too fine, especially with a finer anti-aliasing filter. This depends on their resolution, the shadow type and quality, and the size of the rendering; higher resolution renderings with fine detail will produce greater jitter. Thus, Normal Maps are often blurred slightly to avoid this jitter, obscuring fine detail.

Making Normal Maps can take any number of routes, from painting in a purpose-built sculpting tool to modeling a high-resolution model to drawing them in existing drawing and paint programs and exporting flat images. ZBrush by Pixelogic is a popular application for digital sculpting, as is Mudbox by Skymatter and modo by Luxology. These applications either work on an imported model from 3ds Max, using UVW coordinates, or on a model started native in them. They are designed to work on models with huge polygon counts, and often in layers of refinement or detail, much like traditional sculpting. The high-detail model is then used to produce or bake Normal Maps for export to 3ds Max, which are then applied to the lower resolution mesh. Alternatively, the high-resolution model can be exported to 3ds Max, and then derive its animation from the lower resolution version. As an alternative to a third-party application like ZBrush, there are also plug-ins for applications like Photoshop from NVIDIA and other companies. For the purposes of this book, and since we will explore texture creation in Photoshop, we will use the NVIDIA plug-in. What this and other plug-ins do is convert the grayscale of a drawn Bump Map to the Tangent Space of a Normal Map, with the added options of using the Alpha channel to determine height data as well.

1. Using the brick material from the last exercise, we'll replace the single-channel Bump map with a Normal Map. In the Material Editor, scroll down in the parameters of the brick material to the Bump slot. Click on the map in the slot to access the Bitmap Parameters.

2. Change the map type by clicking on the Bitmap button, and choosing Normal Bump from the Material/Map Browser. A Replace Map dialog box pops up asking if you want to make the old map a sub-map or discard it. In this case, we could use the old Bump map as an additional map in the Normal Bump map to add additional detail to the brick, or discard it. For this exercise, discard the old map so the Normal Map's effect is clearly visible (see Figure 7.19).

3. In the Normal Bump parameters, click on the slot labeled None next to Normal Map. This will again pull up the Material/Map Browser, allowing you to choose the full range of maps for the Normal Map; choose Bitmap (see Figure 7.20).

4. When the Open Map dialog pops up, browse to the Assets folder on the CD for this chapter and choose *BB common running stretchers-N.dds,* which is a generic normal bump map for Boral Bricks in a common running bond with stretcher courses (see Figure 7.21).

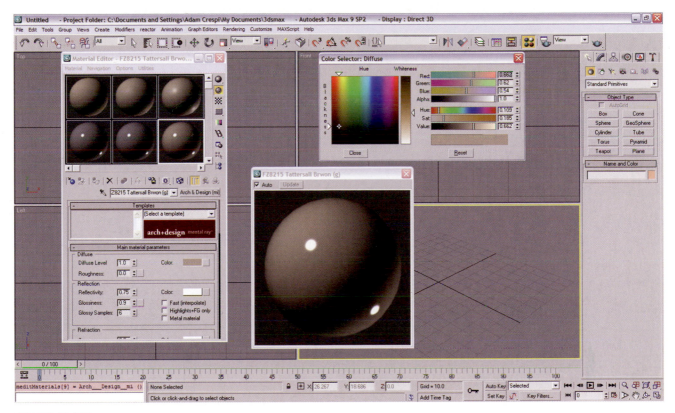

COLOR PLATE 1.1

The paint colors from Chapter 7 in various sheen levels, ready for insertion into the Material Library.

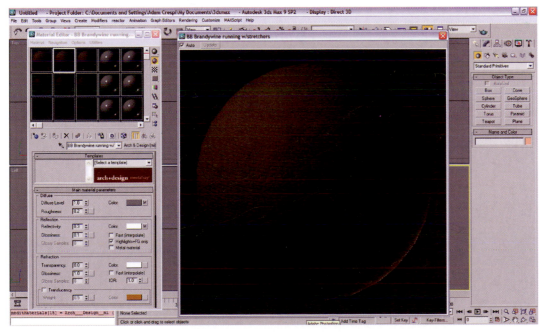

COLOR PLATE 1.2

The various brick materials from Chapter 7, with an enlargement of the Boral Brick Brandywine bricks, shown in a running bond with stretcher courses. Note that the small scale of the bricks in the sample is due to the Real World map Size being used for all of the texture maps.

COLOR PLATE 1.3

The Boral Brick Brandywine bricks shown in color plate 1.2 as applied to a sample wall.

COLOR PLATE 1.4

The completed Walker Zanger Seagrass tile from Section C of Chapter 8.

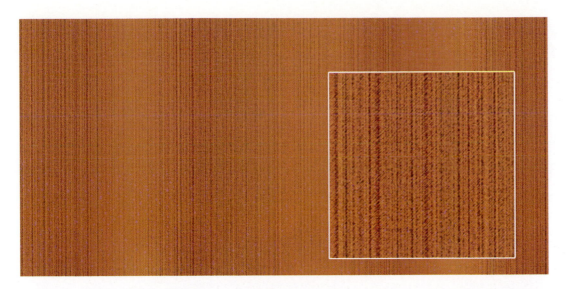

COLOR PLATE 1.5
The quarternsawn oak from Section E of Chapter 8, before applying the Liquify filter. The enlarged image in the lower right corner of the wood shows the crosscut hatching.

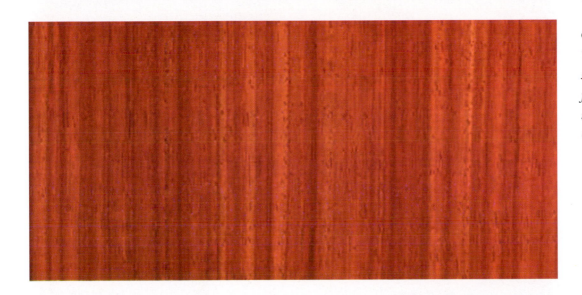

COLOR PLATE 1.6
The padauk sample used for reference in Section E of Chapter 8

COLOR PLATE 1.7
The final padauk texture from Chapter 8, including knots and waving grain, ready for cutting and pasting in an unwrap template as part of a material.

COLOR PLATE 1.8

The test pavilion used in Section B of Chapter 9, rendered using the Mental Ray Daylight System.

COLOR PLATE 1.9

The completed interior lighting from Section C of Chapter 9.

COLOR PLATE 1.10

Figure 10.13 showing color bounce between adjacent objects in the scene due to the use of Global Illumination and Final Gather.

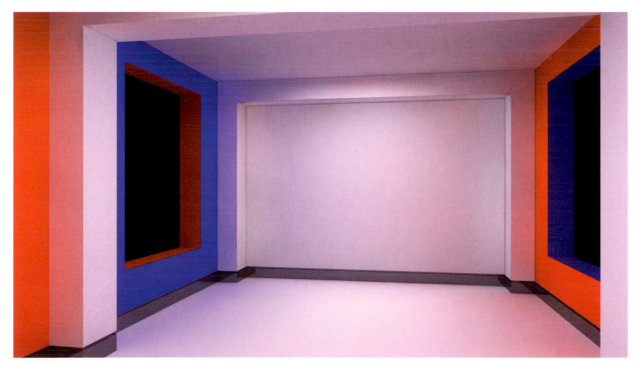

COLOR PLATE 1.11

The rendered modified Cornell box showing color bounce between adjacent objects.

COLOR PLATE 1.12

The rendered grass from Section A of Chapter 11.

COLOR PLATE 1.13

The rendered area rug from Section B of Chapter 11 shown on a carpet tile floor.

COLOR PLATE 1.14

Color correcting and adding grain to the rendered image in Autodesk Combustion.

COLOR PLATE 1.15

The final store image without post processing.

COLOR PLATE 1.16

The final image of the store after post effects and color correction.

COLOR PLATE 1.17
The store seen from the hallway near one of the dressing rooms.

COLOR PLATE 1.18
The store seen from camera location 1 as drawn in Chapter 2.

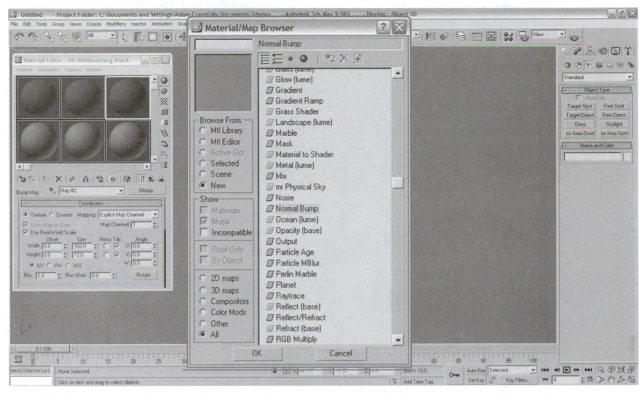

FIGURE 7.19

Changing the bump map to a Normal Bump map type.

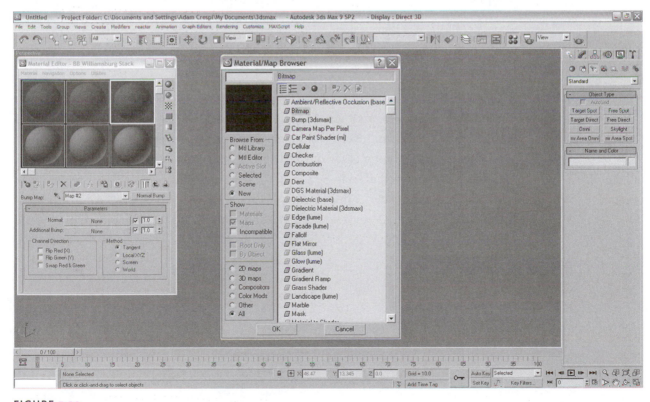

FIGURE 7.20

Selecting the map that will be the Normal Map.

BONUS EXERCISE: Making a normal map in Photoshop

---

1. Draw a grayscale Bump Map as you usually would, starting with a 50% gray if the surface will have both up and down contours. For the NVIDIA export to work properly, the image must be square (see Figure 7.22).

2. If you desire, paint a height map in the Alpha channel as a grayscale (see Figure 7.23).

3. Go to File > Save As . . . and choose DDS from the available formats. This will pull up the NVIDIA Normal Map dialog. While a considerable number of options are available, a Normal Map can be easily exported by changing a few settings. Make sure that the map is set to 2D Texture, and then click on the Normal Map Settings. In the Normal Map Settings, make sure that Convert To Tangent Space Normal Map is checked, and the samples are set to 4. If you painted a height map in the Alpha channel, set the Height Map from Alpha Channel option. Name the map as a Normal Map to separate it from the single-channel bump maps (see Figure 7.24).

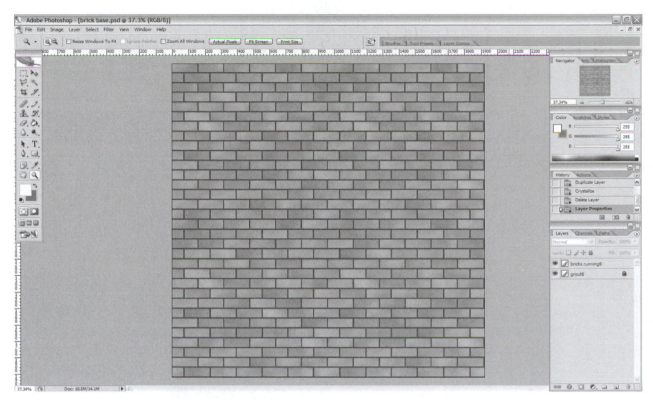

FIGURE 7.22

The base grayscale drawing.

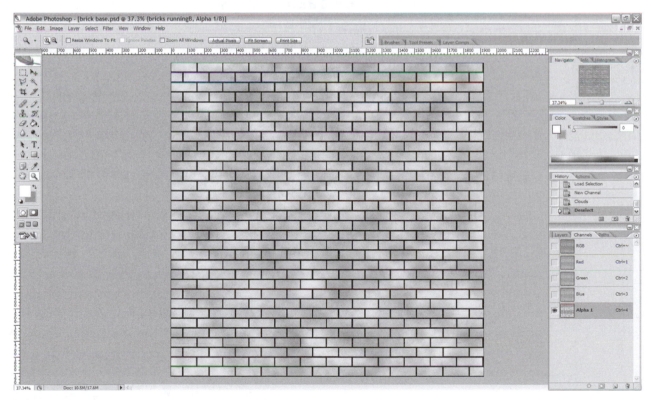

FIGURE 7.23

The height map painted in the Alpha channel.

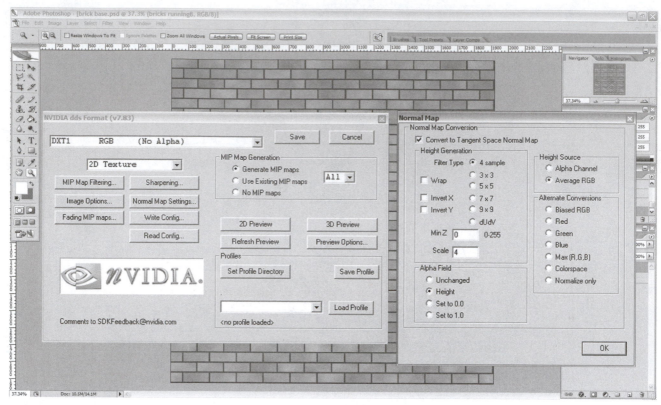

FIGURE 7.24

The export settings in the NVIDIA Normal Map dialog.

SECTION C: SUBSURFACE TREATMENTS

EXERCISE 3:   Subsurface scatter

Subsurface scatter (SSS) is the bouncing of light within but not out of a material such as skin, marble, milk, jade, and so on. SSS helps achieve realism and light in a rendering, allowing objects that might otherwise appear too heavy to sit lighter in an image. As an example, the ARCO floor lamp by Achille Castiglioni with its solid Carrara marble base can easily be dull and heavy in an image. My client was *not* appreciative when I did that. (Note to selves: do not make pristine luminous white stone look dull and gray—use subsurface scatter.)

As part of mental ray, 3ds Max includes several SSS materials that work for skin, leather, marble, and other uses. There are two broad categories: living or formerly living materials, and naturally occurring ones. Skin, and by extension leather, are or were living, marble is not. Skin has an epidermal layer on top, which is lightest in color, and dermal and subdermal layers underneath, which are darker and more saturated. There are also additional layers of specularity, which allow both broad shine blooms and sharp pin highlights. Physical materials have fewer controls than skin; these concern the transmission and reflectance of light in and across the surface.

LEATHER

1. Start 3ds Max or choose File > Reset from the top menu to begin with a clean scene.

2. Press F10 or choose Rendering > Render from the top menu to pull up the Render Scene dialog. Scroll down to the bottom of the Common tab, and open the Assign Renderer rollout. Choose mental ray for the production renderer; the Material Editor is locked to the production renderer by default.

3. Press M to bring up the Material Editor. Click on any open sample sphere to make it the active material.

4. Click on the button marked Standard to change the material type from Standard to Subsurface Scatter—Fast Skin. With a few color changes, this will look like rich brown leather (see Figure 7.25).

5. There are only four or five dozen parameters to tweak in the SSS Fast Skin if you really want to get into them; we can get fairly nice results with a few changes. First, start by changing the Overall Diffuse Coloration to an RGB of 234,118,72. This will color the material deep rust.

FIGURE 7.25

Changing the material type to SSS—Fast Skin.

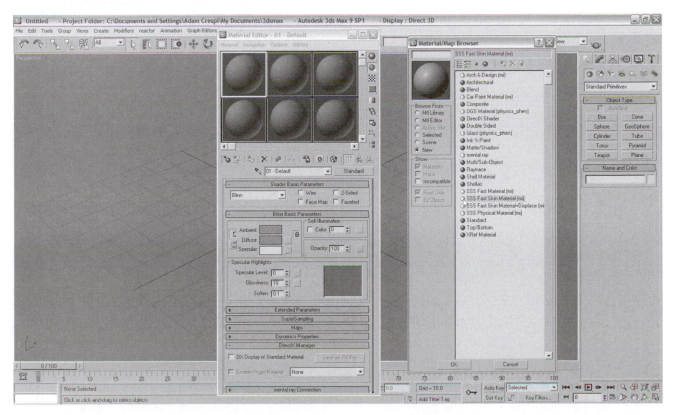

6. Next, change the Unscattered Diffuse Color to 49,34,7 to add a brown undertone.

7. Set the Subdermal Layer Scatter Color to 60,45,15; this will add a yellow to the brown.

8. Lastly, set the Back Surface Scatter Color to 130,90,20; this will let the edges render a little brighter and warmer.

9. Reduce Shininess #2 to 15, to spread the highlight across the surface.

10. Test render the material in a scene.

All of the parameters edited in the preceding steps can also be driven by maps as needed instead of a solid color, and the material also has slots for Bump or Normal Bump if needed. Often I'll unwrap a leather object, such as a seat or seatback, and then use the diffuse color to derive the other scatter color maps. Maps that determine the amount of scatter or shine can be grayscale.

MARBLE

1. Start 3ds Max or choose File > Reset from the top menu to begin with a clean scene.

2. Press F10 or choose Rendering > Render from the top menu to pull up the Render Scene dialog. Scroll down to the bottom of the Common tab, and open the Assign Renderer rollout. Choose mental ray for the production renderer; the Material Editor is locked to the production renderer by default.

3. Press M to bring up the Material Editor. Click on any open sample sphere to make it the active material.

4. Click on the button marked Standard to change the material type from Standard to Subsurface Scatter—Fast Material. This SSS material has parameters similar to the SSS Skin, but not as much depth in the diffuse and specular components. It is a basic SSS material suitable for inorganic substances, or substances that have been carved from a larger block of material and hence do not have the layering from outside to inside like skin (see Figure 7.26).

5. For this example, we'll make a white Carrara marble. Click on the map slot next to the Overall Diffuse Coloration, and choose Bitmap in the Material/Map Browser. Browse to the Assets folder for this chapter and choose *Carrara marble-C.jpg*.

FIGURE 7.26
*Changing the
material type to
SSS—Fast for use
as marble.*

6. Return to the root of the material. For a solid material like this, or other stones with similar qualities, the Unscattered Diffuse Color, Front Surface Scatter Color, and Back Surface Scatter Color should be related, getting lighter and less saturated from front to back in the material. As this is a near white stone, make the Unscattered Diffuse Color 245,245,230, the Front Surface Scatter Color 250,250,245, and the Back Surface Scatter Color 255,255,252. This will let the stone be luminous at the back scatter edges.

7. As always, test the material in a scene; do not rely on the sample spheres to tell the whole story. You may find that as the material gets lighter in color, you will need to increase the brightness of the Ambient/Extra Lighting swatch. This color is set at 0,0,0 by default, and only a small brightness boost is usually required to brighten the material. More than a fifty-point luminance increase will start to reduce the effectiveness of shadows cast on the materials and will appear to be emitting light.

8. Scroll down to the Specular Reflection rollout in the material parameters. For a polished marble, increase the Shininess to anywhere from 65 to 90, and bring the Specular Color closer to white. For duller materials, lower the Shininess and bring the Specular Color closer to a lighter version of the Unscattered Diffuse Color.

SECTION D: GLASS

INTRODUCTION: Thoughts on making glass

Glass has always been a bit difficult to make in 3D. Plenty of options, from Raytrace maps to Raytrace materials, allow us to fake it using highly shiny, non-reflective materials and fake reflections; the list is quite long. The general trend recently seems to be to make it behave like true glass with as much control over reflection and refraction as possible, then throw enough computing power at it to finally render. This is somewhat of a brute-force approach and may waste time and processing power that could be better used to bounce light or cast shadows or work in more detail. A better approach is to consider the lighting that the glass will be seen in and tailor the material to it.

Glass is a chameleon; its appearance changes depending on the angle of viewing, dirt, whether it's outside or inside, reflective or clear, and many other factors. As an example, in a building where the surface area of the glass is a small fraction of the surface area of the building's walls, the windows are deep gray voids when seen from the outside in daylight. At night, with the lights on, the same building's glass disappears completely. In interior renderings, glass ranges from the skim of a reflection across a lake surface to a swarm of butterflies in the colors of the room, flitting in front of a green-tinted sky. (Visualization professionals' note: if the previous sentence seemed a bit over the top, it was purposefully so. To a client's ears, it is far better to talk in terms of butterflies than BRDF graphs and Fresnel reflections.) If this all sounds like we need to make a unique glass for every project, I'm not saying that. Just make a few types of glass that will work in most situations, and then deal with customized glass on a case-by-case basis.

EXERCISE 4: Clear exterior glass

This exercise focuses on making clear residential glass for use in buildings where the window area is a small fraction of the wall area, as found in much of the production housing in the United States today. This glass will be suitable for both day and night renderings from a camera outside of the structure. Although it may sound too specific, this glass will be suitable for use where the whole building is being shown, such as a typical front perspective or elevation used for marketing purposes. This glass will not be good to use in interior renderings, close-up renderings, or in areas where highly reflective or refractive glass is desired.

1. Start 3ds Max or choose File > Reset from the top menu to begin with a clean scene.

2. Press F10 or choose Rendering > Render from the top menu to pull up the Render Scene dialog. Scroll down to the bottom of the Common tab, and open the Assign Renderer rollout. Choose mental ray for the production renderer; the Material Editor is locked to the production renderer by default.

3. Press M to bring up the Material Editor. Click on any open sample sphere to make it the active material.

4. Click on the button marked Standard to change the material type from Standard to Arch & Design. We will begin by using one of the existing glass templates and reducing the refraction and reflection, then adding a little covering color.

5. Pull down the list of templates and choose the Glass (Thin Geometry) template. As the caption next to it says, this glass is made for single-sided objects and does not do any refraction (see Figure 7.27).

6. The default diffuse color for this glass is black, which will leave your windows looking very dark. Click on the color swatch, and change the color to an RGB of 25,20,30. This will leave the windows slightly indigo, as well as let a hint of the inside detail show through. (Using this glass also makes the assumption that even for an exterior-only rendering, you have at least modeled bare interior rooms to bounce the light; walls, floors, and ceilings are sufficient.)

FIGURE 7.27
Changing the material to the Glass (Thin Geometry) template.

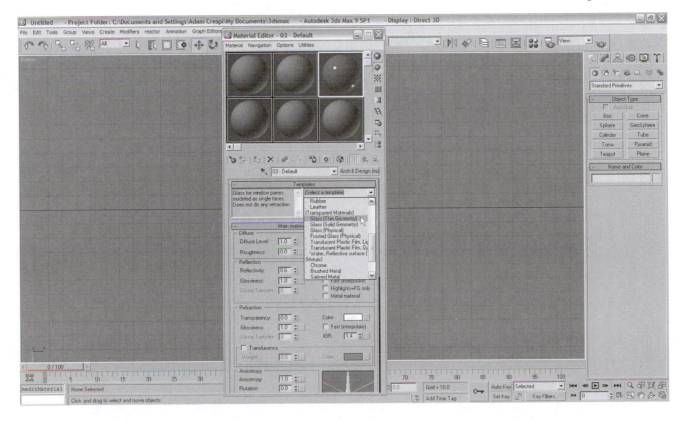

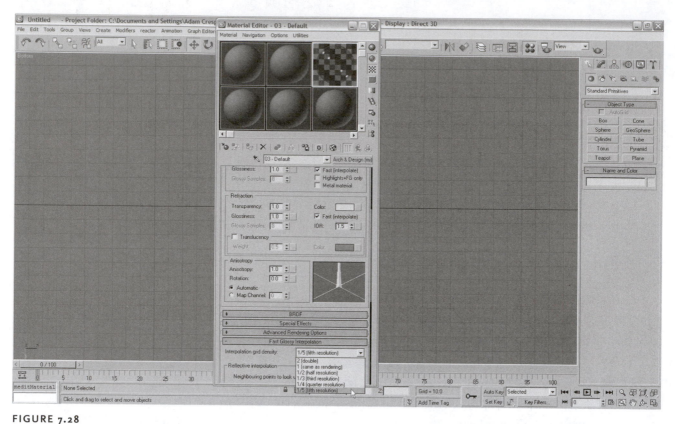

FIGURE 7.28

Setting the Fast Glossy Interpolation to reduce rendering time.

7. Reduce the Reflection from 1.0 to 0.75, and check Fast (Interpolate).

8. Scroll down to the Fast Glossy Interpolation rollout and set the interpolation to ⅕ resolution (see Figure 7.28).

9. Name this material Glass Clear Exterior Small, or per your naming conventions, and place it in your glass material library.

EXERCISE 5:   Clear glass with a green edge using a multi/sub-object material

1. Working in the file from the previous exercise, click on an unused sample sphere in the Material Editor.

2. Click on the button marked Standard to change the material type from Standard to Multi/Sub-Object. A Multi/Sub-Object material allows multiple complete materials to be assigned to polygons of an object, such as the edge of glass and the face. Alternately, you can click on a current material (such as the glass from the previous exercise) and change the type from Arch & Design to Multi/Sub-Object

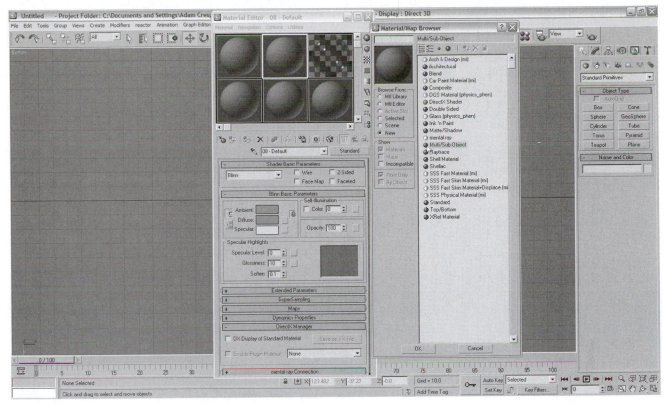

FIGURE 7.29

Changing a default material to a Multi/Sub-Object material.

material. 3ds Max will ask if you wish to keep the old material as a submaterial or discard; choose Keep and the material will occupy the first slot in the Multi/Sub-Object material. For this exercise, proceed with a new material as outlined, as the glass will have a slightly different character (see Figure 7.29).

3. Change the number of submaterials to 2 by clicking on the Set Number button and entering 2 (see Figure 7.30).

4. Click on the material slot for ID 1, and change the material type to Arch & Design.

5. Choose the Glass (Solid Geometry) template.

6. Name this material Glass Green Edge, and change the diffuse color to 0,0.25,0.1.

7. Check Fast (Interpolate) in the Reflection section, and set the resolution to ¼.

8. The green edge glass is ready for use. We have made it green, and reduced the reflection rendering time significantly. Click on the Go to Parent button to return to the root material.

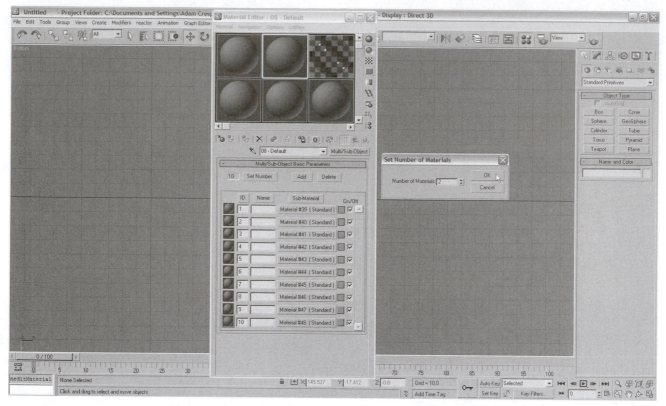

FIGURE 7.30

Setting the number of submaterials to 2.

9. Click on the material slot for ID 2, and change the material type to Arch & Design.

10. Choose the Glass (Solid Geometry) template.

11. Name this glass Glass Clear.

12. Change the color swatch in the Refraction section to 0.825,0.925,0.185, which will give it a slight green tint that works well with the green edge. Click on the Go to Parent button to return to the root material.

13. Add this material to your glass material library.

SECTION E: CONCLUSION

Despite legions of animators working in white or gray scenes, the world is actually made of colorful stuff—materials with unique characteristics that shape light and color. As a visualization artist, it is your job to present the materials that a client is buying at ruinous expense as faithfully as possible. There are literally dozens of ways to make materials in 3ds Max; we have covered merely a few in this chapter. The important lesson, thus, is not to copy slavishly the templates that everyone else has, but instead to customize them and make them your own. The morning light in your loft rendering will not spill down the generic concrete wall that comes with the program and capture the romance you had in your head. You will need to craft your own concrete for that situation, so that the light will spill and caress concrete that only you can provide to your client.

Making materials and libraries is an exercise in pronunciation. The more you pronounce the components of the material as distinct elements and then craft each of them, the closer to the real thing they will appear. As I have seen with countless students, the more the vision of *cool* in someone's head is shared with others, the closer the final result will be to that original *cool*. Lastly, look at the real world for inspiration, and not just the Internet version of it. Get out into the actual sunlight even though it may sting, and look at the real stuff. As design does not exist in a vacuum, materials do not exist in the computer except in an abstracted version that needs a good dose of reality. Good hunting.

CHAPTER 8 Painting Textures

SECTION A: DRAWING MAPS

I am a fan of painting my own textures for my models. Why go through the headache when there are so many textures available, you ask? The answer has two parts. First, most of the commonly available textures are photos of materials. Second, the photo of the material inherently includes lighting and shadows, as well as reflections. (Note: the word *texture* in computer-generated imagery is a generic term, referring to any part of a material governed by some form of raster-based imagery or procedurally generated pattern or event. In 3ds Max, textures are referred to as maps, different from Mapping or UVW Mapping or Unwrapping. To avoid confusion, we will refer to the map that governs the main color of the material in general light as the Color or Diffuse Color, and the map that governs the local small surface texture of a material as the Bump.)

While starting with a photo of an actual material sounds great, too often, as in almost always, photos found in texture libraries or other places are taken of too small an area of the material. Let's look at a case study. Although this reasoning can be applied to any unit masonry or unit applied surface, we'll examine mosaic tile. A typical installation of said material may cover several dozen or even hundreds of square feet. We expect to see a slight variation in the color of each tile covering walls, floors, or other surfaces. In fact, this slight variation is almost always carefully designed by the manufacturer so that the surface is perceived as a rich, nearly homogeneous whole well worth the money paid. Alternatively, if the color is exactly uniform from piece to piece, there will still be a slight variation in surface texture between each piece within the context of the mass-produced whole. Handmade items have even more variation within the general body.

Given the hue and saturation variations within the field of the material to be used, two things need to happen in order to accurately display the material in the generated image. First, the sample used as the texture should be big enough that no discernable pattern repeats unnaturally in the field. "Big enough" in this case is not a reference to image resolution, as many photos used as textures are quite large, but instead to the number of units of tile or brick or other module shown. Take as a more specific example 1″ × 1″ mosaic tile, featured in a blend of three colors. As shown in Figure 8.1, with only four rows of four tiles in the sample, the pattern repeats frequently. This phenomenon, common in amateur renderings, is called *tiling*, and textures are said to *tile* badly in such cases.

While the picture of the tiles may be stunning, it is simply not big enough. Repeating the image will yield undesirable results as shown in Figure 8.2, where the tiling produces diagonal stripes in what should have been a random mosaic. (For scale reference, the tiles are 2″ × 2″, and the biped is 5′8″ tall.)

FIGURE 8.1

A small random pattern that will tile badly.

Single square of the pattern

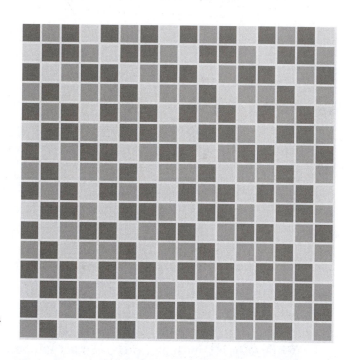

Pattern repeated 4 by 4

FIGURE 8.2

The pattern repeated on a surface and tiling badly.

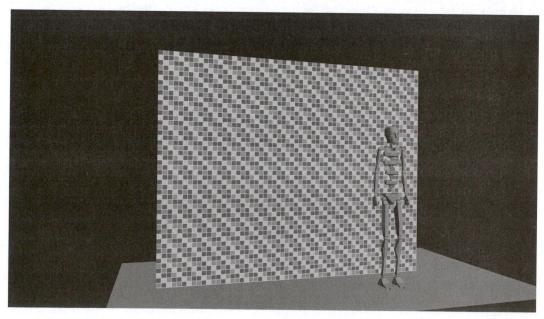

Lighting and color in light is the second major reason I avoid using photos for textures. A photo is inherently that; a snapshot of a surface or condition including the lighting present at the time as viewed through the constraints and interpretation of a lens. What this means for generated imagery is that the material has lighting baked in, or included, that does not match the lighting in the scene. Additionally, it is notoriously difficult, if not impossible, to remove or repaint the lighting in a texture to match that of a scene. The eye looks for subtle clues as to the believability of an image; we willingly suspend disbelief in a representation of reality only when the subtleties we expect to see are present. As a rule in the real world, surfaces do not exhibit double lighting, so neither should generated imagery.

Compounding the lighting and color issues built into photography used for textures is that of perspective. Just as photos have light and color baked in, they also have perspective baked in. No matter how square to a surface a camera is placed, distortion is imparted by the lens, the field of view, and the distance from the camera to the surface. Cropping a photo so that the apparent module repeats is not a solution to this problem. The only way to avoid baked-in perspective in a texture is to draw the texture from scratch.

SECTION B: PLANNING YOUR DRAWING

You need to look at several factors before drawing a map from scratch. As outlined in Section A, a map should be drawn so that there are enough units shown that the randomness stays random; that it does not visibly tile. Thus, the first thing to consider is the size of the unit being drawn in real-world measurements, and how many units are likely to appear on a given surface. Recall the mosaic tile mentioned earlier. Mosaic tile usually measures $\frac{1}{2}'' \times \frac{1}{2}''$, $1'' \times 1''$, and $2'' \times 2''$, with the occasional tile family featured at $1\frac{1}{2}'' \times 1\frac{1}{2}''$ or another odd size. Even a small application, such as a kitchen backsplash, could conceivably have several hundred tiles. A large wall in a restaurant or bar could have several thousand tiles. Add to this the possibility of customization offered by many manufacturers, allowing for blends by percentage of as many tiles as the designer wishes to specify. What you as a visualization specialist must decide then, is how big to draw the map in order to provide proper randomness and seamless tiling.

I often assign a pixel-to-the-inch ratio for easy math in whatever application I am drawing in. The following exercises use Adobe Systems' Photoshop; I also use Adobe Systems' Illustrator on occasion. For this example, let's assume a mosaic of $1'' \times 1''$ tiles, with the possibility of needing a four-color blend. Considering that I am likely to see this tile surface from several feet away at the closest, the tiles do not need to be too large, but I will need an area of several square feet of them to show the proper randomness. (Where do I derive the seemingly arbitrary "several feet" from? As explained in Chapter 2 on setting up a camera, we always want to look diagonally across the longest view of a space. Hence, as the surface gets more perpendicular to our view, it will be farther from the camera in most cases. Surfaces that are close to the camera will be more parallel to the view and hence show less detail. Unless the camera is sitting behind a column or wall with said tile, the tile we need to worry about will be several feet away.) Since we are not scrutinizing our tile at the distance we hold a book to our eyes, the detail is somewhat lost and the color and general surface texture (bump) and shine come into play more. Thus, I will assign a size of 40 pixels to the inch as a working ratio, so I can construct the map with the correctly sized tile and grout. I try to pick ratios that are easily divisible into whole numbers, so that grout can be evenly placed and any necessary wiggle can be accommodated within a given range. For larger tile, I may use a smaller ratio; this will also depend on the amount of color or surface variation within each tile or unit.

Once we have picked the ratio, the next step is to calculate the size of the map. With our 1″ × 1″ mosaic example, we will need at least 4 square feet of tile and perhaps more depending on the application. Without being excessive, I usually construct a map that will work in a situation such as an entry or signage wall in a corporate or hotel lobby or behind a cash/wrap desk in a retail space. Figuring a rough size of eight by ten feet of surface needing tile, I will test the map on a box of this size. If the map works on this, it will definitely work in a residential kitchen or a smaller space. I test my brick maps on a forty-foot wall that is twenty feet tall; the map should tile well in full light in this circumstance. Thus it will be suitable for wainscoting or general use on production housing or on a corporate or retail structure. Given the 40 pixels to the inch ratio, and figuring roughly ⅛″ grout between tiles on a 24″ × 24″ map, this ratio yields a document size of 1080 pixels on a side, a very manageable size.

For a larger tile, such as 12″ × 12″ ceramic floor tile, a ratio of 10 or 20 pixels to the inch usually works well. Again, as with the smaller tiles, we need to look at the variation in color within and between each tile, as well as the difference between colors of each tile. For example, a map of 12″ × 12″ glazed white tiles may only need to have five tiles by five tiles, for a total of 25 square feet, with each tile drawn at 10 pixels to the inch. However, a map of multicolored Indian slate may need to have ten tiles by ten tiles, each drawn at 20 pixels to the inch. The white tiles may only have slight variations in surface detail, while the slate may include gold, green, blue, rust, charcoal, and copper tones, with each tile often having several blended color areas. With this general idea of pixel-to-the-inch ratio and accounting for variation, one can reasonably draw almost any map of a unit applied or constructed surface so that it will tile seamlessly and be repeatable over a large area.

SECTION C: PAINTING TILE

EXERCISE 1:   Mosaic tile

As previously outlined, when drawing maps we need to consider the size of the area the material will be applied to, as well as the size of each unit and the variation within and between each piece. For this example, we'll draw 1″ × 1″ mosaic tiles, such as those found in the American Olean, Dal-Tile, or Walker Zanger catalogs. Usually, tiles come in families, with each family having several available colors following the same pattern of variation and placement.

When drawing maps, just as when modeling fixtures or any other product, it is important to model a specific piece from a specific manufacturer, rather than a generic that you conjure up. The difference is often subtle, but clients have a knack for homing in on little details that you thought were small enough to overlook. Additionally, we visualization professionals need to take every opportunity to build up our libraries at someone else's expense if at all possible. Many of my clients return to me precisely because of my libraries; they know that what they will see in the rendered image will be exactly what they have specified and that no one else has the exact same library.

For this exercise, we will paint the Walker Zanger 1″ × 1″ mosaic field in Seagrass, from their Paradigm line of mosaic tiles (see Figure 8.3). As this tile is available at this size in seven other colors, we'll design this map to be flexible enough to generate all of the variations. Additionally, the techniques we will use are easily adapted to generate the other sizes and patterns of tile in this line. We'll draw this map at 40 pixels to the inch, with a ⅛″ grout line between tiles, in a 24″ × 24″ pattern; this yields a map of 1080 pixels on each side.

FIGURE 8.3

Walker Zanger Seagrass tile shown in a 1″ × 1″ mosaic.

1. Open Adobe Photoshop and go to File > New and start a new drawing of 2000 × 2000 pixels (see Figure 8.4). This will be our base drawing to generate tonal variations, from which we will cut and paste the tiles.

2. Set your foreground color to a brightness of 70% with no saturation, and the background color to a brightness of 50%, also with no saturation (see Figure 8.5). I recommend drawing maps like these initially in grayscale (in an RGB color mode), as the subtleties in the shading show better when they are not confused by color. We'll add the color later.

3. From the top menu, choose Filter > Render > Clouds. This will generate a random cloud pattern that will help us add variation within each tile.

4. Click on the Rectangular marquee tool or hit M, and set the Style to be a Fixed Size of 40 pixels by 40 pixels. Set your marquee down anywhere within the clouds. Click on the Zoom tool or hit Z and draw a window around your marquee (see Figure 8.6).

5. When comparing the amount of variation in the marquee to the amount of variation in each tile in the sample image, we can see that our clouds do not phase at a fine enough detail to accurately reproduce the tile. We can proceed in one of two ways: use a higher pixel-to-the-inch ratio, or downsize the clouds before cut-

FIGURE 8.4
Starting the new document in Adobe Photoshop.

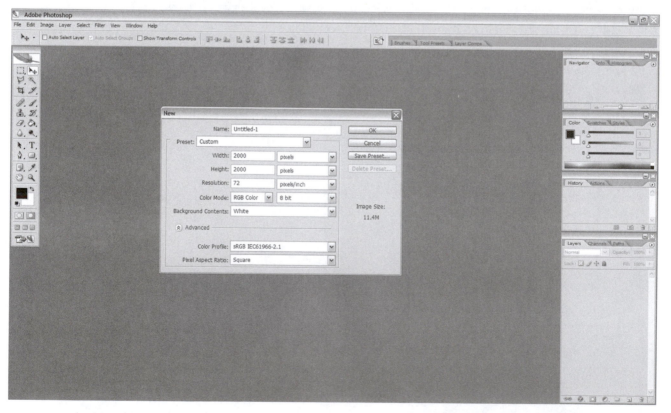

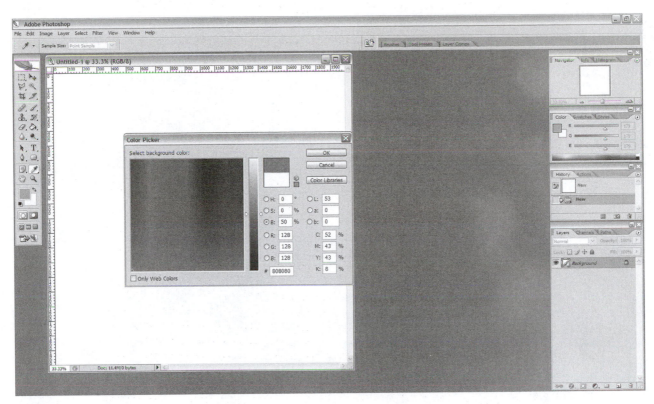

FIGURE 8.5

Changing the foreground and background colors using the color picker.

FIGURE 8.6

The 40 × 40 marquee showing too little variation within the selection.

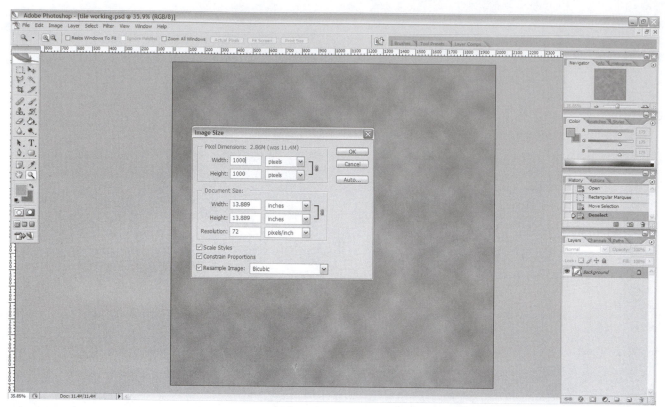

FIGURE 8.7

Resizing the image to increase cloud density.

ting out our tiles. We don't want to generate an excessively large map, as these are 1″ × 1″ tiles, and as previously mentioned, we are likely to see them straight on at several feet away at the closest, so we'll downsize the clouds. From your top menu, choose Image > Image Size. In the Image Size dialog, set the size of the image to 1000 × 1000 pixels and click OK (see Figure 8.7).

6. Now try placing your Rectangular marquee on the image and observe the amount of variation within the selection area. This is much more in line with the variation in the sample image.

7. Deselect everything by hitting Ctrl + D or going to the top menu and choosing Select > Deselect.

8. Now we need to add direction, or grain, and sharper distinctions between colors in the clouds before we cut our tiles. On the top menu, go to Filter > Brush Strokes > Accented Edges, and set your values as shown in Figure 8.8.

Note:
This is a technique I often use, rather than hand-painting each tile. You will most likely want to experiment with the various filters available in Photoshop for uses such as this. Often a combination will work, and everyone's eye and choice is different. Relax and play around—you might find something cool.

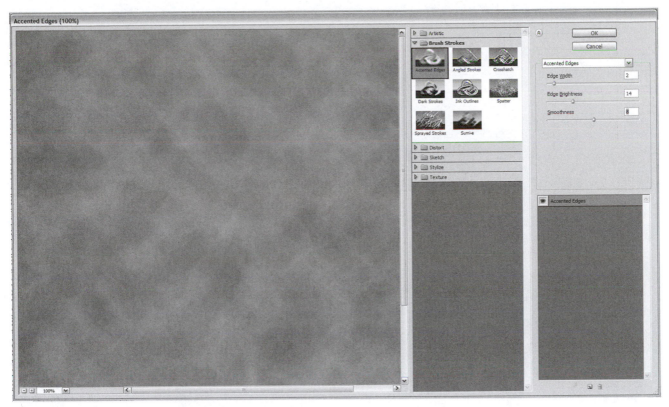

FIGURE 8.8
*Applying the
Accented Edges
filter to the clouds.*

9. Now we need to squeeze down this image just a bit to add a little grain to the stone. Go back to Image > Image Size, and change the image to 1000 pixels wide by 800 pixels tall. Although this may not yet look like the sample image, we have laid the foundations for a seamlessly tiling map.

10. Choose your Rectangular marquee tool again, and place it anywhere within the image. Copy the selection to the clipboard by choosing Edit > Copy from the top menu, or hitting Ctrl + C.

11. Go to File > New or hit Ctrl + N, and set the new image size to 1080 × 1080 pixels, as an RGB color image (see Figure 8.9).

12. Paste the clipboard contents into this new image by choosing Edit > Paste from the top menu or hitting Ctrl + V. Don't worry about where it lands—we'll position the tiles later.

13. Repeat steps 10 and 12 another 144 times. It should take about 10 minutes or so. Flex your fingers if your hand cramps.

14. Go to Edit > Preferences > Guides, Grid and Slices and change your grid to every 5 pixels, with one subdivision (see Figure 8.10). We're going to lay out the tiles by snapping them to the grid, so in this case we've made the grid spacing equal to the

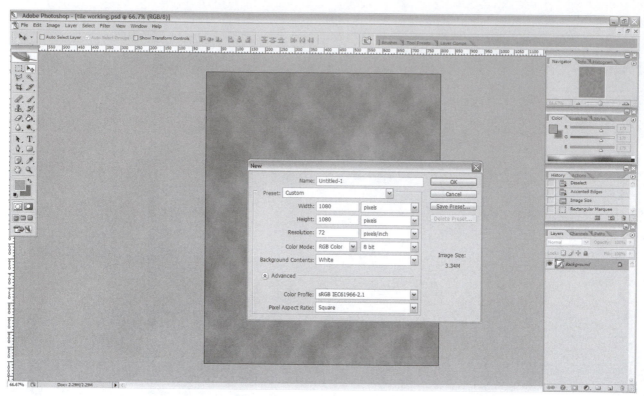

FIGURE 8.9

Starting the new document to place the tiles.

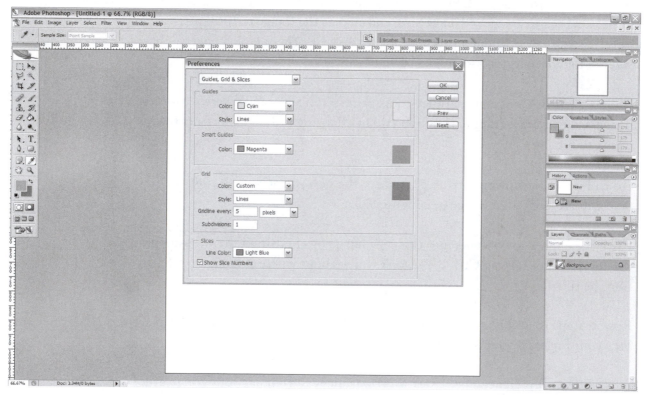

FIGURE 8.10

Setting the grid sizes in the Preferences dialog.

grout width between each tile. We cannot set the subdivisions lower than 1, so we'll leave them there and stay out of their way.

15. Choose the Move tool from the toolbar or press V, and on the Tool Properties at the top of the application, check Auto Select Layer.

16. Go to View > Show > Grid, and turn on the grid.

17. Using your Move tool, grab and position the tiles starting in the upper left corner, and working down and across to end with a 12 × 12 tile grid (see Figure 8.11). Each tile should have one grid space between, or 5 pixels. You may want to zoom in by using the Zoom tool on the toolbar or hitting Z.

18. Now we are ready to collapse the tiles into a layer, while keeping the grout separate for further manipulation. On the Layers palette, scroll down to the bottom and turn off the Background Layer by clicking on the Layer Visibility icon next to the thumbnail.

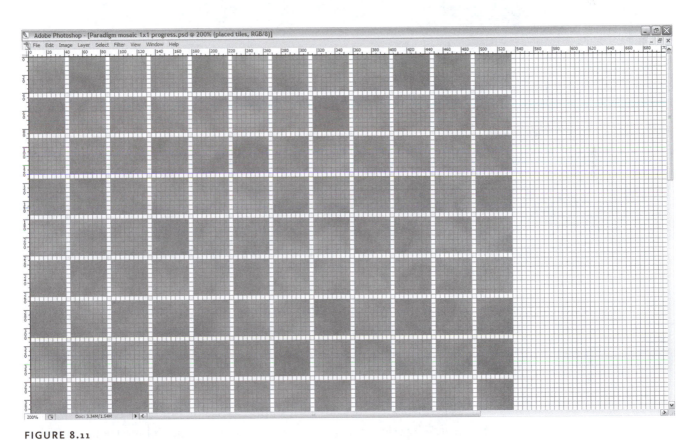

FIGURE 8.11
The 144 tiles in the mosaic.

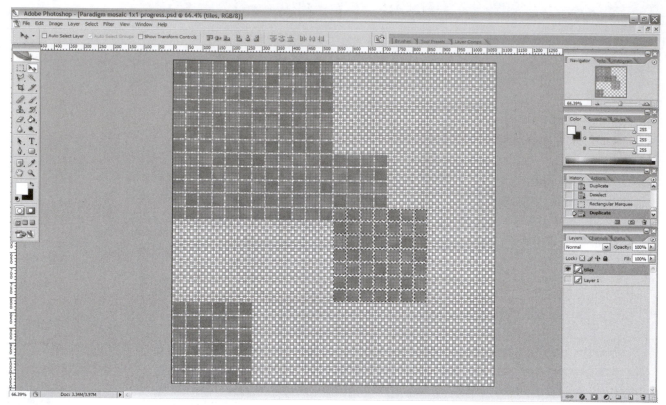

FIGURE 8.12

Cloning portions of the tiles to preserve randomness; cloned sections are shown partially placed.

19. Next click on the Palette options arrow on the upper right corner of the Layer palette, and choose Merge Visible; this is also available by choosing Layer > Merge Visible from the top menu, or hitting Ctrl + Shift + E on the keyboard. For clarity in the illustration, the grid is hidden; you can do this by either choosing View > Show > Grid from the top menu or Ctrl + ' on the keyboard.

20. Change to the Rectangular marquee tool again and select a group of nine or sixteen tiles from the positioned tiles (see Figure 8.12). We'll use this selection to enlarge the coverage of the tiles while still preserving the apparent randomness of the overall texture.

21. Switch to the Move tool, and while holding Shift, drag the selected tiles into the empty space adjacent to the other tiles. Repeat this twice more, landing the cloned tiles as randomly as possible, while still following the layout we've established. Repeat this step as needed to fill in the whole canvas.

22. The canvas is filled with tiles, all with similar variation but laid randomly with no visible repeat. The trick is to grab random sections of tiles, clone them, and occasionally overlap placed tiles with new sections, aligned on the grid, of course (see Figure 8.13).

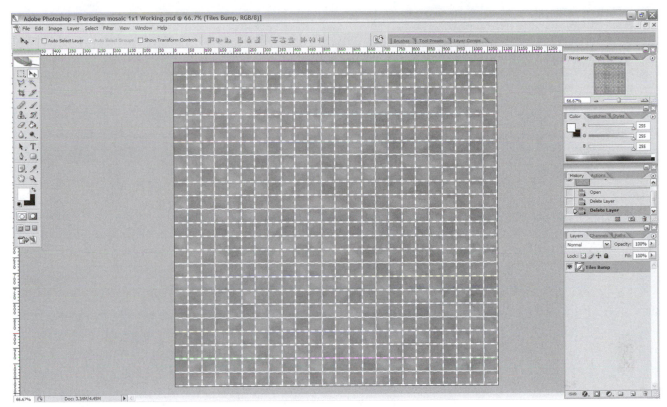

FIGURE 8.13
The completed random mosaic, ready for grout and color application.

23. At this point, our map is ready for additional coloration and saving of selected components. Other maps with more complex patterns or differently contoured tile may require more editing (see the Bonus Steps in Section F). This map will be used to generate all of the colors in the family of tiles, as well as common family maps for bump, shine, and reflection masking. Naming and organization is crucial when creating maps; so take a moment to organize and name this working drawing.

Note:
When drawing maps and organizing materials, I organize them by manufacturer for easy cataloging. I use a two-letter designation for each manufacturer as a prefix for the material and the maps; for example, SW for Sherwin-Williams, WZ for Walker Zanger, DT for Dal-Tile, BB for Boral Bricks, and so on. Working Photoshop documents are named for the manufacturer and the product family plus Working in the title.

To rename a layer in Photoshop, double-click on the layer name in the Layer palette. As we will be producing multiple maps from this working drawing, name the background layer Grout Bump and the tiles layer Tiles Bump (see Figure 8.14).

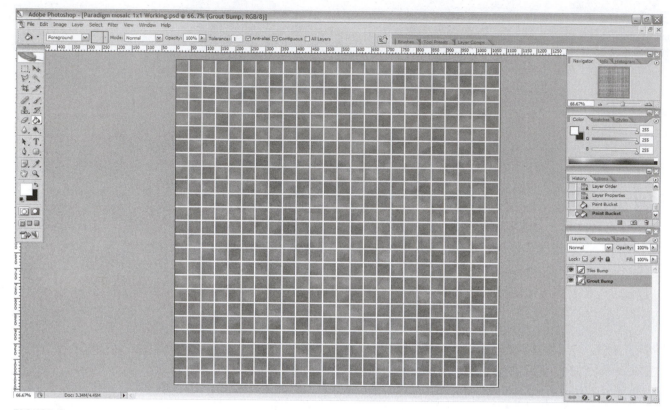

FIGURE 8.14

Naming and organizing layers while creating them.

24. Change the color of the Grout Bump layer to a darker gray than the tiles. Choose Image > Adjustments > Brightness and Contrast from the top menu (see Figure 8.15). In this example, the grout has been darkened by 100 points and the contrast increased by 30 points.

25. Go to File > Save As . . . and save this image as a 24-bit Targa file. Name this file *WZ Paradigm 1×1-B.tga,* and save it in a folder containing your tile maps.

Note:
This is a generic Bump map that will work with any of the Paradigm line in a 1″ × 1″ mosaic, hence the name WZ Paradigm 1×1-B.tga. *I usually name generic maps like the Bump for the family of the products, and then each color of the product will also have that color in the name. For example, the Seagrass tile we'll make next will be named* WZ Paradigm Seagrass 1×1-C.tga; *the Flannel would be named* WZ Paradigm Flannel 1×1-C.tga, *and so on.*

I try to name files such as these maps so that by looking at a list view of a directory, I can tell what maps I have and where they are intended to be used. In general, you should assume that maps will be drawn at a large size, and that previewing or viewing them in an application will take more time than you are willing to wait. Hence, a clear, logical naming structure that allows for a descriptive list view is an advantage in that it does not interrupt your workflow and thought process.

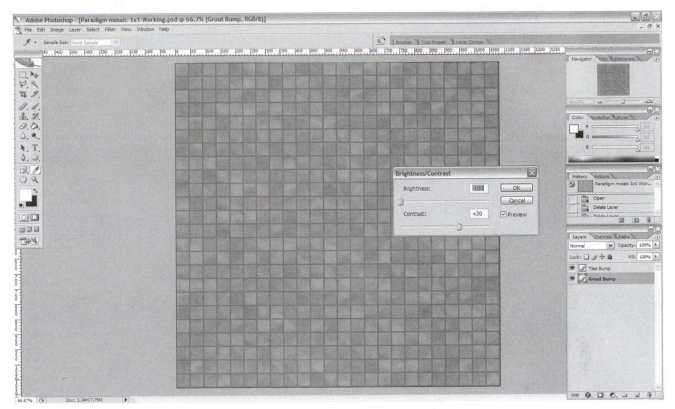

FIGURE 8.15

*Adjusting the
brightness and
contrast on the
grout so that it is
darker and hence
appears recessed
from the tiles.*

26. At this point, we are ready to construct the color map for the Seagrass mosaic tile, as well as any others we may need. The first step when constructing a color map is to look at the sample image (if there is one) at a very high magnification. Often there are details that do not need to be in a Bump map that are part of a Color map or a Shininess map, such as flecking, streaking, glinting, or glittering in a composite, and so on. The Seagrass tile has a dark flecking in the general pattern, as well as light dots or splotching. We'll use several techniques to achieve this look. Start by creating a new layer by choosing Layer > New . . . , hitting Shift + Ctrl + N on the keyboard, or by clicking on the New Layer button on the Layers palette.

27. Now we are going to generate a random pattern with a Grain filter, and then use different colors in the resulting grain to select small areas of color to form the dark flecking. Fill Layer 1 with 50% gray by choosing Edit > Fill . . . from the top menu or Shift + F5 on the keyboard. In the drop-down menu in the Contents section, choose 50% Gray (see Figure 8.16). This will be a scratch layer in this document; if you want to name it as such, feel free to do so.

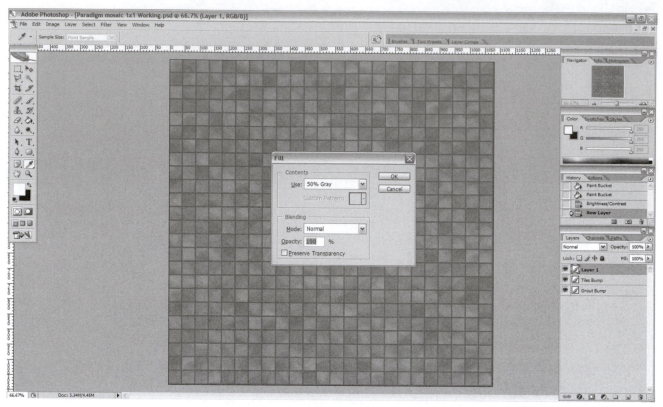

FIGURE 8.16

Filling the new layer with a 50% gray prior to applying the grain.

28. Choose Filter > Texture > Grain from the top menu. When the Filter editing dialog pops up, set the Grain Type to Enlarged, with an Intensity of 80–85, and a Contrast of 70–75 (see Figure 8.17). We want distinct but not sharp dots of color in a random pattern that is the same proportion and scale of the dark flecking in the tile. When using a technique such as this, you may find that you need to repeat the grain and selection steps a few times to get the right look; but don't panic. There is always a little trial and error in this sort of thing.

29. On the toolbar, select the Magic Wand tool, or press W on the keyboard. Set the Tolerance to 10 or so, turn off Contiguous, and turn on Anti-alias. Select one of the dots of color and look for a scattering of selection marquees as shown in Figure 8.18.

30. Create a new layer, and fill the selection with Render Clouds that phase between grays with a Brightness of 20% and 40%, with no Saturation. Name this layer Seagrass dark flecking01.

31. Set the Blending mode of this new layer to Multiply, and pull down the opacity to 30% or so.

32. Repeat steps 26–31 once more, but vary all of the numbers by 10–20%. We want scattered dark flecks that have randomness in their intensity and distribution. Name the second flecking layer Seagrass dark flecking02.

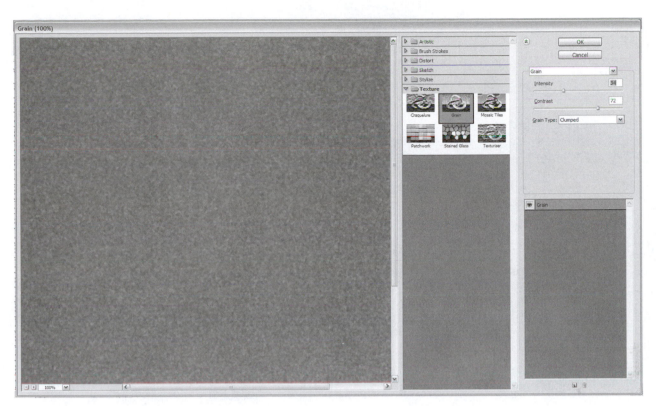

FIGURE 8.17

The grain pattern on the gray.

FIGURE 8.18

Selecting color ranges in the grain pattern to add speckling in the tile.

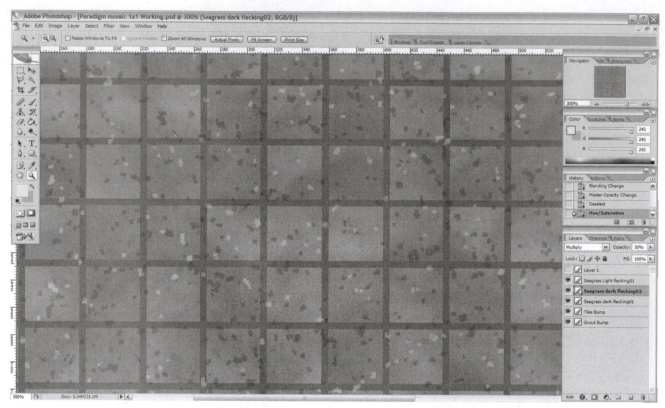

FIGURE 8.19

The dark and light flecking patterns overlaid on the tile.

33. Repeat steps 26–31 again, but this time change the grain type to Clumped (see Figure 8.19). This variation of grain size and pattern will produce the lighter splotches on the tile. Substitute grays of 75% and 95% for the dark grays in step 30. Additionally, change the Blending mode of this layer to Hard Light with an opacity of 65%. Name this layer Seagrass light flecking01.

34. At this point, the map is almost ready for color. The last step before coloring is to make sure that none of the flecking crosses a grout line. On the Layers palette, highlight the Tile Bump layer, and then hold Ctrl and click on the Layer Preview window with the left mouse button. This should select all of the tiles, leaving the grout unselected. Invert the selection by choosing Select > Inverse from the top menu or pressing Ctrl + Shift + I on the keyboard. Now only the spaces between the tiles should be selected (see Figure 8.20).

35. Highlight each of the three flecking layers, and press Delete on the keyboard. This will clear any of the flecking out of the grout if it landed there during the Magic Wand selection. When the flecking is cleared from the grout spaces, go to Select > Deselect or press Ctrl + D to deselect everything.

36. Highlight the Tile Bump layer, and drag it over the New Layer button on the Layers palette. This will create a copy of that layer. Name this copy Seagrass tile color.

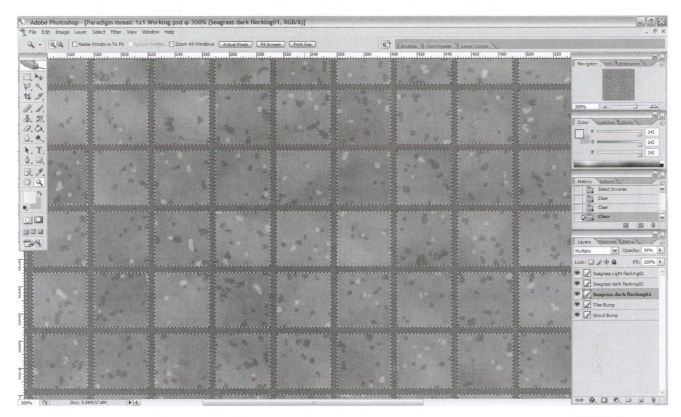

FIGURE 8.20

Cleaning up the flecking in the grout by using an inverted selection of the tiles.

37. Open the reference photo of the Seagrass tile in Photoshop. Resize both windows so you can see the map you are constructing and the reference side by side (see Figure 8.21).

38. We need to colorize this tile, and then add the variations found in the reference. Making sure that the Seagrass tile color layer is selected, go to Image > Adjustments > Hue/Saturation, and check Colorize in the Hue/Saturation dialog (see Figure 8.22). Adjust the Hue, Saturation, and Lightness sliders to match the image as well as possible.

39. This will at least produce an approximate match to the reference; however, it needs more work. What distinguishes a material such as this is the complexity and occurrence of color within each tile. To do this, we'll use the Replace tool in the Image > Adjustments menu. When the dialog is up, select one of the dark areas; we need to replace some of the yellow with gray (see Figure 8.23).

40. Repeat step 39 several times until the proportion of light and dark, gray, tan, charcoal, and straw colored tiles matches the reference. Again, this may take a bit of trial and error; keep trying different colors and combinations until you are satisfied (see Figure 8.24).

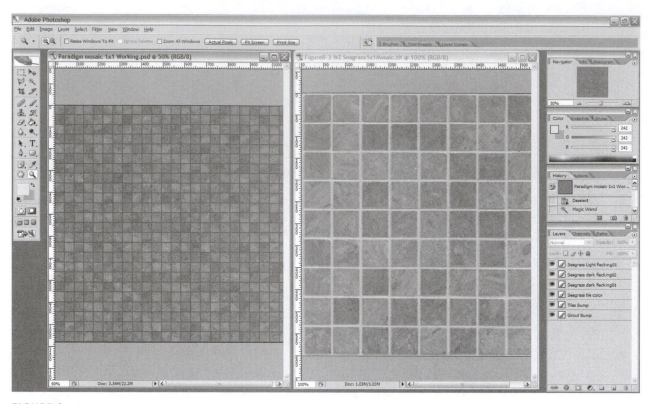

FIGURE 8.21

The new and reference documents open and ready to match the tile color.

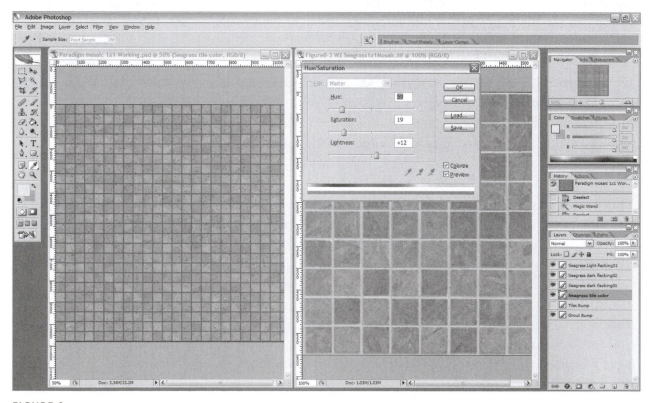

FIGURE 8.22

Colorizing the tile to match the sample.

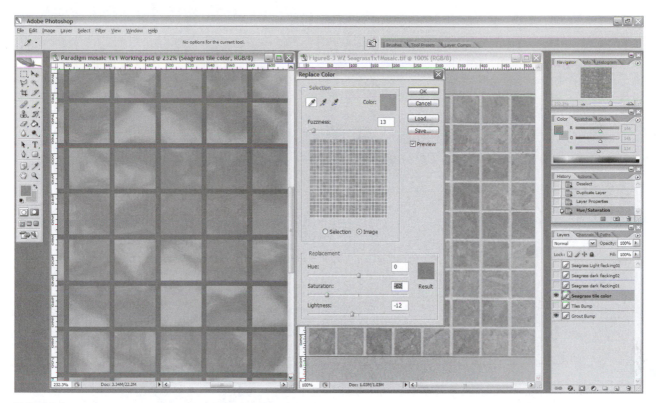

FIGURE 8.23

Using the Replace tool to change colors in the tile.

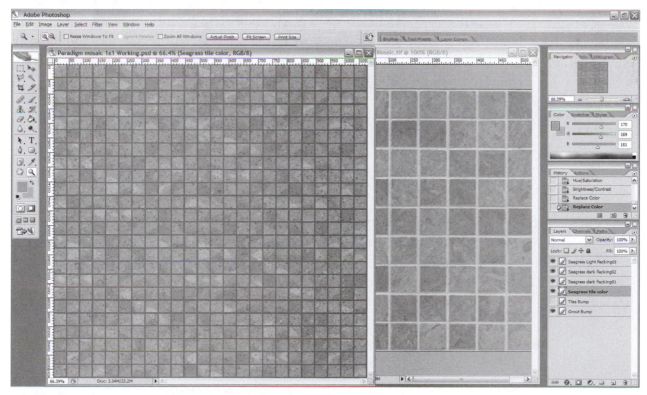

FIGURE 8.24

The tile color after using the Replace tool several times.

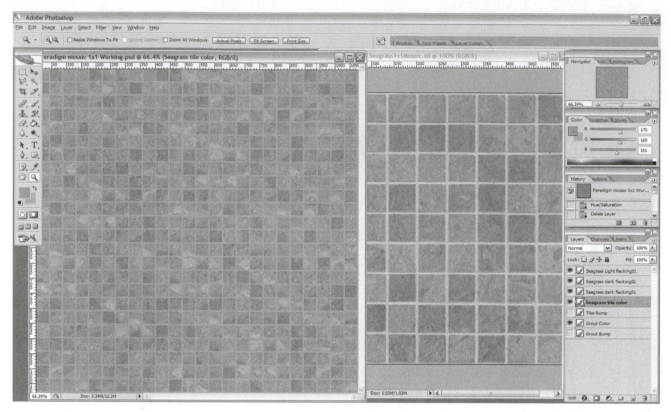

FIGURE 8.25

The completed tile color map.

41. Select the Grout Bump layer and make a copy of it. Name this copy Seagrass grout color. Fill this layer with a light gray, approximately 20%. If the Seagrass tile color layer appears too dark or light next to the grout when compared to the sample, adjust it using the Hue/Saturation dialog (see Figure 8.25). (Colors can always be adjusted slightly with the Hue/Saturation tool if needed.)

42. Go to File > Save As . . . and save the color layers as *WZ Paradigm Seagrass 1 × 1-C.tga* in your Tile Maps folder.

43. At this point, if needed, the other colors available in the Paradigm family for this size tile can be easily generated with these same methods. Before doing so, it is a good idea to organize this working drawing. On the Layers palette, click on the Create a new group button at the bottom. Name this group Seagrass tile mosaic.

44. Drag all of the color layers into this new group, checking to see that the order stays intact (see Figure 8.26).

45. Repeat step 44, naming the group Paradigm mosaic bump. Drag the bump layers into this new group. Save your file.

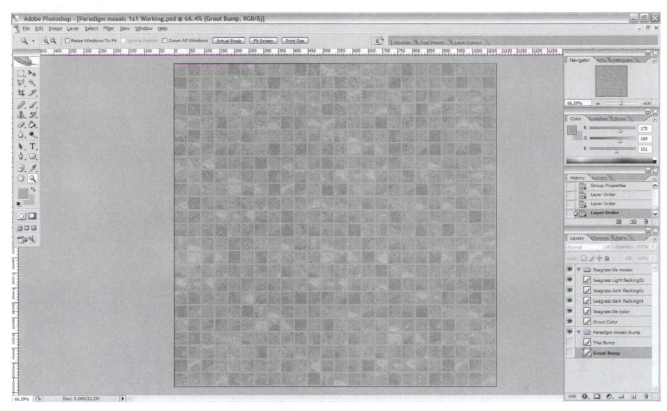

FIGURE 8.26
Organizing the tile layers in groups.

Note:

This working file will help generate all of the Paradigm family of tiles offered at this size. For files such as this, where one tile may be generated at a time, I'll name this file WZ Paradigm mosaic 1 × 1 Working.psd, and place it one directory down in my Tile Maps folder. This way, I won't accidentally load the PSD instead of a tile map, and I'll have it for future use and editing. Other working drawings in the Paradigm family might be WZ Paradigm small brick Working.psd or WZ Paradigm large brick Working.psd.

FIGURE 8.27
A reference image of granite panels.

SECTION D: GENERATING STONE

EXERCISE 2: Stone

In this exercise, we will draw granite using a method suitable for generating several different types of stone. Figure 8.27 is a reference for creating our stone. This tutorial consists of two main parts: construction of the pattern of the crystalline structure and matrix in the stone, followed by an application of color dependent on the topology of an unwrapped object. The second part concerning the application of the stone also features the stone as applied to a panelized construction such as the cladding of a building.

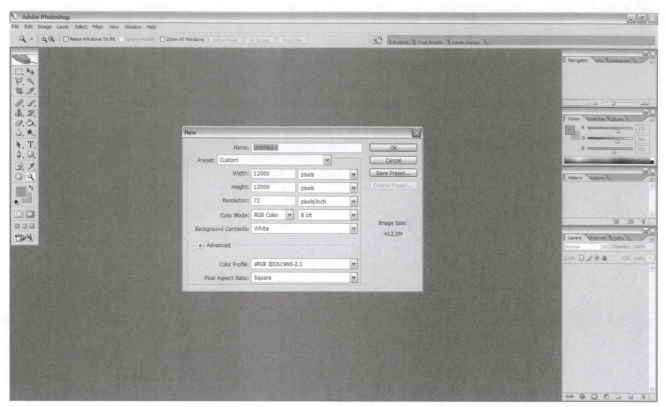

FIGURE 8.28

*Starting the new
document for the
stone at 12000 ×
12000 pixels.*

GRANITE, PART 1: THE BASE STONE

1. First, we need to simulate the general structure of the granite. Granite is an igneous rock, formed from cooling lava or magma pockets, and its structure is fairly uniform and blended, with blotchy variations between tones. To establish this general structure, we'll use Render Clouds, drawn big and scaled down. Start a new document by choosing File > New . . . from the top menu, or pressing Ctrl + N, and creating a document that is 12000 × 12000 pixels (see Figure 8.28).

    Note:
    This is a huge document, and these initial steps may bog down less powerful computers temporarily. You may want to close any other applications currently running to free up system resources.

2. From the Color Picker dialog, set the foreground color to RGB of 205,205,205, and the background color to 140,140,140.

3. From the top menu, choose Filter > Render > Clouds. This should cloud the entire document.

4. From the top menu, choose Image > Image Size, and resize the document to 2000 × 2000 pixels (see Figure 8.29). We started with the large document and

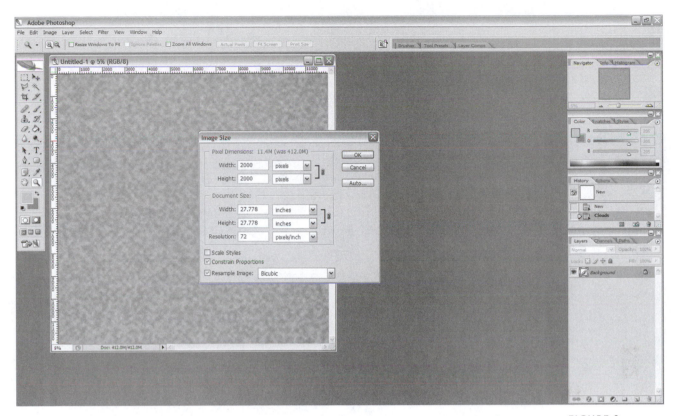

FIGURE 8.29
Resizing the image to 2000 × 2000 pixels once the clouds have been generated.

reduced it once the clouds were generated to produce a higher density of clouding within a manageable document size.

5. From the top menu, choose Filter > Pixelate > Facet. This will transform the smooth blending of the clouds into a faceted stonelike structure. Repeat this step once (see Figure 8.30).

6. Rename the background layer Matrix by double-clicking on the layer name on the Layers palette. Create a new layer below the Matrix layer named Base Color.

7. Fill the Base Color layer with the base color of the stone in the medium and light areas, in this case a warm gray with RGB of 204,196,188. Set the Blending mode of the Matrix layer to Color Burn at 100% opacity. Note: Depending on the type of stone and the variation within the matrix, you may want to fill the Base Color layer with Render Clouds instead of a solid. Set the foreground color as outlined in step 2, and then set the background color to a brighter version of the foreground color. Use the Render Clouds filter to fill the Base Color layer and adjust accordingly per your reference image (see Figure 8.31).

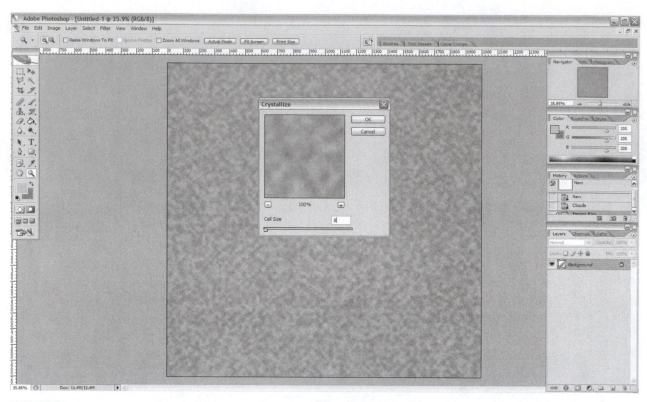

FIGURE 8.30

Applying the Pixelate filter to the clouds to crystallize and add facets to the structure.

FIGURE 8.31

The Matrix layer as a color burn over the clouds.

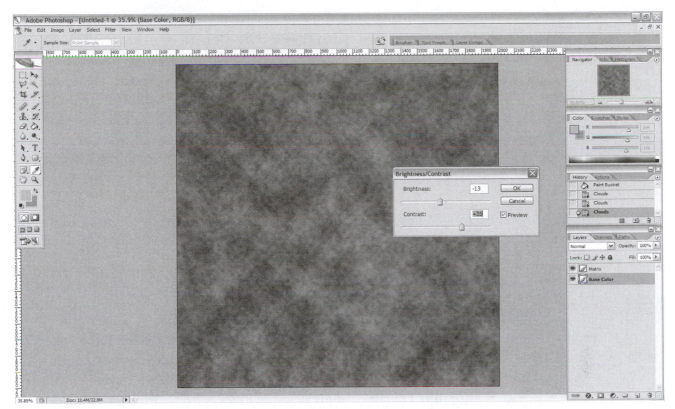

FIGURE 8.32

Adjusting the brightness and contrast of the base layer to add depth to the stone colors.

8. Different stones have different light to dark variation and intensities, so the amount of adjusting in this step will vary depending on the stone you are drawing. The granite reference photo shows a variation between a fairly dark charcoal, and warm and neutral light gray. From the top menu, choose Image > Adjustments > Brightness/Contrast, and decrease the Brightness by 13 and increase the Contrast by 35 (see Figure 8.32). By choosing grays close in value for the Render Clouds and adjusting later, we achieve a constant change in color over the image. If colors used for Render Clouds are too far apart in value, the image tends to have large areas of flat color that are awkward to adjust later.

9. At this point, the matrix and basic colors are in place. Now we'll construct the flecking of other stones that adds sparkle and personality to the granite. Create a new layer above the Matrix layer. This layer does not need a name as it will be a scratch layer. Fill the new layer with a 50% Gray by choosing Edit > Fill . . . from the top menu and selecting 50% Gray in the Use . . . drop-down menu, or by pressing Shift + F5.

10. With the new scratch layer highlighted on the Layers palette, go to Filter > Texture > Grain on the top menu. Choose the enlarged grain type, with an intensity of about 30 and a contrast of about 15.

11. Select the Magic Wand tool from the toolbar, or press W. Set the Tolerance to 12, and select one of the green splotches in the grain pattern.

12. Create another new layer named Flecking01, and fill the selection with a gold color (or other color based on a different reference image), with RGB of 185,170,135.

13. On the top menu, choose Select > Deselect, or press Ctrl + D. Go to Filter > Pixelate > Facet, applying the Facet filter to the Flecking01 layer so that it matches the crystalline feel of the other layers.

14. If necessitated by the reference image, repeat steps 10–13, choosing a different color to select from the grain. This will allow generation of multiple flecks as needed.

15. Save this document as *Granite working.psd*. This stone is now ready for use as a base texture, or as a color map for even-colored stone.

GRANITE, PART 2: APPLICATION AND ADDITIONAL COLORATION

This section of the tutorial requires a UVW template rendered from an unwrapped object. The granite constructed previously will form a base for specific sections in the Unwrap, which will then have additional color applied.

1. Open the *Granite working.psd* or continue from the previous tutorial.

2. Open the rendered unwrap template from 3ds Max. For this tutorial, open the *Counter and Bar Unwrap Template.tga* file in the Chapter 8 Assets folder (see Figures 8.33 and 8.34).

FIGURE 8.33
The countertop and bar top rendered from 3ds Max.

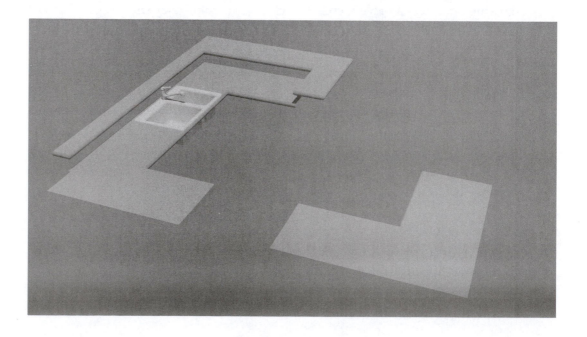

CHAPTER 8 : PAINTING TEXTURES

FIGURE 8.34
*The unwrap template
for the countertop
as exported from
3ds Max.*

3. In the *Granite working.psd,* go to Layer > Merge Visible on the top menu, or press Shift + Ctrl + E.

    Note:
    Do not save over the working version of the granite or you will lose your layer structure.

4. With the Move tool, drag the flattened granite across to the Unwrap Template document.

5. The granite as copied into the Unwrap Template is far too big for the stone's structure to be accurate. Scale down the stone by using the Transform Handles option on the Move tool, or by choosing Edit > Transform > Scale from the top menu. The scale of this stone depends on the area it is covering as well as the size of the Unwrap Template. For this countertop, scale the stone down to approximately one-third of its original size, so that the matrix looks proportionate on the template when compared with the reference image (see Figure 8.35). Be sure to hold the Shift key while scaling to maintain uniform proportion.

6. For easy reading and organization, drag the template layer above the stone layer in the Layers palette. Name the template layer Template, and the stone layer Stone Base.

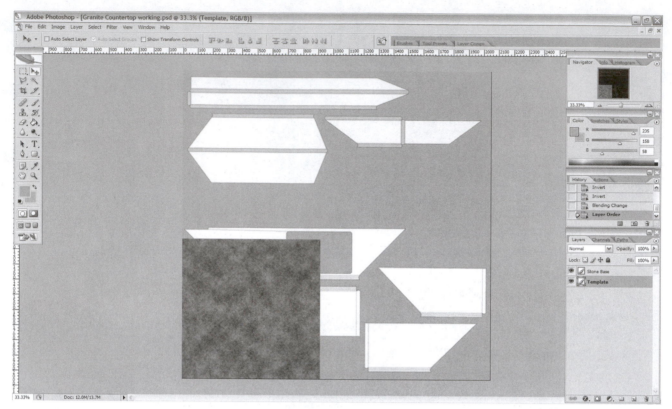

FIGURE 8.35

The granite base dragged onto the unwrapped counter and scaled down.

7. Press Ctrl + I to invert the colors of the Template layer, and set the Blending mode to Multiply Mode Opacity. This will allow anything under the template to show through while overlaying the mesh lines on the texture.

8. Lock the Template layer by clicking on the Lock button on the Layers palette.

9. Using the Move tool, click on the stone and hold the Alt key while dragging the stone across the document. This will clone the stone on a new layer. Cover all of the template parts using this method. When the stone overlaps another part of the template, use the selection lasso, polygonal lasso, or marquee tool to select and delete the overlapping area before continuing. If the stone is not big enough to cover a part of the template without a seam, leave an overlap of stone at the seam (see Figure 8.36).

10. In areas where the stone copies are overlapping at a seam on the template, use the Eraser tool with a large sponge brush to irregularly erase some of the overlapping layer. This will blend the two sections to eliminate the seam.

FIGURE 8.36

The stone panel, cloned and roughly cropped around each section of the countertop.

11. Merge the stone layers into one layer by turning off the Template layer on the Layers palette, and then choosing Layer > Merge Visible from the top menu, or pressing Ctrl + Shift + E. Name the resulting stone layer Stone Base. At this point, you can save the stone out as a separate map for use in a material in 3ds Max if a homogeneously colored stone is needed. The next steps concern adding color banding to the stone if needed.

12. Create a new layer on top of the Stone Base layer, and turn on the Template layer if it is not visible. Name this new layer Stone Banding.

13. This step may take a few tries to get the right look. Using a combination of brushes, add color banding or areas of varying color across the elements of the countertops. Be sure to stay consistent on the size and quality of the variations so that the pieces of stone look like they were either cut from the same slab or chosen to be together.

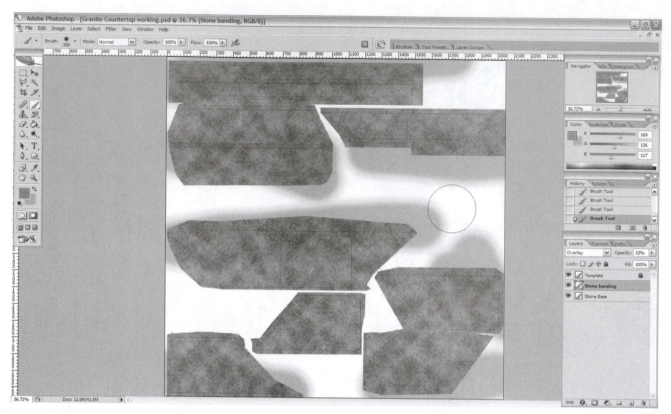

FIGURE 8.37

The stone with banding painted on.

14. Set the Blending mode of the Stone Banding layer to Overlay, and adjust the opacity for the desired result. Alternatively, try moving the Stone Base layer above the Stone Banding layer and setting the Blending mode of Stone Base to Multiply or Overlay (see Figure 8.37).

15. Save this document as *Granite Countertop working.psd* in your Stone Maps directory. Turn off the Template layer again and save this file as *Granite Countertop-C.tga,* at 24-bit depth.

SECTION E: WOOD PATTERNS

EXERCISE 3: Wood

As with metallic finishes, mosaics, and complex stone veneers, we can be easily overwhelmed by the complexity of color and subtlety in wood. To simplify the process, the first step in constructing a complex material is to separate the color from the pattern. With a wood, the starting point is the grain, which will give us a basis for the color map, as well as a shine and bump, depending on how finely finished the sample needs to be. As with previous tutorials, the map we draw will start with a grayscale simulation of the pattern and randomness of the material.

Section A explained that textures found on the Internet or in texture libraries are often too small in terms of the physical area shown. The image may be several thousand pixels on a side, but too often the area of wood shown is only several inches by several inches. Additionally, as wood is often polished to a high shine, it is nearly impossible to get a photo of wood without some baked-in lighting. Hence, the aim of drawing wood from scratch is to remove the lighting present in the image and provide a sample that can be used on a large panel or piece of furniture or casework at the right scale.

This tutorial is divided into two sections, each featuring a different wood. Figures 8.38 and 8.39 are provided as photo references in creating the wood. After completing these exercises, you will have a large sample of wood for general use in mapping on furniture or casework, or for further editing to produce flooring or other patterned application.

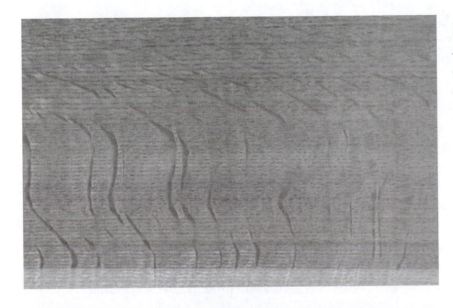

FIGURE 8.38
A reference image of quartersawn oak.

FIGURE 8.39
A reference image of crosscut oak showing a different grain.

FIGURE 8.40

Starting the new document.

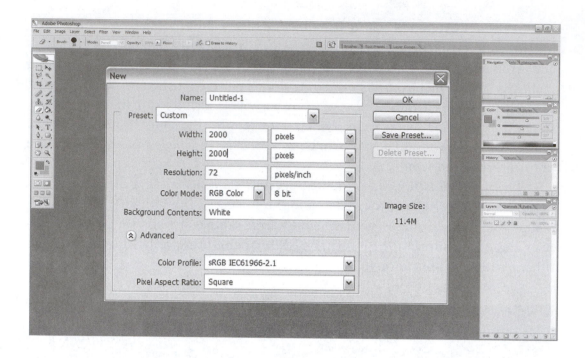

WOOD, PART 1: POLISHED QUARTERSAWN OAK

1. In Photoshop, start a new document that is 2000 × 2000 pixels, 8-bit, with a square pixel aspect ratio (see Figure 8.40).

2. Fill this image with 50% gray by hitting Shift + F5, or choosing Edit > Fill from the top menu, and then selecting 50% Gray in the Contents section.

3. From the top menu, choose Filter > Texture > Grain. When the Filter dialog appears, change the grain type to vertical. Take the Contrast down to 0 and the Intensity to 20–25 (see Figure 8.41). This will produce an even grain pattern in a gray field.

4. Choose the Brush tool and pick a round brush somewhere between 275 and 325 pixels, with hardness set to 0 (see Figure 8.42). In the document, right-click to access the Brush dialog; alternatively, the < and > keys will enlarge or reduce the brush size. Brush options are also found at the top of the screen, just below the top menu. Set the opacity of this brush to 50%.

5. Brush several lines along the length of the document, keeping them roughly but not perfectly vertical. Add additional color depth by changing the brush size, opacity, and color by 10–15% up and down. Start with a foreground RGB color around 130,130,130, or roughly a 50% gray. The purpose of this step is to somewhat but not totally obscure some of the grain to approximate the growth rings of hard and soft woods.

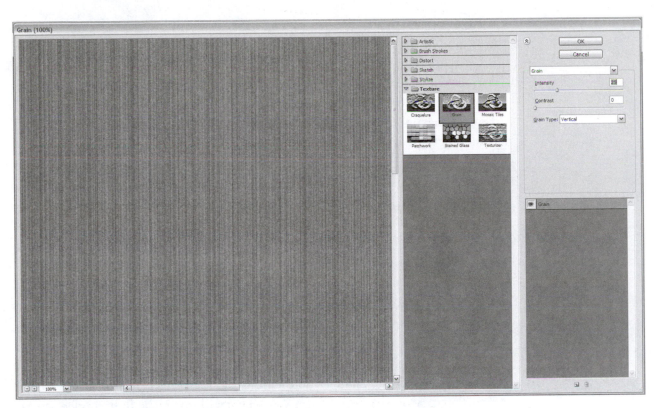

FIGURE 8.41

The vertical grain applied to the 50% gray.

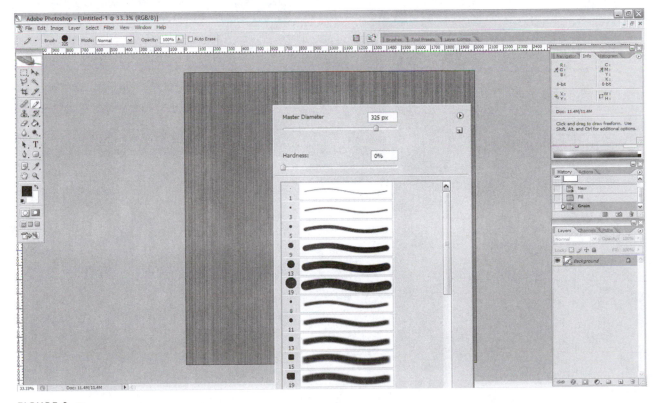

FIGURE 8.42

Setting the diameter and hardness of the brush.

6. Create a copy of this layer by choosing Layer > Duplicate layer . . . or dragging the layer onto the New Layer button in the Layers palette.

7. With the copy of Layer 0 selected, go to Filter > Brush Strokes > Angled Strokes, and apply the filter with a Direction Balance of about 55, a Stroke Length of about 20, and a Sharpness of 7 or so (see Figure 8.43). There is a little wiggle room in values such as these to allow tuning of the look and feel of the drawing.

8. The previous steps added an angled pattern over the grain, but the image is too muddy; it lacks contrast between hard and soft woods within the sample. Go to Image > Adjustments > Brightness/Contrast, and increase the contrast and brightness of this layer until only some of the angled strokes remain on an otherwise fairly solid field (see Figure 8.44).

9. Go to Image > Adjustments > Invert, or press Ctrl + I, and invert the colors of this layer. This will leave white strokes on a dark background, simulating the striations in the wood that run counter to the grain.

10. On the Layers palette, change the Blending mode of this layer to Linear Dodge, with an opacity of 25% (see Figure 8.45). This will make the light angled strokes become apparent over the dark grain lines.

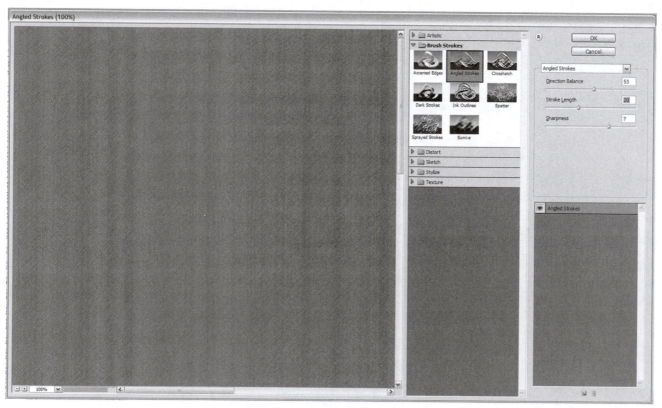

FIGURE 8.43

Applying the angled strokes to the clone of the grain layer.

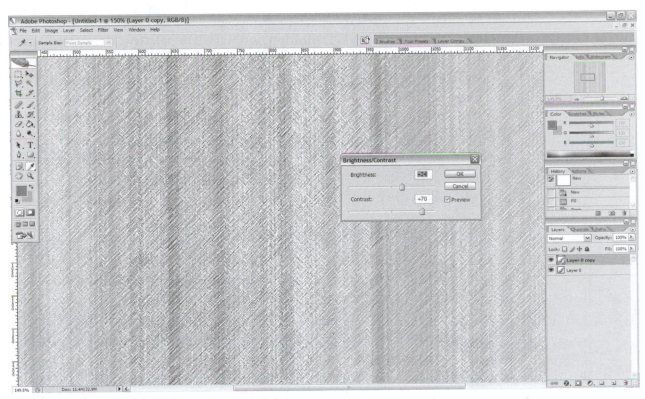

FIGURE 8.44

Increasing the brightness and contrast of the angled strokes so that they will provide a subtle cross-grain highlight.

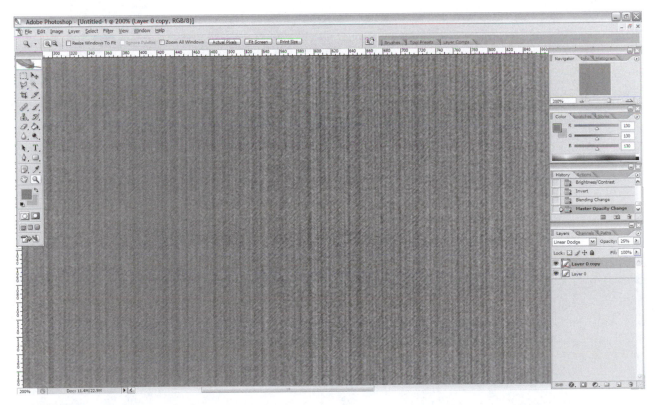

FIGURE 8.45

The angled cross-grain highlights over the straight grain.

11. At this point, the wood is ready for color. Create a new layer underneath the others by clicking the New Layer button on the Layers palette, or pressing Shift + Ctrl + N, or choosing Layer > New . . . on the top menu. On the Layers palette, drag this layer below the other two. This will be the color layer of the wood.

12. Set the foreground color to a warm tan matching the color of the lighter parts of the reference image. This color should tend toward being less saturated and lighter than the color in the reference image, so adjust as needed. As an example, the color shown has RGB values of 193,174,144. Fill the bottom layer with this color by using either the Paint Bucket or the Edit > Fill . . . command.

13. Set the Blending mode of the original grain layer to Color Burn, with an opacity of about 90%. The image should be fairly close to the reference image. With luck, the overlay of the high contrast cross-grain layer will produce banding and looping similar to actual wood.

14. At this point, the wood map is ready for final color adjustment and grain enhancing. Highlight the top layer in the Layers palette. On the top menu, go to Layer > New Adjustment Layer, and choose Brightness/Contrast as the type. Adjust the brightness and contrast of the wood map until it matches the general tones of the reference image (see Figure 8.46). If additional adjustment is needed, use another Adjustment layer set to Hue/Saturation, and adjust accordingly.

FIGURE 8.46
Adjusting the wood using Hue/Saturation and Brightness/ Contrast adjustment layers.

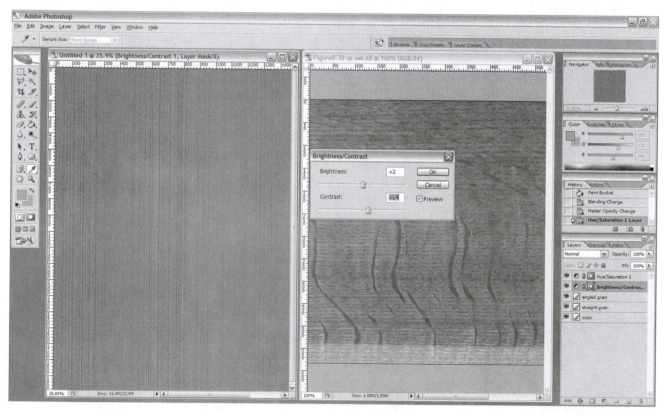

15. The base map for this oak is complete for use as a color map or for further editing into a panelized or assembled construction. At this point, you can save this Photoshop file as *Oak Quartersawn working.psd,* and then save as a Targa file named *Oak Quartersawn-C.tga,* set to 24-bit.

BONUS STEPS

1. Try drawing different configurations of the map using various brush sizes and colors in step 5.

2. Add additional coloring by painting on dark and light color variations on the bottom color layer.

3. Flatten the map and use the Liquify filter to add some waviness to the grain as shown in Figure 8.39. Use a very big brush (500–600 pixels wide) with a low pressure, and gently distort the grain (see Figure 8.47). Play with it, and don't be afraid to mess around until it looks right.

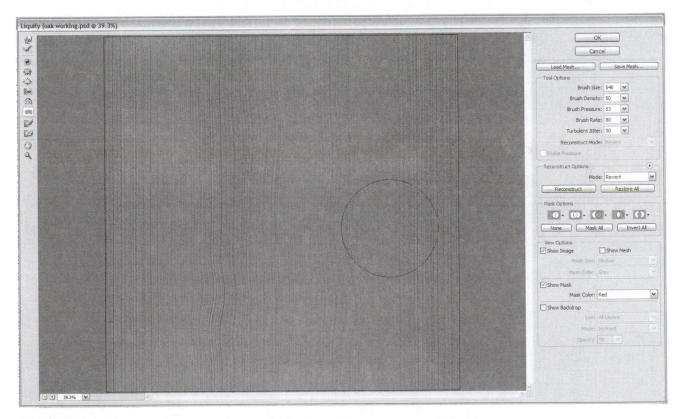

FIGURE 8.47

The Liquify filter used to add waviness to the wood grain.

FIGURE 8.48

A reference image of padauk.

WOOD, PART 2: POLISHED PADAUK

1. Before getting started, take a look at the reference image of padauk (see Figure 8.48). Now, open a new document that is 100 × 100 pixels, 8-bit, RGB. Fill this document with 50% gray.

2. Go to Filter > Texture > Grain and choose Vertical Grain, with an Intensity of about 25 and a Contrast of about 20.

3. On the top menu go to Image > Image Size and change the size of the document to 2000 × 2000 pixels (see Figure 8.49). (Note the extreme blurring of the grain from the resizing.)

4. This will provide the base color striping in the wood, which is the difference between heartwood and sapwood. From the top menu, choose Filter > Blur > Motion Blur. Set the Angle to 90 and the Distance to about 350 (see Figure 8.50).

5. Rename the Background layer to Base Stripes. Create a new layer below it called Base Color.

6. Set the foreground color to a light orange/tan, with RGB values around 210,170,135. Fill the Base Color layer with this color.

7. On the Layers palette, change the Blending mode of the Base Stripes layer to Color Burn, with an opacity of about 95%. This should produce a stripe pattern varying between deep purple, burnt orange, blond, and other hues.

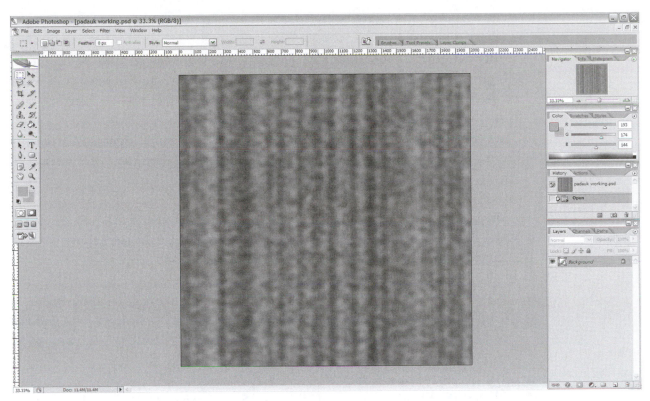

FIGURE 8.49

The resized vertical grain at 2000 × 2000 pixels.

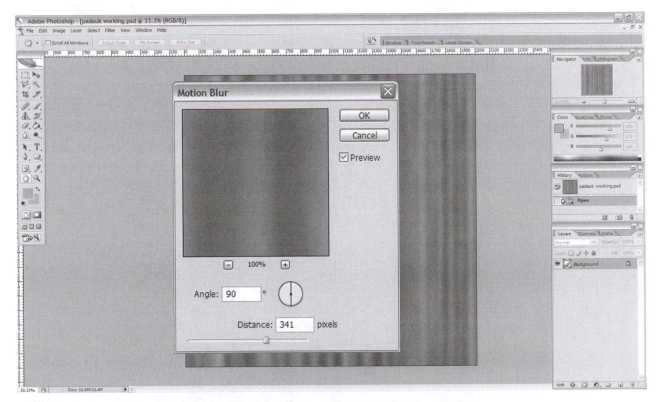

FIGURE 8.50

Applying the motion blur to the grain which smoothes out the grain while preserving the color variation.

8. Create a new layer on top of the Base Stripes layer called Growth Rings.

9. Fill the Growth Rings layer with 50% gray, and then choose Filter > Texture > Grain from the top menu. Use the Vertical Grain, with an Intensity of 25 and a Contrast of 25 or so.

10. Set the Blending mode of the Growth Rings layer to Hard Light at 15% opacity (see Figure 8.51). This will add fine dark stripes simulating some of the seasonal growth rings in the tree.

11. Drag the Growth Rings layer onto the New Layer button on the Layers palette to make a copy of this layer. Alternatively, hold Alt and drag the layer above Growth Rings to clone the layer. Name this new layer Heartwood Striping.

12. With the Heartwood Striping layer selected, choose Image > Adjustment > Brightness/Contrast from the top menu. Increase the brightness by 40 and the contrast by 60 or so. Most of the layer should be white to light gray, with some striping remaining.

13. Change the Blending mode of Heartwood Striping to Color Burn with an opacity of 60%.

FIGURE 8.51
The working wood sample shown with base stripes and growth rings overlaid on the base color.

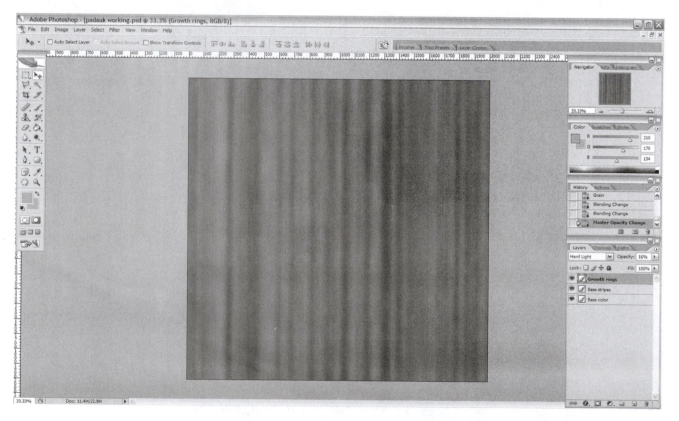

CHAPTER 8 : PAINTING TEXTURES

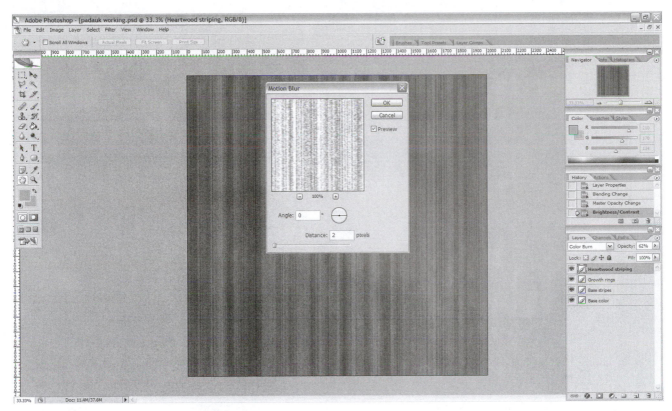

FIGURE 8.52
The motion blur applied to the Heartwood Striping layer.

14. Go to Filter > Blur > Motion Blur on the top menu, and set the Angle to 0 and the Direction to 2 pixels. This will blur the small dots in the grain while leaving the dark striping intact (see Figure 8.52).

15. Create another new layer on top of the Heartwood Striping layer, and name it Pores. Fill this layer with a brighter and more saturated version of the base color.

16. On the top menu, Choose Filter > Noise > Add Noise, and add a Gaussian Noise at 5%, with the Monochromatic option checked (see Figure 8.53).

17. Set the Blending mode of the Pores layer to Multiply at 50% opacity.

18. The base map of the padauk is now complete. Save this file as *Padauk working.psd* in your Wood Maps directory.

19. Go to Layer > Flatten Image on the top menu, or press Ctrl + Shift + E, and flatten this image into one layer. Make sure you have saved the layered version before this step.

20. On the top menu, choose Filter > Liquify. When the Liquify dialog pops up, set the Brush Size to 500, the Brush Density to 15, and the Brush Pressure to 15 or so. Use the brush set to Forward Warp and add subtle waviness to the grain. This

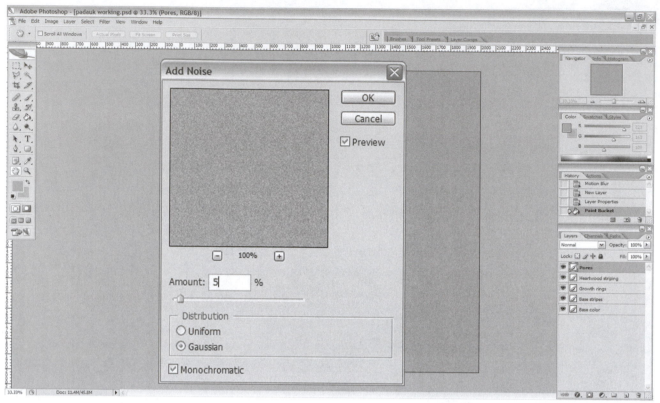

FIGURE 8.53

Adding the Gaussian noise to the Pores layer.

may take a few tries to get the hang of it; there is a Reconstruct All button on the right side of the interface should you require it.

21. Once you have added variation to the grain consistent to your reference image, save this file in your Wood Maps directory as *Padauk1-C.tga,* set to 24-bit depth. You may want to repeat the flatten and Liquify process two or three times to make a selection of matching but varied woods to avoid repeat occurrences of a particular wave or grain (see Figure 8.54).

FIGURE 8.54

The final wood image with wave and knots added using the Liquify filter.

SECTION F: CARPETS AND RUGS

EXERCISE 4: Carpets

Like many materials, carpet or carpet tile as shown in a three-dimensional rendering is really about a pattern that we expect to see on that type of surface, or in that particular area or zone. Unless we are six inches from it, we cannot see the fibers in the weave, and even at three feet away, the eye starts to swim when focusing on the loops. Hence, carpet can be drawn as a general pattern of randomized color in small dots, and then if needed have a weave or tile pattern overlaid.

EXERCISE 5: Rugs

This tutorial covers drawing rug maps for use where a rug has not been specified from a manufacturer. There are many fine makers of rugs around the globe that can probably provide something that perfectly fits the design, and at a lower price than a custom-designed rug. However, as generated renderings are often produced long before exact product specifications are made, being able to conjure a rug in short order is extremely useful. Additionally, and this chiefly concerns the stroking of a client's delicate ego, being able to say that the rug shown in the rendering was custom-designed for them always wins the visualization artist serious points.

1. Open a new document that is proportionate to the rug desired. To avoid excessively large maps, create one inch of map for every foot of rug. For this example, we'll make a 6′ × 9′ rug for use in a lobby or waiting area. Hence, the new drawing should be 6″ × 9″; setting the resolution at 150 pixels per inch will produce an adequately sized map (see Figure 8.55).

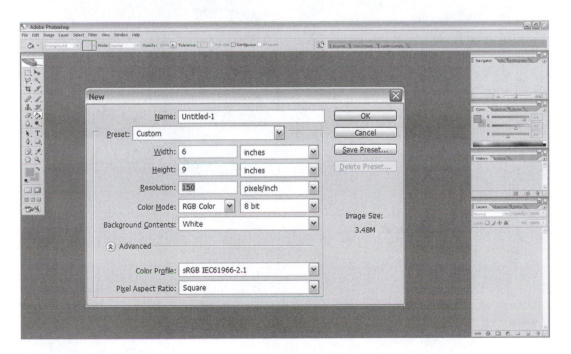

FIGURE 8.55
Starting the new rug document.

2.   Rename the Background layer to Color on the Layers palette.

3.   Draw the color pattern of the rug using whatever tools you wish. For a simple geometric or abstract rug, use the marquee tool and the Paint Bucket to fill areas. Unless you are drawing a white rug, make sure that the document is filled with color (see Figure 8.56). Let loose with your inner rug designer and have a little fun here.

4.   As you can see from the examples in step 3, the possibilities are endless. Let your inner weaver come forth and design! When the Color layer is drawn to your liking, create a new layer above it named Weave.

5.   Fill the Weave layer with 50% gray, and then unleash the filters! Some examples of different weave patterns are outlined next.

5a. For a horizontal weave, go to Filter > Texture > Grain, and set the Grain Type to Horizontal, with an Intensity of 30 and a Contrast of 15. Set the Blending mode of the Weave layer to Hard Light at an opacity of 100%. Blur the weave a bit by choosing Filter > Blur > Gaussian Blur from the top menu, and use a Radius of 1.25 (see Figure 8.57).

FIGURE 8.56

A geometric pattern drawn for the color of the rug.

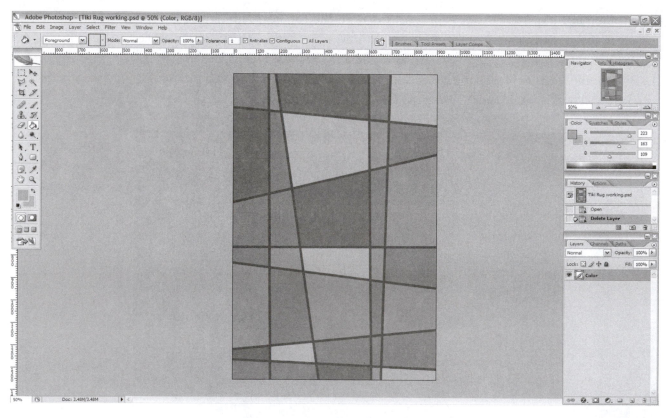

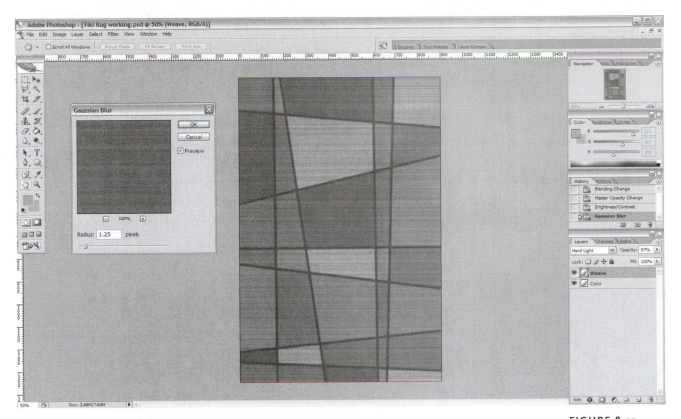

FIGURE 8.57
*The Weave layer
with a horizontal
grain and a
Gaussian blur
applied to soften
the grain.*

5b. For a nondirectional "nubbly" or looped weave, go to Filter > Pixelate > Pointillize on the top menu. Set the Cell Size to 5, the smallest. Desaturate the Weave layer after applying the filter. Move the Color layer above the Weave layer, and set the Blending mode to Multiply or Color Burn. This will undoubtedly require experimentation, so play around with the Blending modes, the layer opacity, and the order of layers until the result works.

5c. For a shaggy, looser weave, go to Filter > Texture > Grain and choose a Clumped Grain type. Set the Intensity to 65 and the Contrast to 45. Zoom out on the drawing to 12.5% size or so, and scale the Weave layer to seven or eight times its original size. Desaturate the Weave layer. (You may want to Sharpen or Sharpen More the Weave layer.) Move the Color layer above the Weave layer, and set the Blending mode to Hard Light or Color Burn. This will undoubtedly require experimentation, so play around with the Blending modes, the layer opacity, and the order of layers until the result works.

6. Highlight the Color layer on the Layers palette, and go to Filter > Blur > Gaussian blur (for the looped weaves) or Filter > Blur > Motion blur for the directional weaves. Add a pixel or two worth of blur to the Color layer to increase the perceived fuzziness of a woven product.

7. Save the document as *Rug working.psd,* or if you are feeling confident in your design ability, give it a fanciful name. Ideally, this name will have little or no connection to the actual rug design, in keeping with industry standard practices for naming colors and textiles.

8. Go to File > Save As . . . on the top menu, and save the rug as *Rug Name-C.tga,* at 24-bit depth. This will be the color map for the rug in 3ds Max.

9. Hide the Color layer and change the Blending mode of the Weave layer to Normal, with 100% opacity. Go to File > Save As . . . on the top menu, and save the rug as *Rug Name-B.tga,* at 24-bit depth. This will be the bump map for the rug in 3ds Max.

BONUS EXERCISE: More complex rugs

Draw a rug that has textural variations as well as color variations by combining different weave patterns and scales. Use the Magic Wand tool to select the color areas of the rug, and then apply the weave generating filters on a different layer.

SECTION G: ADDING AGE OVERLAYS

EXERCISE 6: Age overlays

Yes, things do occasionally show their age in renderings. There are two kinds of wear to add to a map, mechanical wear and gravity or water-based wear. Of these, mechanical wear is the more desirable. In this realm fall antiqued surfaces, the scratches and dings so prized for their earthiness, the patina of thousands of fingers on a surface. Gravity or water-based wear is not always as desirable. Often things are stained by leaks, soiled by sprinklers, or discolored by a constant battle with the elements. However, some airborne water-based wear is useful occasionally. For example, an antique sideboard may show a patina of darkening in the corners of the door frames, or a reclaimed wood floor may be stained by years of river mud. On any of the maps you have drawn, once you cut them to fit an unwrap template, you can add dirt and patina.

1. Open the *Dresser Unwrap Template.psd* from the Assets folder for this chapter. This is an unwrapped antique Shaker dresser that has already had wood grain applied from a sample similar to the one generated in earlier exercises. On the Layers palette, create a new layer and name it Patina Dark. Rather than trying to paint all of the wear on one layer, add the patina a bit at a time, so that it can be easily adjusted (see Figure 8.58). (This image focuses on the drawers and surrounding frames.)

FIGURE 8.58
*The unwrap
template and wood
images for the
dresser.*

2. Switch to the Brush tool, and choose a dark brown foreground color.

3. On the Layers palette, press Ctrl and click on the thumbnail window for the UVW Template layer. This will constrain a selection to the filled parts of the layer.

4. Set the Brush tool to Airbrush, at 20% opacity, with a Blending mode of Multiply.

5. In long fluid strokes, add darkness around the edges of the panels and trim, making sure to leave the middle open. This is only the first layer, so go lightly. Make sure that the strokes are not quite perfect; that there is a little wiggle here and there (see Figure 8.59).

6. Repeat this process twice more, naming the new layers Patina Medium and Patina Light. Each time, reduce the opacity of the brush by 5%, and lighten the foreground color by 20 points.

7. As you brush the successive layers, make sure to spread each one toward the middle of the panel a little more, so that as it is all painted, the outer 15 to 20% of each panel is a "patina zone."

FIGURE 8.59

Painting on the patina and darkening of the wood, slowly and in layers.

8. Create another new layer on top of the Patina Dark layers, and name this one Patina Rubbed.

9. Set the foreground color to a deep gold, and the Blending mode to Soft Light at 15% opacity. On the top of the dresser, paint in the center of the panel and at the front edge some lightening of the finish. This should be a golden rub, from years of clothing being set on top and pulled off (see Figure 8.60). As before, work in very faint strokes and layer them on to simulate time-based wear.

10. Save a copy of this image as *Dresser Antique-C.tga* in your furniture library maps folder.

FIGURE 8.60
Painting the brighter area of the wood using a brush set to Soft Light.

SECTION H: CONCLUSION

We can produce perfection in the 3ds Max world, where corners are exactly ninety degrees, walls are plumb forever, and bathroom tiles are laid in exact rows as far as the eye can see. However, just because we can create perfection, it doesn't mean we should. Like uniformly shimmering blond hair, a too perfect rendering does not ring true either. When constructing a visualization, it is the artist's job to add small amounts of randomness that come from using manufactured materials to build buildings. It is the human element of the equation that adds realism to a rendering. The ability to analyze and deconstruct a coherent whole into component parts for reconstruction and replication is a critical skill. As shown in the section on creating tile, we can and should make a distinction between quality of workmanship and material variance. We do not want our images to show shoddy construction, but rather the variation of color seen in a crowd of faces; the differences in personality of siblings, not strangers.

CHAPTER **9** Lighting

SECTION A: ACCURATE LIGHTING

*S*unbeams are sexy. People like shiny objects. Show them the money. These primary concepts of visualization depend on many factors, from camera placement to proper modeling techniques to good material design. These factors, in turn, each depend on one thing being done successfully in the scene: lighting. Without good lighting, there is no depth in the shadows, polished floors do not shine, and sofas do not bask in golden light. In badly lit scenes, colors are blown out or sallow, details are lost in murkiness, and expensive furniture floats flaccidly above the floor.

When designing the lighting for a space or a building, it is better to design the mood of the scene rather than looking at the exact bulbs or luminaries to be used. To create a mood, we will borrow from the world of cinematography and motion pictures. Design the lighting in terms of highlights, midtones, and shadows; talk about the transparency or opacity of the shadows. When I discuss lighting with a client or in class, we talk about the way people should feel when they see the image or animation. The color, derived from the lighting, determines the mood the audience feels before anything happens. The quality of the shadows, how they spread or stay sharp, can bring a feeling of crisp precision or soft luxury to an image. We talk about the richness and complexity of dappled shadows from trees in front of a window or the soft pooling of light on tables in a restaurant.

The overriding guideline for lighting, aside from sunbeams being sexy, is that that lighting should be complex and varied, with all of the subtlety and drama that we expect to see. As an example, the corner of a building should never have even lighting from side to side; move the sun so that one side is brighter and one is darker. This will define the corner and lengthen shadows on the darker side, adding depth. Sunbeams that reach across a space, slinking on the floor and over the furniture to climb the opposing wall, have much more visual power than those that simply leave yellow parallelograms on the rug. Can lights should leave soft puddles of light on the floor and parabolic arcs on the walls, adding rhythms of light and shadow to the scene.

One of the exercises I have my classes do, and I do myself for clients, is to write a descriptive brief of the lighting, shadows, and overall mood of the scene. It is notoriously difficult to draw lighting as the light fades across a surface; it is far easier to draw the shadows, assuming that the space is evenly lit to start. For this reason, I often skip the step of creating a concept drawing for the lighting. In this case, it is better to have a thousand words than a picture, as people respond to the romance of the described space. This brief will, of course, talk about the materials and character of the design, as those and the lighting are intertwined. Here is an example brief written for the retail renovation featured in this book.

The store is set in a renovated brick retail building, whose strength and character is a vital part of the interior design. Rough original brick walls ripple in golden sunbeams as they stand in warm contrast to the smooth white plaster of the ceiling and new walls. The luminous plaster in turn showcases the depth of the glossy finish of the display casework as it sparkles in the light. Recessed can lights leave pools of warm light on the polished concrete floor, while halogen track lighting bathes the clothing on display in a bright pure light. The store is a symphony of contrast and subtlety, the dark sparkling wood and charcoal-stained concrete rich and luxurious next to the calm of the plaster. Brushed steel and aluminum accents and fixtures add a crisp, precise touch while flush jet black baseboards with brushed steel reveals provide a solid datum from which the finely tooled cabinetry springs.

In this chapter, we explore the creation of sunlight and artificial lighting in a building and on the exterior of a building. This lighting will utilize 3ds Max's Standard and Photometric lights, as well as the new mental ray (mr) daylight system.

SECTION B: EXTERIOR LIGHTING AND DAYLIGHT

EXERCISE 1:   Full sunlight

1.   Open *Basic Sunlight.max* from the Assets folder for this chapter. This is a simple pavilion on a podium, inspired by the clean modern lines of Mies van der Rohe and Philip Johnson (see Figure 9.1).

2.   Our first lighting scenario is full sunlight, which we will create using the mental ray daylight system. The daylight system allows for easy creation of sunlight in interior and exterior renderings. Press F10 or choose Rendering > Render from the top menu. When the Render Scene dialog pops up, scroll down to the bottom of the Common tab, and open the rollout labeled Assign Renderer. Assign mental ray as the rendering engine for Production (see Figure 9.2).

3.   In a Top or Perspective view where the XY plane is visible, choose Create > Light Daylight System from the top menu. Alternatively, using the Command panel, click on the Create tab, and then the Systems button, and finally the Daylight object. Click and drag in the scene to place a compass rose (see Figure 9.3).

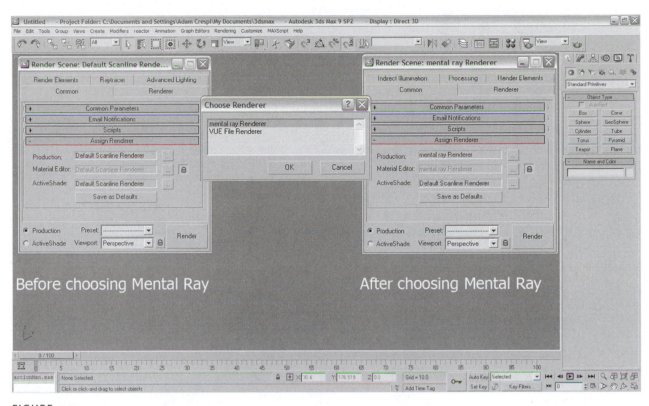

FIGURE 9.1

The starting model of the pavilion.

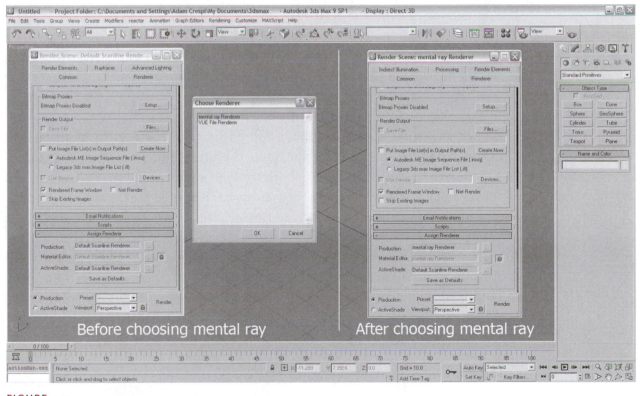

FIGURE 9.2

Changing the production renderer to mental ray.

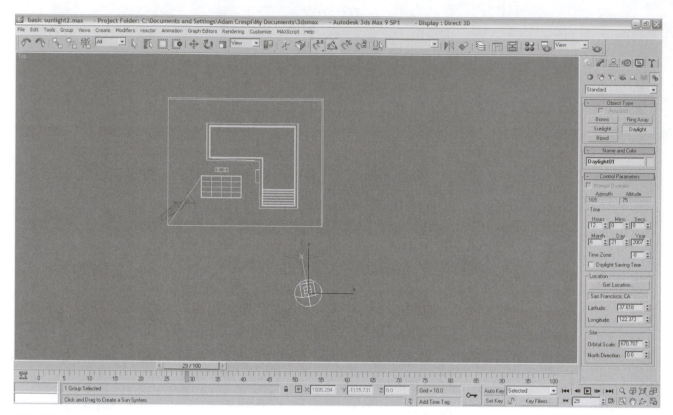

FIGURE 9.3

The daylight system including the sun, sky, and compass rose.

4. The daylight system includes three types of lights: Standard, IES (Illuminating Engineering Society, the recognized technical authority and publisher of lighting standards for use in design), and mental ray. In this exercise, we will focus on the mental ray lights. Switch to the Modifier panel, and under the drop-down menus for the Sunlight and Skylight, choose mr Sun and mr Sky, respectively (see Figure 9.4).

5. A daylight system creates the sun at a desired position, as well as the bounced light in the atmosphere opposite the sun, using the Sky. While this can be done manually, the daylight system controls both through a unified interface. Additionally, the daylight system provides easy-to-use controls for setting the sun at a particular time of day, date, month, year, and geographic location. For example, a house being constructed in Seattle can be rendered with the angle, color, shading, and quality of light that is found in Seattle. We'll assume that our building is set in Los Angeles, California, and will be rendered on September 25, 2007, at 10:00 a.m. On the Modifier panel, click on the Setup button under the Daylight Parameters rollout, and when the Control Parameters appear, choose Get Location. On the Geographic Location pop-up, choose Los Angeles, California, from the list (see Figure 9.5). Alternatively, you can click on the map to choose a location; there is a check box to snap to the nearest large city if desired.

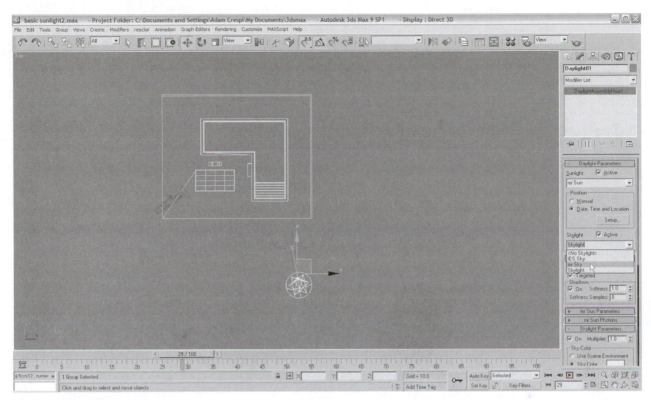

FIGURE 9.4

Changing the daylight system to use mental ray.

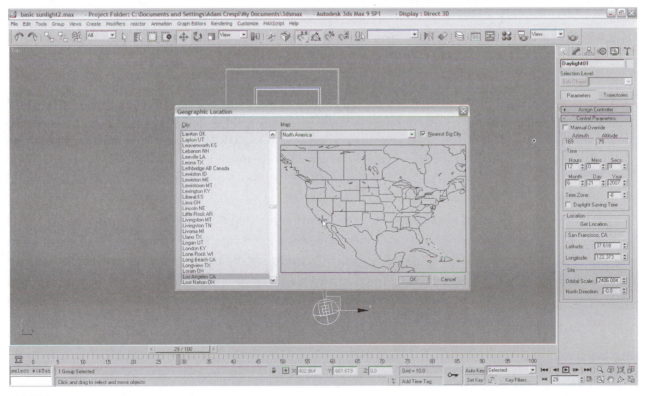

FIGURE 9.5

Setting the daylight system to a specific locale.

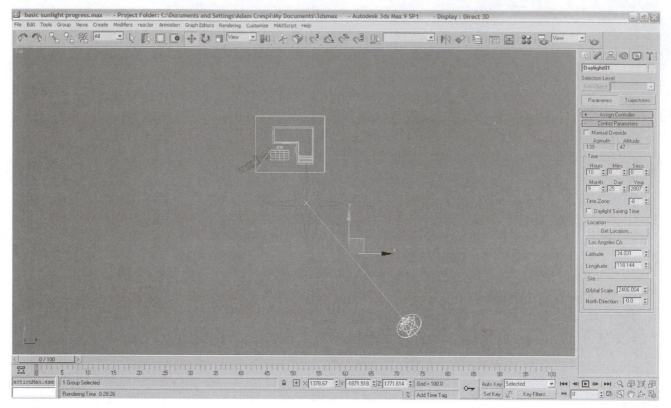

FIGURE 9.6

The daylight system set to a specific date and time.

6. On the Control Parameters, set the time and date to 10:00 a.m. on September 25, 2007. The time is recorded in a twenty-four hour cycle; keep this in mind when inputting times after noon. Check the box for Daylight Savings Time, as this is observed in California (see Figure 9.6).

7. The daylight system using the mental ray Sky and Sun requires a Physical Sky shader in the environment map to add the bounced sky color to the scene. Additionally, as the sun is physically correct, it requires Logarithmic Exposure with daylight compensation to be turned on to avoid overexposing or blowing out the scene. If you wish to see your scene rendered in blinding white, test render before you turn these features on. When the Sun and Sky were switched to mental ray, a notification should have popped up announcing the need for and the insertion of the Physical Sky shader. If this did not happen, press 8 or choose Rendering > Environment from the top menu. On the Environment dialog, click on the Environment Map slot to access the Material/Map Browser. When the Material/Map Browser pops up, double-click on Physical Sky from the shader list. At this time, you do not need to edit any of the parameters for the Physical Sky, as it is designed to interact with the chosen sunlight. If need be, a background image can be added into the Physical Sky shader.

Note:

Free maps, such as the Physical Sky shader, can be edited by dragging the map across to an open slot in the Material Editor. When the map is dragged over to the Material Editor, choose Instance when the Clone dialog appears. This way any changes made in the Material Editor will be reflected in the scene as well. As an example, drag the Physical Sky shader from the Environment dialog to the Material Editor as an instance. Click on the map slot near the top labeled None, and add a custom background map, such as a photo montage of a building's surroundings. Additional controls can be accessed here as well to change the Physical Sky if a stylized look is desired for the rendering.

8. In the Environment dialog, change the Exposure Control to Logarithmic by selecting Logarithmic Exposure Control from the drop-down menu. Check the Exterior Daylight box to avoid the aforementioned scene incineration (see Figure 9.7). Logarithmic Exposure allows light in a high dynamic range to function properly, such as the bright and dark tone of sunlight and shadow. Additionally, it can be used to adjust the brightness and contrast of an image. For now, leave the Logarithmic Exposure Control settings at their defaults.

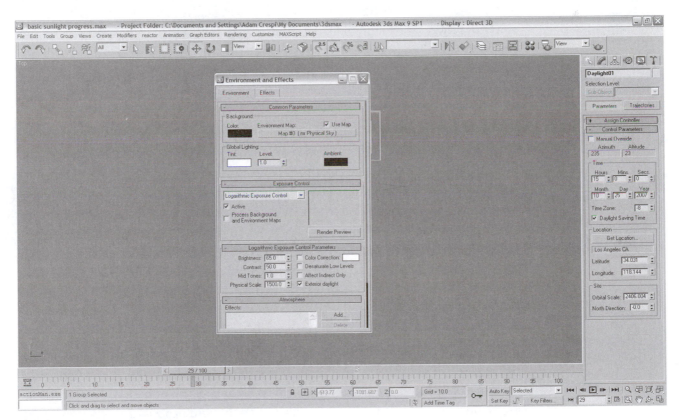

FIGURE 9.7

Logarithmic Exposure adjusting for exterior daylight.

FIGURE 9.8
The first test render of the daylight.

9. Press C for Camera, and choose Ext Camera from the list that appears. Test render the scene by pressing F10 to call up the Render Scene dialog, and then press Enter to render (see Figure 9.8). Alternatively, press F9 for a Quick Render. (Note that occasionally Quick Render may render the previous viewport if the Render Scene dialog is still open and another viewport is listed in the Viewport drop-down menu.)

10. At this point, you should have fairly realistic daylight. However, it is by default very crisp, with deep, nearly black shadows. We can do several things to change this look, depending on the quality of the rendering desired. Usually for exteriors, clients like to see their building in full sunlight, with crisp shadows to show off whatever details are present. Rule three of design visualization, *Show them the money,* especially applies here when tuning the sun and shadows. Extra corners cost extra dollars, as do panel joints, stucco over foam trim, board and batten, overhanging eaves, wrought iron accents, and on and on. One of the first things to do is slightly soften the shadows, so that even small detail shadows have a subtle variance in brightness across the shadow. On the Modifier panel, with the daylight system selected, scroll down to the mr Sun Basic Parameters rollout. In the Shadows section, increase Shadow Softness to 1.25 (see Figure 9.9). This will increase the edge softness of the shadows, allowing more depth in the lighting. If shadows close to the camera appear jagged, increase Softness Samples to 12 or higher. As with many of the numbers I give you, no one value is exactly right. Tweak the shadows to get the look you want that best shows the building you have.

FIGURE 9.9
*Close-up view
of the shadow
showing the
softened edge.*

11. Aside from the shadow quality and softness, the other major variable to experiment with is haze. Haze accounts for the particulate water and other matter found in the air; by adjusting it, you can simulate the light quality found in various locales. The current settings for our daylight system are for a fall morning in Los Angeles, California. The sunlight in Southern California at this time of the year has a slightly flat, brassy quality to it, with long sunbeams that reach across surfaces. There is often a little haze in the air, which refracts the light. Scroll down on the Modifier panel to the mr Sky Parameters. By default the Inherit from mr Sky box is checked in the Sun Parameters; this makes it easy to adjust the system without tuning each component. The Haze number has a range of 0 to 15, with 0 being a clear sky and 15 being extremely overcast. Increase the haze to 3, and test render again (see Figure 9.10). There should be a slight brassy haze to the air and the sky, which will reflect as warmth on the building and a slight lightening of the shadows. The shadow area under the main platform will still be dark in the center, but a little more light will bounce into the shadows.

12. The Horizon Parameters allow the generic horizon and ground to be tuned as needed. Typically, I either use background photos of the site as part of the Physical Sky shader or additional geometry, terrain, and foliage to obscure the horizon line. The horizon is not an ideal way to end the view, as it will clearly show the edges of the geometry in the scene. It's more useful to simulate the change in color of the sky as it gets closer to the horizon. In the Horizon Parameters, increase Blur to 0.25, and decrease Height to −1.0 (see Figure 9.11). This will blur the line between sky and ground, as well as lowering the ground line below at least some of the geometry.

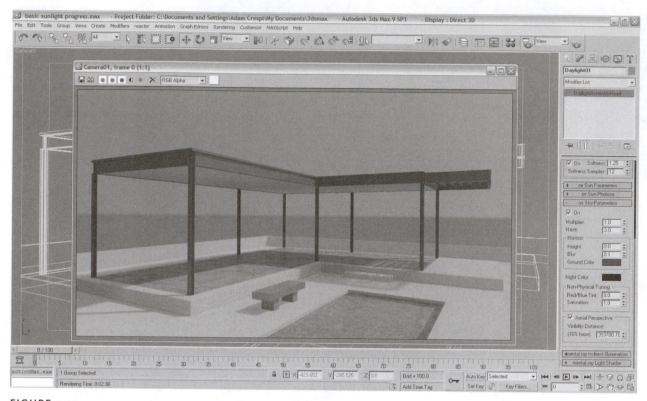

FIGURE 9.10

The increased haze on the Modifier panel and a render test.

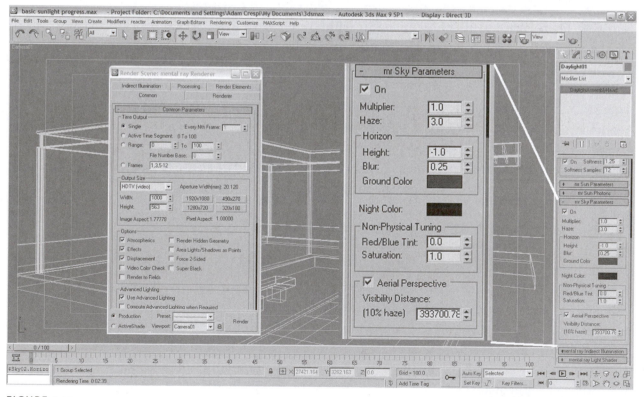

FIGURE 9.11

Lowering and blurring the horizon.

FIGURE 9.12
*Exterior sunlight
using the daylight
system.*

13. The exterior sunlight is complete; ready for additional background, model, foliage, or anything else the rendering needs. Test render again as needed to verify the desired look (see Figure 9.12). Step 14 illustrates the customization of the daylight system for a more stylized rendering.

14. If the angle of the sun as dictated by the time and date of the daylight system does not suit the building, change to Manual from Date, Time, and Location in the Daylight Parameters on the Modifier panel. This will allow you to move the sun and sky as desired. To move the sun and sky, select the Assembly Head and move it as you would any other 3ds Max object. If you move the compass, the daylight assembly will go with it, maintaining its relative position.

SECTION C: INTERIOR LIGHTING

EXERCISE 2:   Standard and photometric lights

There are two different types of lights in 3ds Max, Standard and Photometric, as previously stated. They share some attributes, such as shadow types and light shapes, but differ in their behavior. In a nutshell, Standard lights are arbitrary, having controls to simulate physical light in a variety of conditions. They do not, however, understand by default that they should behave like true physical lights. Photometric lights are modeled on true physical light sources. They inherently understand that they are, and behave like, true lights, and they can be used to simulate distinct color temperatures, bulb types, and photometric webs of true light sources. As mental ray is a global illumination solution, it will play nicely with both types of lights, and they can be freely mixed in the scene. As a caveat, Standard lights are inherently brighter by default than Photometrics. Additionally, the use of a sun will decrease or mute the effectiveness of interior lights, either Standard or Photometric.

In this exercise, we will light the building used in the previous exercise with interior lights. We will explore the use of both Standard and Photometric lights in a scene, while designing the light to have as much visual impact as possible. The counterpart to the sexy sunbeams for interior lighting is that light should pool, slink, puddle, and bathe.

1. Open *Basic Interior Light.max* from the Assets folder for this chapter. This is a simple pavilion on a podium, inspired by the clean modern lines of Mies van der Rohe and Philip Johnson (see Figure 9.13). Notice that the light fixture geometry is placed before the lighting.

2. Our first lighting scenario is full interior light, which we will create using the mental ray renderer. Press F10 or choose Rendering > Render from the top menu. When the Render Scene dialog pops up, scroll down to the bottom of the Common tab, and open the rollout labeled Assign Renderer. Assign mental ray as the rendering engine for Production (see Figure 9.14).

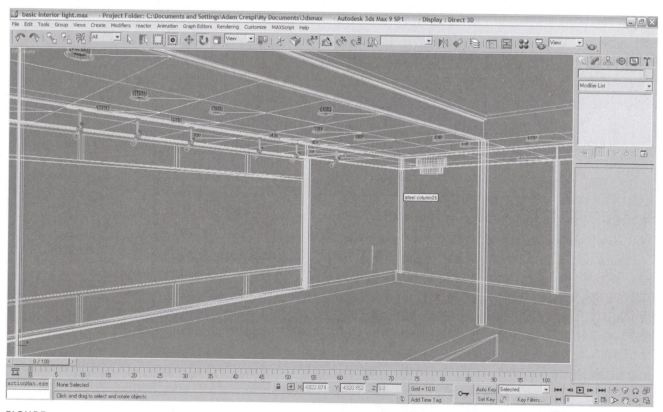

FIGURE 9.13

The starting scene ready for lighting.

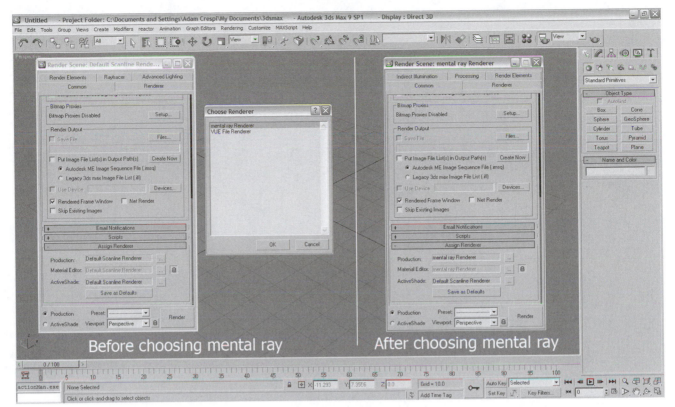

Before choosing mental ray · After choosing mental ray

FIGURE 9.14

Changing the production renderer to mental ray.

3. Press T to switch to Top view. On the Command panel, click on the Create tab, and then the Lights button. When lighting an interior I first turn on all of the down lights; these are the recessed can lights and surface mount ceiling fixtures. I do this so that the general mood of the room is established, generating the areas of light and dark, and showing me any areas needing non–source-based lighting. For recessed can lights, I prefer to use Photometric lights, as they fall off in a natural way. Then I mix Photometric and Standard lights for the surface mount and directed fixtures, as these often need a perceived greater brightness because they often are aimed at important features or found in key areas. In the example model, the can lights provide general illumination for the space, while the track lighting is aimed at the largest wall to highlight the art, and the chandelier is a focal point of the entry. Thus, the chandelier should be bright, the can-lit areas should be more subdued, and the track lighting should be bright as well. In the Lights section, drop down the menu that reads Standard, and choose Photometric. Click on the Free Point button, and click in the middle of one of the can lights to create the light (see Figure 9.15). Right-click to stop creating lights.

4. The Photometric lights come in four basic flavors: Point, Linear, and Area, as well as the daylight components. We created a Free Point light, which as the name suggests, emits light from one point. This light is useful for fixtures like the recessed can lights, where the bulb can be considered one point that emits light. The Linear lights emit light from a line, and hence are terrific for linear fixtures

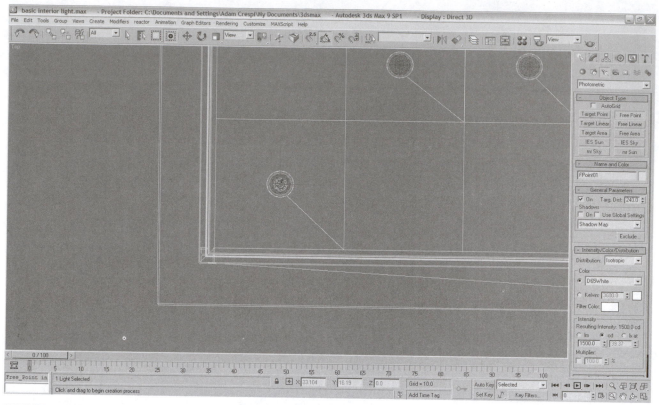

FIGURE 9.15

The Photometric Free Point light set in a can light.

such as office lighting or cove lights. Finally, the Area lights emit light from a user-defined rectangular area, and thus are suited for diffused light sources such as those found in drop ceilings; I also use them under cabinetry if it has under-mounted lights that make it visually float above the floor. Zoom in on the Free Point light, and make sure that it is centered on the light bulb in the can light (see Figure 9.16).

5. Press F for Front view, and move the Free Point light up so that it is just below the bulb geometry (see Figure 9.17). It is important to not submerge the light object in the geometry, as this will lead to excessive render times and odd results. The viewer will not be able to tell that the light is coming from below the bulb versus from the bulb anyhow; as long as the fixture appears to emit something like the light we expect to see, you'll be fine.

6. With the Free Point light still selected, go to the Modifier panel. The default Distribution for Free Point lights is Isotropic, meaning that the light emits in all directions equally. This is physically impossible, as the bulbs must be plugged or screwed in somehow. However, the lights work quite well for our purposes since it is difficult to tell the difference between a perfect distribution and one from a naked bulb, especially a typical incandescent bulb. For our can lights, however, the intent of the fixture is to focus the light down in a cone, creating circles of light on the floor and parabolic arcs of light on the wall; thus we need to change how

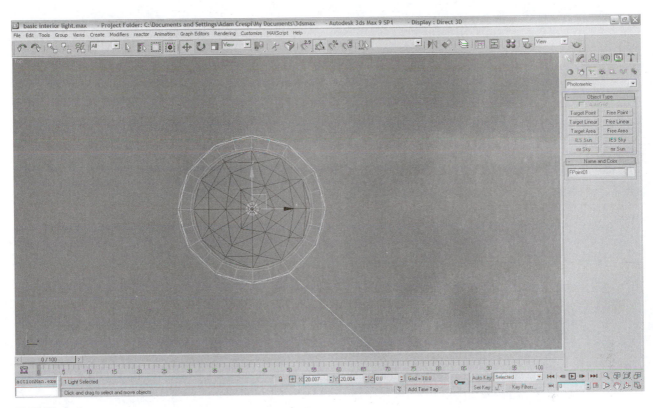

FIGURE 9.16

The Free Point light centered on the can light bulb.

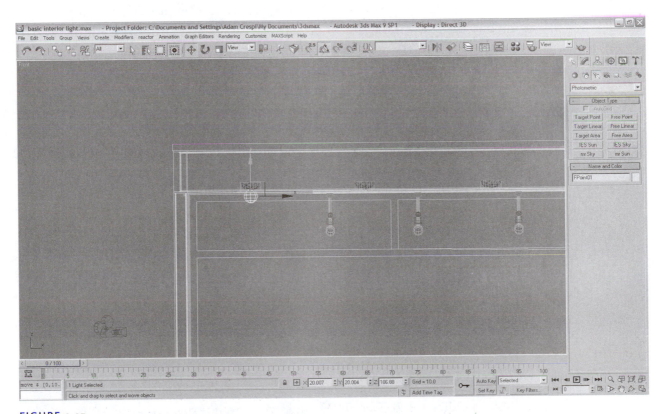

FIGURE 9.17

The Free Point light positioned just below the bulb geometry.

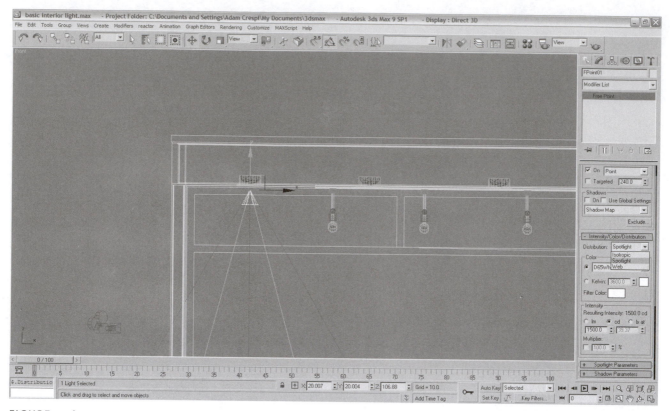

FIGURE 9.18

The Free Point light set to spotlight distribution for proper puddles and bathing.

the Free Point light emits light in the scene. In the Intensity/Color/Distribution rollout, drop down the list for the Distribution and choose Spotlight instead of Isotropic. The light takes on a cone shape, aimed at the floor (see Figure 9.18).

7. We are going to configure this light as a generic can light bulb, suitable for most situations where a distinct bulb has not been specified. Photometric lights have templates for many common bulb colors and types built into the light parameters. Still in the Intensity/Color/Distribution rollout, drop down the list next to Color, and choose Daylight Fluorescent (see Figure 9.19). This will add a slightly warm cast to the light without being excessive, allowing whites to read as white, and any halogen bulbs such as those in the track lighting to stand in warm, bright contrast.

8. Scroll down to the Spotlight Parameters rollout on the Modifier panel, and increase Falloff to 75 degrees (see Figure 9.20). The default Hotspot of 30 degrees will work nicely for most can lights, but the default Falloff of 60 degrees will leave a harsh circle of light on most floors. A light's hotspot is the area in which the light has 100% strength, while the falloff number denotes where the light falls off to 0% strength. As the difference in degrees between the numbers increases, the light will have a softer edge. Because can lights are generally soft (remember, pool, slink, puddle, and bathe), these values work well in most situations. Name this Free Point light Can Light Bulb01.

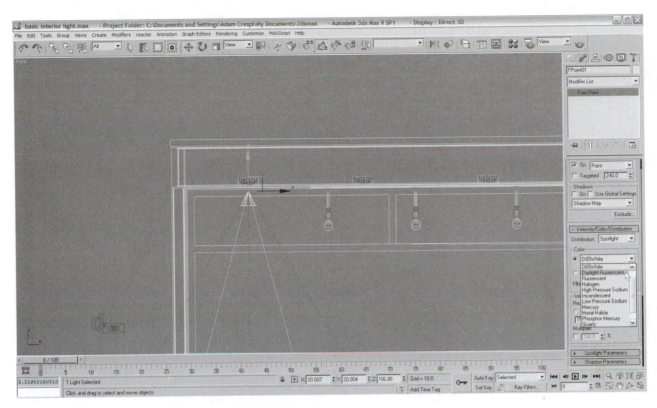

FIGURE 9.19

Adding a warm cast to the light bulb using a template.

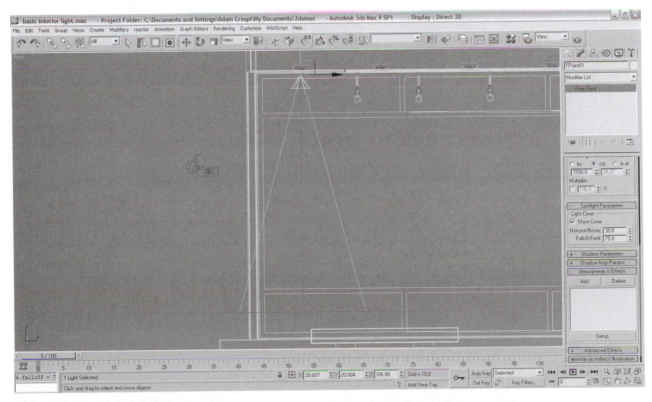

FIGURE 9.20

The configured bulb showing the hotspot and falloff.

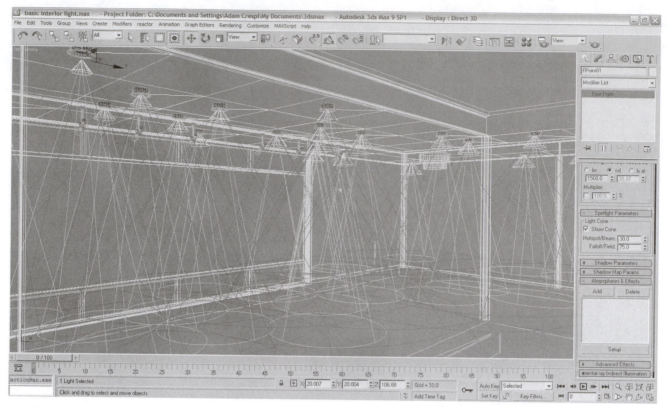

FIGURE 9.21

The Free Point light cloned to all similar light fixtures.

9.   At this point, the typical can light bulb is ready to copy to the other fixtures. In the Top view, press the spacebar to enable the Selection Lock, and then switch to Move, hold Shift, and clone the light to the next fixture, snapping to the center of the bulb. Clone this Free Point light to all of the can lights as instances (see Figure 9.21).

10. As you may have noticed, we have adjusted the distribution of the light, how it emits, as well as the softness of the cone of light, but we have not adjusted the intensity of the light yet. Rather than tune one light to look right, only to clone it and find out it needs further adjusting, I prefer to place all similar lights as instances and establish a general scene brightness level first. As each type of light is an instance, adjusting the lighting in the scene becomes a matter of changing one light per type. Press C for Camera, and choose Int Camera from the list of cameras. Press F9 to Quick Render the scene and see the lighting (see Figure 9.22).

11. As the test render shows, there is a rhythm of dark and light areas in the scene; however, the general amount of illumination is too low. With any one of the instances of the Can Light Bulb selected, go to the Modifier panel and scroll down to the Intensity/Color/Distribution rollout. The default candle power, or candela, is 1500 cd. This is more than a 100-watt incandescent bulb, and often less than the candela from a bulb that might be used in a fixture like this. Increase the candelas to 3000 cd and press F9 to test render again (see Figure 9.23).

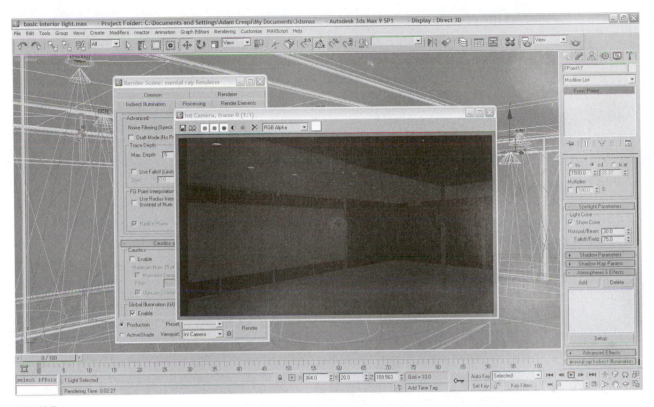

FIGURE 9.22

The first test rendering showing low illumination.

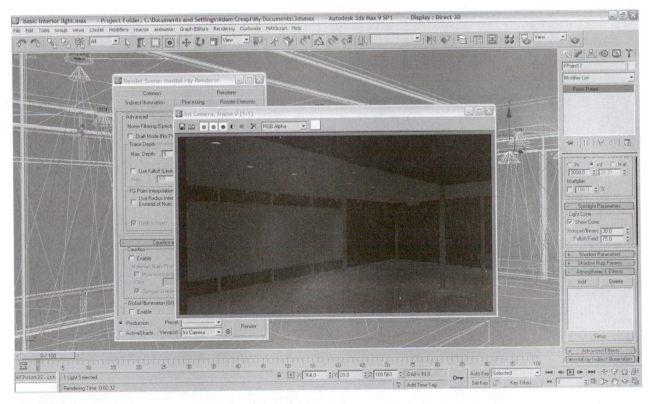

FIGURE 9.23

Another test rendering showing increased illumination levels.

12. The space should be generally evenly lit, although it still may be a bit dark. Press 8 to access the Environment dialog, or choose Rendering > Environment from the top menu. In the Environment dialog, in the Logarithmic Exposure Controls, increase the brightness to 75. (If you did not do the previous exercise, drop down the Exposure Control menu and choose Logarithmic Exposure. Logarithmic Exposure is designed for scenes with a high dynamic range, mapping the physical values to RGB values.) This will brighten the scene and make the whites whiter but still leave some shading and shadows.

13. Before tuning the look further, let's add the lights to the chandelier in the entry. On the Command panel, click on the Create tab, the Lights button, and finally on the mr Area Omni button. Although the chandelier has several bulbs, we can light this using one light source, as the bulbs are close enough to be perceived as one. The mr Area Omni has precise controls for limiting the amount and spread of the light, so we can stop the chandelier from adversely affecting the rest of the scene. Click in the middle of the chandelier once to create an mr Area Omni, then right-click to stop creating lights (see Figure 9.24).

14. Press F to switch to the Front view, and move the light up into the chandelier, roughly in the center (see Figure 9.25).

FIGURE 9.24

The mr Area Omni placed in the chandelier.

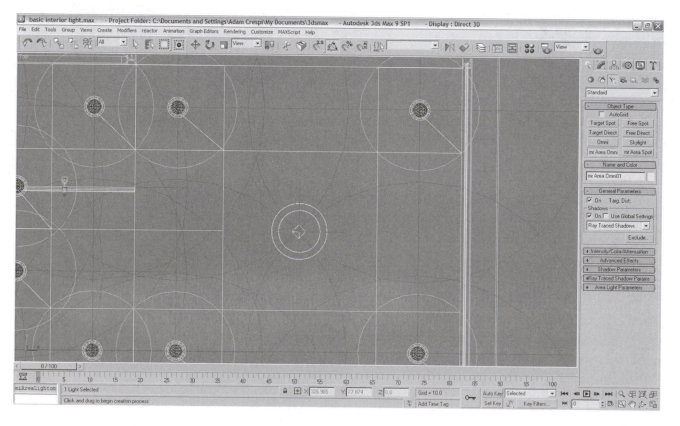

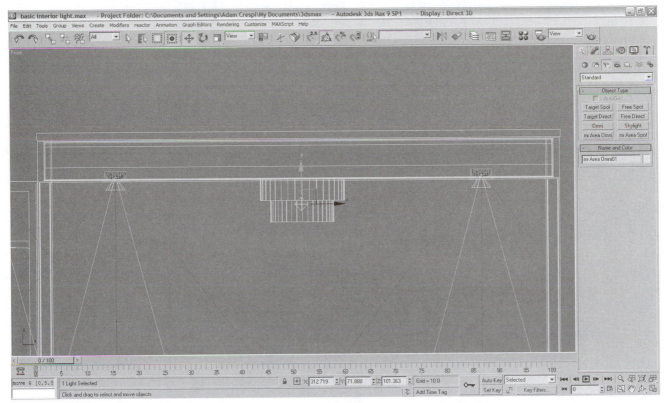

FIGURE 9.25
The mr Area Omni centered in the chandelier in a Front view.

15. With the mr Area Omni selected, go to the Modifier panel, and scroll down to the Intensity/Color/Attenuation rollout. Chandeliers such as this cast shadows that are fuzzy and spread away from the light source. We don't notice the shadows from the chandelier as much as the radial spread and falloff of the light from it. Hence, the specific arbitrary controls found in a 3ds Max Standard light are usually better suited to accent lights such as these. Turn on the Far Attenuation for this light by clicking on the check box next to Use (see Figure 9.26).

16. The ranges on the Near and Far Attenuation are in scene units and delineate absolute radii at which the light starts or stops. (I rarely use Near Attenuation; those who produce digital explosions and their accompanying shockwaves may find this feature more useful. However, most clients do not like to see their buildings exploding.) Set the Start of the Far Attenuation to 24 and the End to 144 (see Figure 9.27). This will make a small bright area on the ceiling, while fading the light to 0% intensity at the End range. (Notice the soft fade of the chandelier light.) Test render your scene again from the Int Camera.

17. The bloom of light should be in the correct place and fade out nicely but is probably still too bright for the fixture. On the Modifier panel, in the Intensity/Color/Attenuation rollout, set the intensity of the light to 0.4. Next, add a tiny bit of warm yellow to the color of the light by clicking on the color swatch next to the intensity number, and decreasing the blue by 10 to 245 and the green to 252.

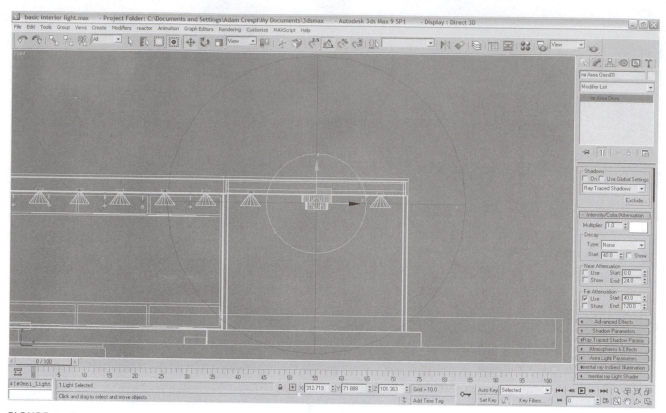

FIGURE 9.26

Far attenuation on the mr Area Omni light.

FIGURE 9.27

The scene rendered with the new attenuation settings.

Computer-generated lights are white by default, and rather dead looking, so it's usually a good idea to warm them up a little. Test render again to see the revised chandelier lighting.

18. The lighting is almost done. We have illuminated the cans, the chandelier, and now are ready for the track lights. Remember, the goal is to get the room generally lit, and then add accent lights such as track lights. These track lights have halogen bulbs, which should produce bright warm washes on the walls. On the Command panel, click on the Create tab, the Lights button, and finally on the mr Area Spot button. The mental ray area spot is an arbitrary light, like the mr Area Omni, and by default has a target when created. Place the head of this light near the head of one of the track lamps (see Figure 9.28).

19. On the Modifier panel, with the mr Area Spot selected, scroll down to the Spotlight Parameters, and set Hotspot to 25 and Falloff to 60 degrees (see Figure 9.29). A light's hotspot is the area where the light is emitted at 100% strength, and the falloff sets the 0% point. As the two numbers get closer, the edge of the light on a surface is sharper; when they are farther apart, the edge of the light is softer. I usually start bulbs such as these track light heads at 25 and 60, and can lights at 30 and 75. The smaller numbers and lower difference for the track head produce a fairly focused circle or ellipse, while the larger numbers and spread for the can light leave a soft puddle of light on the floor.

FIGURE 9.28
The mr Area Spot placed near the track light head with the target aimed toward the wall.

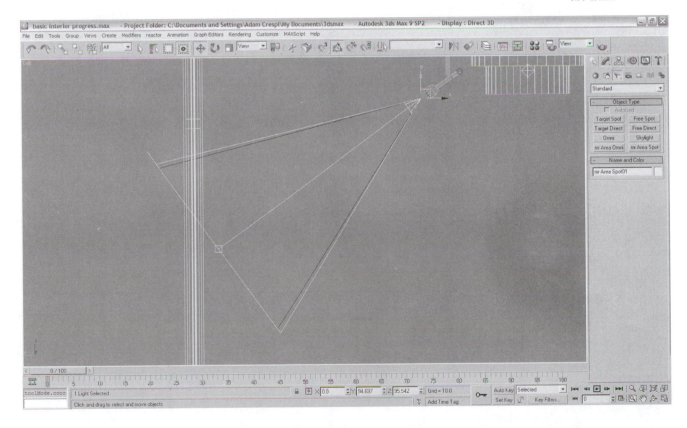

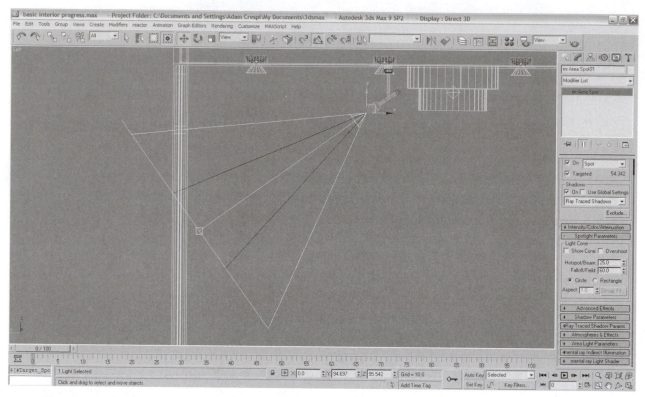

FIGURE 9.29

The track light showing hotspot and falloff.

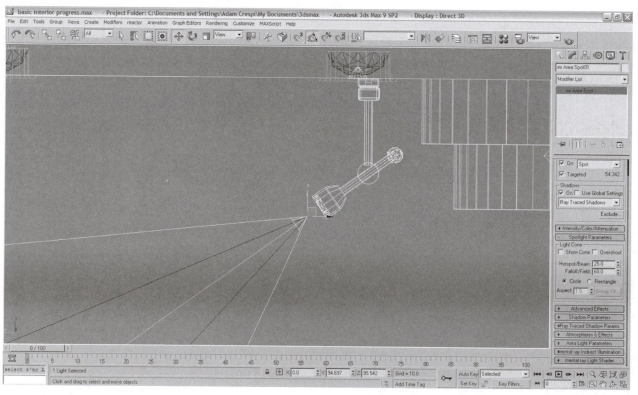

FIGURE 9.30

Close-up of the track head showing light placement.

20. Check in a Top and Front viewport to make sure that the spotlight is aligned on the center of the bulb geometry, positioned just in front of it. You can either do this manually or use the Align tool on the Main Toolbar (see Figure 9.30).

21. With the mr Area Spot head selected, click on the Select and Link button on the main toolbar. A dotted line should follow the Select and Link cursor; click on the track lamp head (see Figure 9.31). The spot is now linked to the track head geometry and will move where it moves. Do the same to link the track head to the shaft and base group.

22. On the top menu, with the track head selected, choose Animation > Constraints > Look at Constraint. Click and drag from the track head group to the Target of the light (see Figure 9.32). This will constrain the track head to always rotate to follow the Target.

23. Go to the Motion tab on the Command panel. Scroll down to the Rotation List, and select the Look At controller. Then scroll down further, and set the Select Look At Axis to Y, and check Flip. This will align the track head to the spotlight. After this, scroll down to the Align to Upnode Axis, and set it to Z (see Figure 9.33). This will ensure that the track head isn't twisted on the base. Additionally, you may need to check the box marked Keep Initial Offset to maintain the correct placement of the light and lamp head.

FIGURE 9.31
Linking the light to the track head.

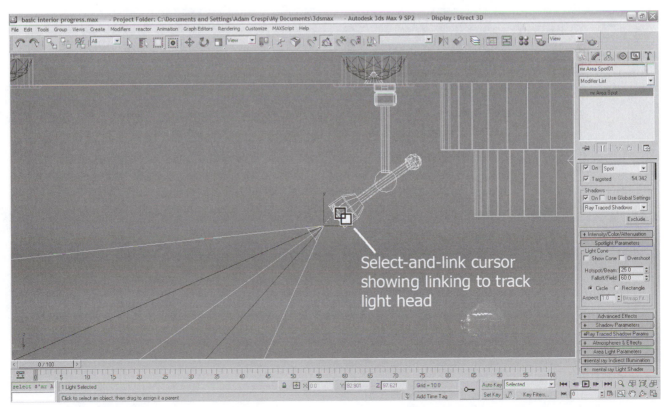

Select-and-link cursor showing linking to track light head

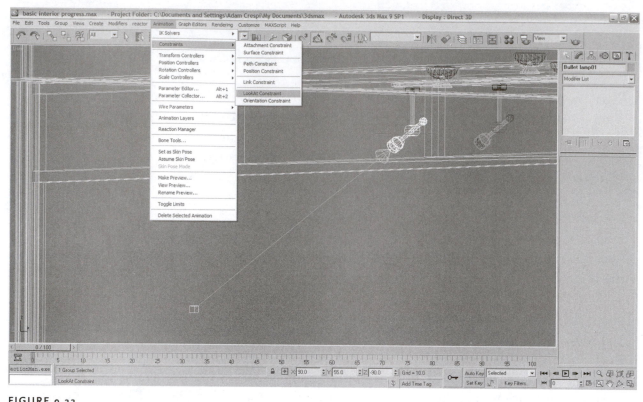

FIGURE 9.32

The Look at Constraint applied to the track head.

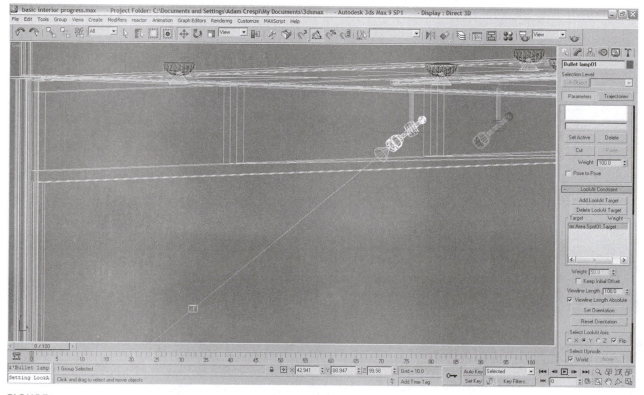

FIGURE 9.33

Setting the Look at Constraint options in the Motion panel.

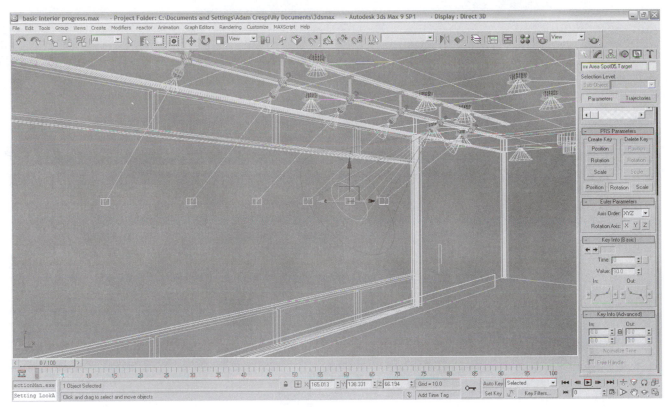

FIGURE 9.34
*The cloned track
heads and lights.*

24. Select the track head, the base, the spotlight, and the target, and clone the objects as instances along the track, making three copies (see Figure 9.34). Space them out evenly to the ends of the track. (You can eyeball this; no need for exact measurement here.)

25. Select the Target of each light, and aim it at the gallery wall. The track head and light should follow the Target (see Figure 9.35). In theory, they may actually be aimed at artwork at some point. That can happen after the lighting level is set.

26. Test render the lighting from the Int Camera. The lighting on the wall is probably too bright, being flat and overexposed where the track lights cross. Reduce the Multiplier on the track lights' spotlights to 0.2 and test render again. You may need to adjust the aim of the lights, the multiplier, or the hotspot and falloff to get a soft look (see Figure 9.36).

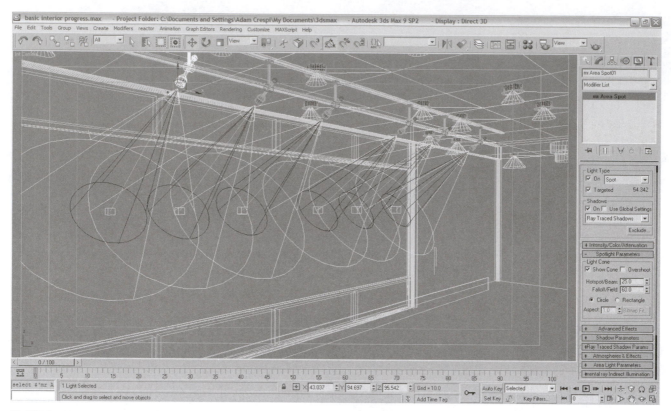

FIGURE 9.35

The lights aimed at the gallery wall.

FIGURE 9.36

The final rendered space.

SECTION D: CONCLUSION

Accurate lighting depends on repeating one mantra over and over, especially when lighting an interior: Lots of Little Lights. Viewers expect to see light coming from fixtures in the scene and matching the intensity a fixture is expected to radiate. What makes lighting successful is the play of light and shadow and the variance in the darkness. Spaces come alive when they are naturally lit; there are always some corners that should be darker to ground the design. Conversely, there are places where a little overexposure and bloom is acceptable; it adds realism to the rendering that a perfect light might not show. Perhaps the biggest instruction for lighting is to relax and let go of some of the precision. Paint with light, style it; massage it around until the space smiles.

CHAPTER 10 Rendering

SECTION A: CHOOSING AND USING A RENDERING ENGINE

Rendering is the actual process of calculating the geometry, the lights, materials, animation, particles, and whatever else comprises the scene to produce the final image. Rendering is an artistic choice, just like modeling methods or the design of a house or store. In 3D, the choice of rendering engine affects how a space looks; it is the renderer that controls the bounce of light, reflection, refraction, shading, shadows, and innumerable other possibilities. If we consider the scene as the world—or the World as 3ds Max calls it—the capabilities of a rendering engine are global controls. Rendering affects everything in the scene on an equal footing; this is important as rendering is a matter of tuning the process until the desired mood is reached.

Many programs support multiple rendering engines as plug-ins, often shipping two or more with the base application. As an example, Autodesk 3ds Max and Autodesk Maya both ship with their native software rendering engine, the Scanline Renderer and the Maya Software engine, respectively, as well as mental images' mental ray. Within 3ds Max, the Scanline Renderer can also work with the included Advanced Lighting plug-ins Radiosity and Light Tracer; these concern themselves with the bouncing of light. Quite a few additional rendering engines are also available, including Cebas' finalRender, Chaos Group's V-Ray, SplutterFish's Brazil, and Pixar's RenderMan. Each has its unique attributes, ways that it excels at handling certain situations, and each rendering engine has its group of zealous supporters who preach the virtues of their particular favorite. Often a rendering engine will gain a strong foothold in a particular industry. Many movie studios use RenderMan and mental ray, many architectural visualization firms use V-Ray, several prominent game studios render cinematics in Brazil, and so forth.

While a best-of-breed approach is good, it is often better for the student or solo visualization practitioner to get to know one rendering engine intimately, then fumble around with several others. As an analogy (and as a surfer), I would rather surf for six months on one board and become familiar with the way it responds to myriad different waves on a personal, intimate level, than switch boards every few weeks and repeat the learning curve. I have never had clients tell me that they didn't like my images because I used this or that software or renderer; clients simply don't care. As long as the ethereal plaster walls and glass tile in my rendering look like the ethereal plaster walls and glass tile they are paying for, they don't care if I had to part the Red Sea or teach my cell phone to make toast.

This book focuses on using the mental ray renderer exclusively. Although you will experience somewhat of a learning curve, it is worth the results in the final rendering. Mental ray is known for the way it handles ray tracing, caustics, subsurface scatter, and global illumination among many other talents. Environment artists, which we in design visualization are, care deeply about such things. The Scanline Renderer in 3ds Max is and always has been quite powerful; I used it for many years on a multitude of projects. However, mental ray simply does a terrific job at letting the light play and dance, so that will be the first artistic choice we will make.

In the following exercises, we will step through enabling the rendering engine, and then setting up some basic parameters to get draft and high-quality renderings. We will do this with an eye toward reuse and library building, so that you will not need to reinvent the wheel on future projects.

EXERCISE 1:   Aliasing and how to avoid it

---

1.   Open *Render Test.max* from the Assets folder for this chapter. This is a simple scene containing several different conditions and details that will allow us to judge the renderings (see Figure 10.1). The design is based somewhat on the Cornell Box, a standard mesh for testing global illumination that has several bright-colored adjacent surfaces and freestanding objects. This test scene has been tailored somewhat as a generic architectural space for our purposes.

2.   Press F10 or choose Rendering > Render from the top menu. This accesses the Render Scene dialog. Press the Render button at the bottom to see the scene render (see Figure 10.2). A line should travel from the top to the bottom of the rendered frame window; this is the scanning of lines and calculation of the rendering, hence the name Scanline Renderer.

3.   The Render Scene dialog has tabs at the top, which access different components of the rendering engine. These tabs will change depending on the engine's operation and features. When the Scanline Renderer is active, the tabs are Common, Renderer, Advanced Lighting, Raytracer, and Render Elements. Two of these tabs, Common and Render Elements, will always be on the Render Scene dialog. The Common tab contains sections that govern the range of time to be rendered, the file size and output, as well as rollouts for e-mail notification, pre- and

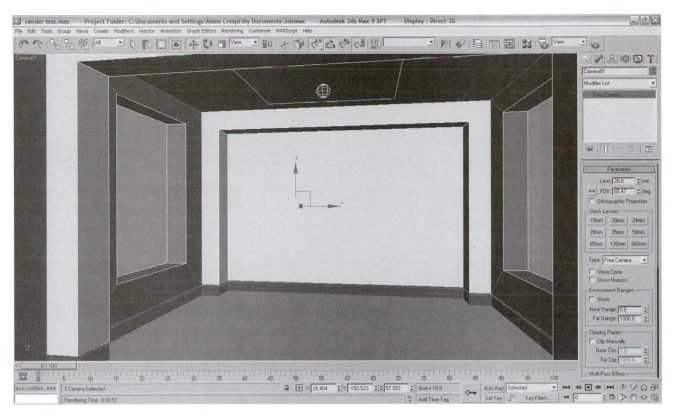

FIGURE 10.1

The starting test scene.

FIGURE 10.2

The scene rendered with the Scanline Renderer.

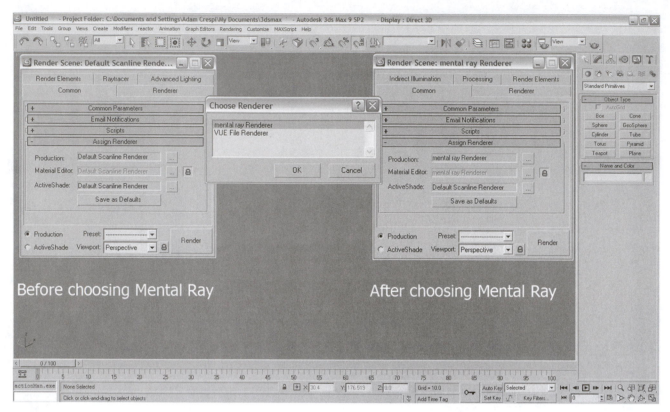

FIGURE 10.3

Setting the production renderer to mental ray.

post-rendering scripts, and assigning rendering engines. Scroll down until you see the Assign Renderer rollout. Open the rollout, and click on the button next to Production. A dialog will pop up that allows the loading of different rendering engines. Choose the mental ray renderer and click OK (see Figure 10.3).

4. The top tabs should now read Indirect Illumination, Processing, Renderer, Common, and Render Elements. Press Render again. Instead of a scanline traveling from top to bottom, you should see squares, or buckets, as they are properly known, spiral around the rendered frame window.

5. On the Common tab, locate the drop-down menu in the Output section. This has presets for many different image formats such as high definition (HD), 35mm, slides, and NTSC (the format of analog television used in the United States, Canada, Mexico, and other countries mostly in the Americas; the format was named for the National Television Standards Committee, the standards body that created it). Choose HD from this list (see Figure 10.4).

6. The buttons to the right of the Output sizes are preset rendering sizes, in pixels. By default these list some of the common sizes for HD format, such as 1920 × 1080 and 1280 × 720. The other sizes provided are derivatives with the same aspect ratio, the width-to-height ratio of the image. Choose 1280 × 720 and press Render again.

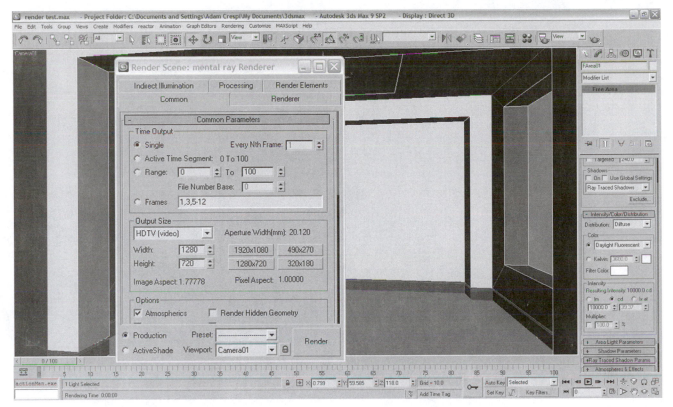

FIGURE 10.4
Setting the output resolution.

7. The image renders with light and shadow, but quite a bit of the detail that is visible in the viewport is jagged or lost in the rendering. This stair-stepping is called aliasing and is a result of displaying edges that are not aligned perfectly horizontally or vertically on pixels that are. Rendering engines control and counter aliased edges with anti-aliasing (surprise!), which is also called sampling. In 3ds Max, using mental ray, the anti-aliasing feature is found on the Renderer tab on the Render Scene dialog, in the Samples per Pixel section. This Samples section is where you control the minimum and maximum number of samples per pixel, along with a filter type, and width and height. We read the samples per pixel as a number, thus the default minimum of 1/4 is actually one sample per four pixels, or a very coarse sample—hence the jaggies in our image. The maximum number governs the ceiling of this range, with a default of four samples per pixel. Set these numbers to a minimum of 1 and a maximum of 16, and test render again. This is approximately the anti-aliasing quality found in the Scanline Renderer (see Figure 10.5).

8. Sampling quality is an artistic choice, as previously mentioned; so is the filter that is used. In the Filter section, set the filter to Mitchell (see Figure 10.6). The Mitchell filter weights the sampling per pixel on a diminished bell curve, adding more weight to the sampling in the center versus the edge. This filter will give crisp lines and fine edges; however some lines may read as too crisp. Test render the scene, but don't close the rendered frame window when the rendering is done.

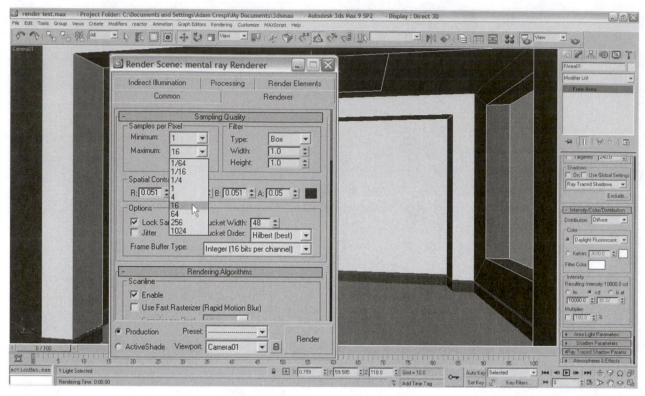

FIGURE 10.5

Setting the sampling quality in the mental ray renderer.

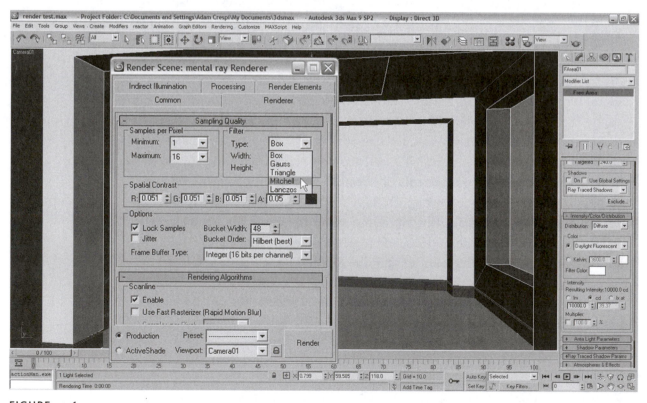

FIGURE 10.6

Setting the filter to Mitchell for crisp lines.

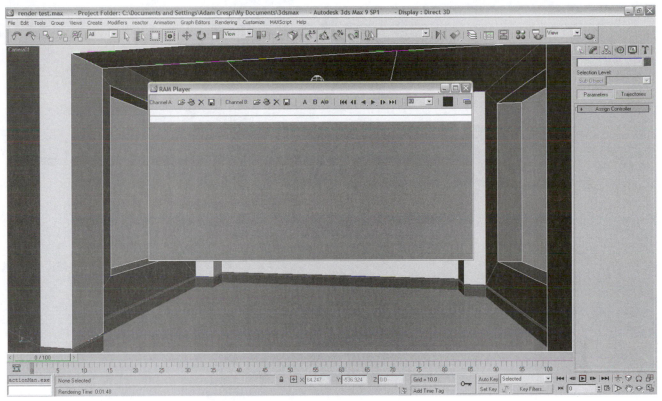

FIGURE 10.7
The RAM Player
now ready to load
images.

9. On the top menu, choose Rendering > RAM Player (see Figure 10.7). This will open the RAM Player, a utility that allows the loading of images or animations into the available memory of the computer. Additionally, two images or sequences can be loaded into channels A and B, allowing side-by-side comparison.

10. On the RAM Player, click on the green teapot in the Channel A section (see Figure 10.8). This will load the last render into Channel A. For clarity in printing, the renderings shown have been adjusted to be brighter by enabling Final Gather in the renderer. (Both the Mitchell and Lanczos images have been included on the accompanying CD as well as an image rendered using the Gauss filter for comparison.)

11. On the Render Scene dialog, change the filter to Lanczos, and test render again. Load this finished frame into the RAM Player in Channel B.

12. Compare the two filters by clicking and dragging in the middle of the image on the RAM Player (see Figure 10.9). The white arrowheads at the top and bottom denote the intersection of the images. The Mitchell filter carries the sampling across the sampling area evenly, resulting in a slightly softer look, but may obscure microfine detail and some subtle surface texture. The Lanczos filter sampling tapers off at the edge of the sampling area, resulting in possibly a crisper image, but raising the likelihood of aliasing at the edges.

Section A: Choosing and Using a Rendering Engine **251**

FIGURE 10.8

The Mitchell-filtered image loaded into the RAM Player.

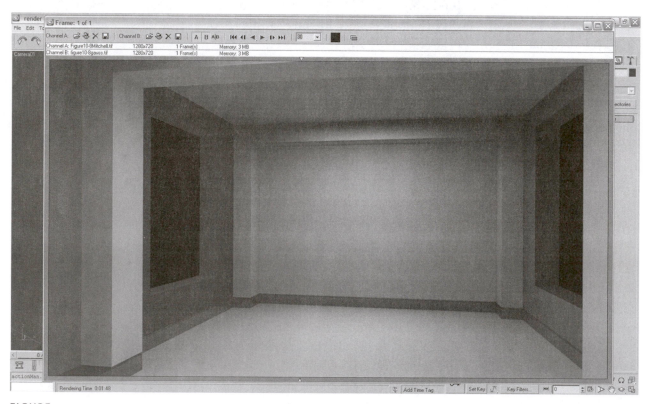

FIGURE 10.9

Both images loaded into the RAM Player for comparison.

13. Both of the aforementioned problems raised by the filters can be countered by adjusting the sampling ranges and the filter width and height. However, you must strike a balance between sampling quality and rendering time; there is never quite enough time. It is imperative to test the rendering quality before time becomes critical; this is the kind of exercise where a render farm becomes highly useful. Try switching back to the Mitchell filter and raising the ranges to a minimum of 4 and a maximum of 16, then test render again (see Figure 10.10). The difference is mainly noticeable along near-horizontal or near-vertical lines, such as the drywall bents between the colored walls. The additional sampling helps reduce aliasing in conditions such as these and the reveal at the top of the baseboard.

Note:

What is a render farm and does it involve pigs, cows, or chickens? Thankfully, a render farm is swine, bovine, and poultry free. It is a network of computers used to distribute rendering across any available processors, versus making one machine do the whole job. 3ds Max comes with Backburner, an excellent render farm utility, which includes Manager, Monitor, and Server applications. In many offices, the workstations are the render farm, the computers being set as slaves when the employees leave. The manager then parses out the frames to the computers, so that when everyone returns to work in the morning, there are directories full of rendered images. Some firms may also have a dedicated farm, several

FIGURE 10.10
The rendered image with sampling raised to 4 and 16.

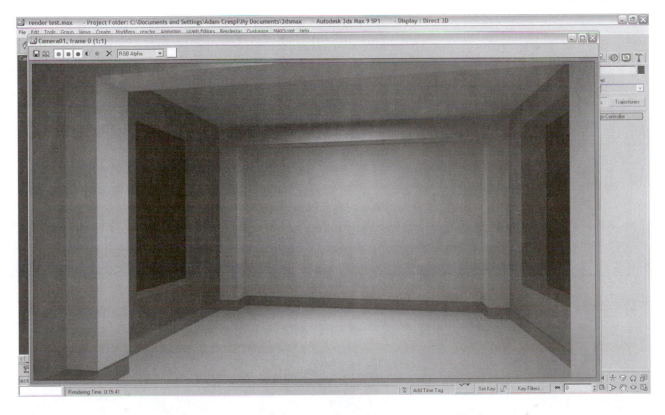

or many computers that were bought solely for rendering. Dedicated machines often have small hard drives, large amounts of memory, inexpensive graphics cards, and fast processors. These can be either standalone boxes or blade servers, whole computers that fit onto a plug-in board and share hard drive and display functions. In many visual effects firms servicing the movie industry, it is not uncommon to have racks full of such blades, and dedicated personnel whose job is to manage and support them.

To set up a Backburner network, follow the instructions that come with 3ds Max; the installation is straightforward and fairly easy. As a caveat, you will need to install a minimum or slave version of 3ds Max on every machine you wish to use as part of your render farm; however, this installation will not require authorization.

14. If the scene still contains jagged areas, try increasing the filter width and height. Try 5 by 5 for the Lanczos, and 5 by 5 for the Mitchell. Remember that as width and height increase, render times will increase, as a larger sample with possible greater variance is being considered. Test render each filter again, and load the resulting images into the RAM Player for comparison.

15. The final influence on the sampling is the contrast. Spatial contrast refers to the colors within each still image. The contrast numbers specify the difference in adjacent pixels as a percentage of a value from 0 to 1.0; pixels that are greater than the specified number per channel are sampled. Those adjacent pixels that are below the threshold relative to each other are not sampled. Try decreasing the RGB samples to 0.3 and test render again.

16. By decreasing the contrast threshold, pixels that are closer in color are sampled, smoothing the color blending across the image. Thus the image appears softer, but at the risk of losing small details or subtle color variations. There is no one right solution for every rendering task, but it is possible to develop a range of solutions that can be applied to varying circumstances. When you feel that the result is an optimum balance of quality, details, and rendering time, save these parameters as a preset. At the bottom of the Render Scene dialog is a drop-down menu for Render Presets. Pull the list down and choose Save Preset. Name this preset Crisp Modern, or another name as part of your naming conventions. As an example, I have presets saved for Soft Black and White, Crisp Modern, Soft Historic, Crisp Interior, and Soft Interior. These function as a base for experimentation with future scenes.

Note:
Render Presets saves every parameter in all of the rendering tabs, including the file output and indirect illumination support files. Saving presets was introduced at this stage to familiarize readers with the concept; however, it may be necessary to modify the saved presets after further exercises.

SECTION B: GLOBAL ILLUMINATION AND FINAL GATHER

EXERCISE 2: Adjusting global illumination

1. Open the *Modern Gallery.max* file from the Assets folder for this chapter. This is a simple modern space with some solid brick walls, some frame and panel steel construction, a plaster ceiling, and large windows (see Figure 10.11). For ease of use, a daylight system has already been set up, with Logarithmic Exposure Control.

2. Press F10 to open the Render Scene dialog. Test render the Camera view by pressing Render. Although the areas in direct sun look reasonable, the portions of the structure in shadow are in deep black shadow, with no bounce of light (see Figure 10.12).

3. Go to the Indirect Illumination tab on the Render Scene dialog and turn on Final Gather and Global Illumination by checking the boxes labeled Enable (see Figure 10.13). This will activate the bounced light in the scene (Global Illumination) and the regathering and smoothing of that light (Final Gather). Test render the scene again.

FIGURE 10.11
The starting modern gallery scene.

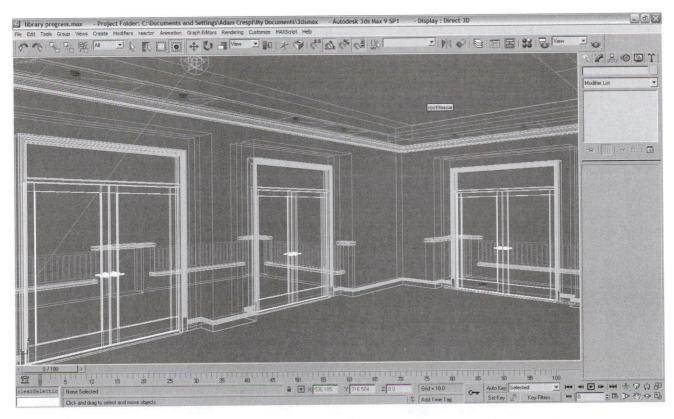

FIGURE 10.12

The rendered image showing black shadows and sunbeams.

FIGURE 10.13

The rendered image showing bounced light and the Render Scene dialog showing the Indirect Illumination tab.

4. When using Global Illumination (GI) and Final Gather (FG), you will most likely work with two different quality settings, one for test rendering and one for final rendering. In the FG section, drop down the Preset list and choose Draft.

5. Mental ray calculates the geometry, checks to see if any linked maps are present and loaded, calculates the Shadow Maps, and then calculates the Global Illumination and Final Gather, in that order. After all of this is done, it will start to process the actual rendering. The stages that take the most time are the FG and the rendering. For the Final Gather, the settings that most affect render times are the Rays per FG Point. Final Gather is an adaptive solution, applying computational power in situations of variable lighting or geometry that bounces light, and economizing on flat, shaded, or fully lit areas. The lower the number of Rays, the faster the rendering, but at a cost of quality. Test render the scene again.

6. 3ds Max displays the Final Gather pass first, to let you preview the rendering and spot any mistakes or issues before taking the possibly longer time to render. The blotchy quality of this pass is a reflection of the number of Rays; higher Rays mean a smoother FG pass, while lower Rays have bigger chunks but render faster. With GI and FG on, light bounces off the floor and up into the space and into the shadows. Light also bounces between adjacent objects and picks up some of their color, which can be seen on surfaces with different colors. As an example, look at the base of the brick planter where it meets the concrete. A tiny bit of red is visible on the concrete from the bricks, and a light bounce is visible on the bricks from the concrete. At the moment, the shadows are still fairly heavy, partially as a result of the clear sunlight from the daylight system. However, we can globally choose to bounce more light into the shadows in the Final Gather settings. On the Render Scene dialog, in the Final Gather settings, increase the Diffuse Bounces to 2 (see Figure 10.14). This will enhance the bounce of light and color in the scene. Test render the scene again.

7. Scroll down to the Global Illumination rollout. This controls globally (for everything in the scene) the global illumination; the bouncing of light. The first number to experiment with here is the Maximum Photons per Sample, set to 500 by default. Increase this number to 5000, switch to the Int Camera, and test render. As the photon number gets higher, the qualities of the light bounces increases, but with a corresponding increase in rendering time.

8. The number you finally settle on for the GI largely depends on the scene itself. Exteriors with small overhangs, leaving much of the façade in full light, may not benefit from greatly increased numbers of photons. However, interior renderings, with a greater number of spaces in closer proximity combined with an increased likelihood of glossier surfaces, may need a much higher number of photons for optimal light bouncing. Save a new Render Preset or modify an existing one after you have tuned the global illumination to your liking.

FIGURE 10.14

The rendered scene showing additional lighting from the Final Gather bounces.

SECTION C: RESOLUTION, FILE OUTPUT, AND FORMATS

As a rule, renderings for print are much larger than renderings for screen display. I usually figure that large prints should be at least 200 dots per inch (dpi), and smaller 8″ × 10″ or 11″ × 17″ prints should be 300 dpi. People are more likely to stand back to view a large print, such as a 24″ × 36″ image, so the lower resolution holds up quite well. Viewers are more likely to leave nose prints on smaller images, holding them right up to their faces for scrutiny worthy of a fluoroscope and a white lab coat. If we figure that one pixel equals one dot, calculating the image size is easy. As an example, I often place a 16″ × 10″ image horizontally on 11″ × 17″ paper, with a title below the image. Sixteen inches times 300 dpi is 4800 dots, or 4800 pixels, giving a final render size of 4800 times 3000 pixels at 300 dpi.

In 3ds Max, under the Rendering command on the top menu, the Print Size Wizard will perform this calculation for you. The caveat with this utility is to make sure that your input size is the image size, not the paper size, or else you will cut off the edges of your image when it prints.

The format you choose for the rendered image depends on where it is going to go after rendering. I always take my images as RPFs (Rich Pixel Format, which allows the inclusion of arbitrary image data in the file along with the RGBA values, such as Z-Depth, Transparency, Velocity, and others; it also supports a full floating-point bit depth, which allows for greater flexibility in color correction and post effects) into Autodesk's Combustion for the application of post effects and color correction, and then render an image for print from there. Actually, images come from Combustion into Adobe Illustrator for branding and labeling, and then finally for print. Your own workflow may vary depending on the tools and knowledge available. For general printing from 3ds Max, the TIF format will work quite well. In the Render Scene dialog, under the File Output section, choose TIF as the format. In the Setup dialog that appears, you can specify bit depth, alpha channel, and even dots per inch.

For onscreen display of an image or an animation, where the image will go after rendering determines the format. Again, I will render a sequence of RPF files for compositing and post effects in Combustion, and from there as uncompressed QuickTime files for editing and DVD authoring in Adobe Premiere and Encore, respectively. If you are simply rendering an animation for exporting straight to VHS or DVD, either an AVI or QuickTime file will do nicely. I always prefer to render uncompressed, performing compression of the animation once at the end in the online edit. 3ds Max can access all of the compression options available to the various formats from the Render Scene dialog if needed. As compression flavors change daily, listing all of the available codecs (compression/decompression algorithms) would not be terribly useful. I recommend rendering a short animation clip and trying various codecs on it to see which one works the best. Above all, test before you are in a deadline crunch.

SECTION D: CONCLUSION

How you render shapes the overall look and feel of the image as much as the lighting. Clients expect a high degree of realism simply because that is becoming the norm in visualization, and on a broader scale in motion picture special effects. Learn the subtleties of your rendering engine of choice, and tune the result to best fit the building. Test, test, test, and test again—the final render should never be a roll of the dice, but rather an application of brute computer power to a problem whose solution you already know.

CHAPTER **11** Hair and How to Make Things Messier

SECTION A: INTRODUCTION TO THE HAIR AND FUR PLUG-IN

Quick! Make a hairy building! I want a fur-covered desk! Drape the windows in hanging moss! Style the pendant lamps in beehives and the task lamps with cornrows! Actually, just a fur rug by the fireplace and a fuzzy throw on the sofa will work nicely . . . and can you fluff up the grass by the front walk and make it more natural looking?

Thankfully, I have had clients make only the last three requests, the furry rug, fuzzy throw, and fluffy grass. I do all of this with the Hair and Fur modifier, which can generate everything from throw fuzz to sweeping expanses of lawn, and incidentally, hair on a person, dog, or monster should the need arise. Hair is a very flexible and powerful tool to have in the visualization artist's toolbox, ranking in importance equal to cloth, and worth devoting time to master.

Why place hair on such a pedestal? In our world of presenting the perfect building perfectly to the perfect client, it is easy to be too perfect. Walls are perfectly straight, floors are perfectly flat, tiles can be precisely laid with exact grout joints, and so on. Even curves can be perfect, as can light and shadows. Thus, any tool that can add an element of randomness, natural flow, or irregularity is a prized possession. The straight line is highlighted by the flowing curve next to it as much as by the sunbeam spilling across on the diagonal.

Hair is actually a render effect, being generated in full at render time. Based on Joe Alter's Shave and a Haircut plug-in, the Hair and Fur plug-in is well integrated into 3ds Max, allowing you, as of release 9, to edit and style hair directly in the viewport. Additionally, hair has a multitude of properties that can be defined by maps, whether bitmaps or procedural textures, so that the hair can range from tiger stripes (on a tiger if needed, or not) to wild grasses to wavy flowing locks on a hero or heroine. Hair also supports dynamics and forces, so should you need fields of wheat waving in the wind, or perhaps furry tiger-striped curtains blowing in the wind, it can be done. In this chapter, as we will be using the Hair plug-in, I will refer to any generated hair as "hair," even if we are making grass or fur. In the context of 3ds

Max, and in the 3D world in general, hair is hair, even if it is green and apparently cut with a lawn mower.

EXERCISE 1: Creating a lawn

For this exercise, we will create a simple grassy hill bounded on two sides by sidewalks. Designing hair for use as grass, hair, fur, fuzz, or any other purpose is somewhat like painting seemingly random texture maps of tile or other material. It is not a totally random jumble, but a series of similar instances that have randomized parameters within precise ranges. A lawn in a visualization is not an overgrown field of weeds; it is an even carpet of grass that has been mowed recently yet does not look like that indoor-outdoor green stuff. It has color variation within a section of the green and yellow hues, generally similar density all over, and visually pleasing curl and wave without flat areas or canine crop circles.

1. Open *lawn start.max* from the Assets folder for this chapter on the CD. This scene has sidewalk squares bounding the aforementioned hill, lights, and a camera (see Figure 11.1). (Notice that the hill has been brushed with the Paint Deform tool found in the Editable Poly so that the ground under the grass is not perfectly smooth and level.) For this exercise, as is typical in this book, we will use the mental ray rendering engine; the parameters have been set up correctly in the scene already.

2. Select the hill by clicking on it in the viewport. On the Modifier panel, drop down the Modifier List and choose Hair and Fur from the World Space Modifiers (see Figure 11.2). Note that Hair and Fur is not an Object Space Modifier as the render effect can control multiple hair and fur modifiers.

3. The first thing to change with hair is the overall scale and cut length, getting the hair in the right size as a broad stroke. On the Modifier panel, scroll up or down until you see the General Parameters rollout. Set the Scale down to around 10 and then the Cut Length to around 45 to 50 (see Figure 11.3). With hair, scale affects the whole hairs' length, from root to tip, while cut length crops the hair at a certain percentage along the shaft. As this is a lawn, we want it to look recently mowed and hence all roughly the same size, appearing to have been cut at the same time.

4. Now that the grass is much shorter, we can reduce the number of hair segments as well. The number of hair segments determines the ability of the hair to curve over its length, and how smooth those curves are. Although we still want some curve to the blades, between anti-aliasing, depth of field, shadow, and distance from the camera, any artifacts will be smoothed over. Reduce the hair segments to 3 for this lawn (see Figure 11.4).

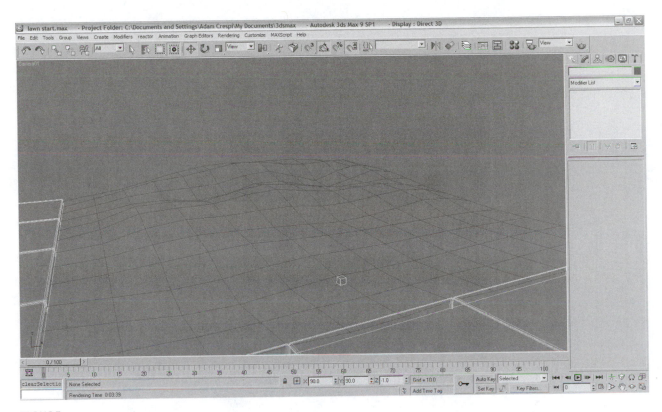

FIGURE 11.1

The starting scene from the camera view.

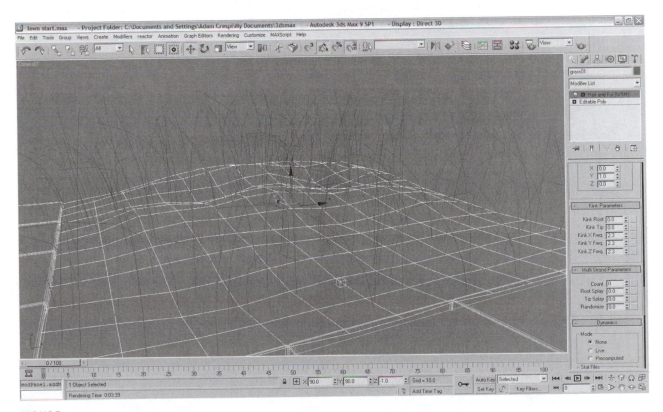

FIGURE 11.2

The Hair and Fur modifier applied to the hill, showing default hair guides.

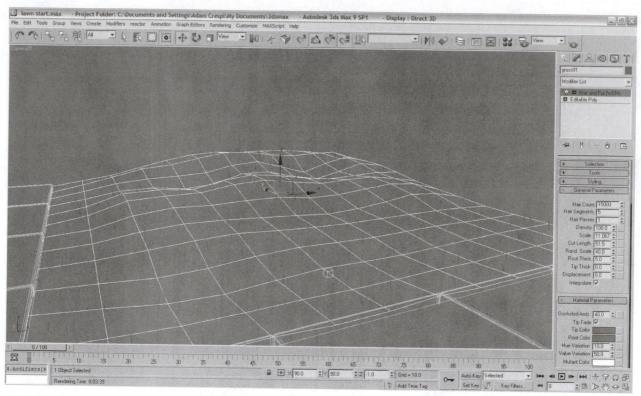

FIGURE 11.3

The hair with the changed scale and cut length.

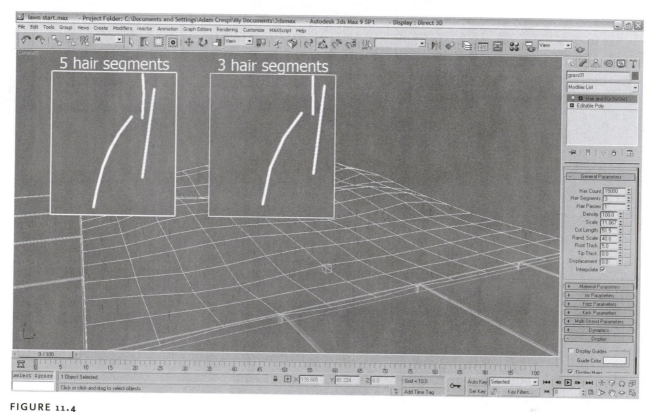

FIGURE 11.4

The hair segments reduced to 3.

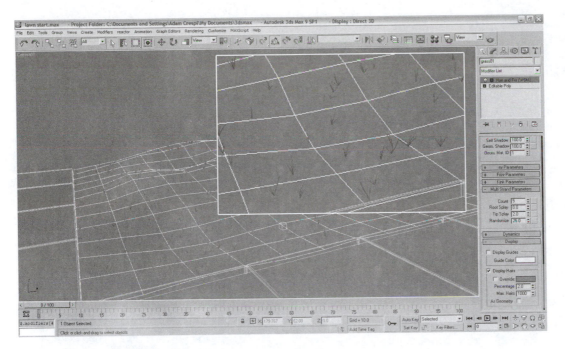

FIGURE 11.5

The Multi-Strand Parameters, showing the clumped hairs.

5. Above Hair Segments in the General Parameters is the Hair Count, which defaults to 15000. In practice, I try to make the hair look fuller in every other way possible before raising this number. The number of hairs in the scene directly affects the rendering time of that scene and can cause render times to lengthen considerably. Additionally, when using Final Gather and Global Illumination, rendering time can increase even more as hair count increases, because hairs start to occlude bounced light and reflect color on each other. Thus, any method of reducing hair count while maintaining the look desired should be explored and experimented with. One technique is to use multi-strand hairs, where each hair growth point sprouts multiple hairs that are considered and rendered as if they were one. Scroll down on the Modifier panel to the Multi-Strand Parameters, increase the Count to 5 and the Tip Splay to around 2, and Randomize to roughly 25 (see Figure 11.5). This will generate five hairs for each hair growth point, spread out the tips to make fan-shaped clumps, and randomize the spread and position of the strands.

6. Test render the scene if you want to see how the hair looks (see Figure 11.6). When dealing with hair, as with particles, we work in small representative percentages that show the overall motion or pattern without swamping the processing power of the computer or graphics card. The rendering then shows the full number of the hairs or particles in the scene.

7. Now that the pattern and length are getting close, it is time to get the material looking more like grass, as well as increasing the coverage on the hill. Scroll up to the Material Parameters and click on the Root Color. Change it to 52,73,19, a dark green, and change the Tip Color to 86,121,31 (see Figure 11.7). This should produce hairs that are dark at the base and lighter at the tip.

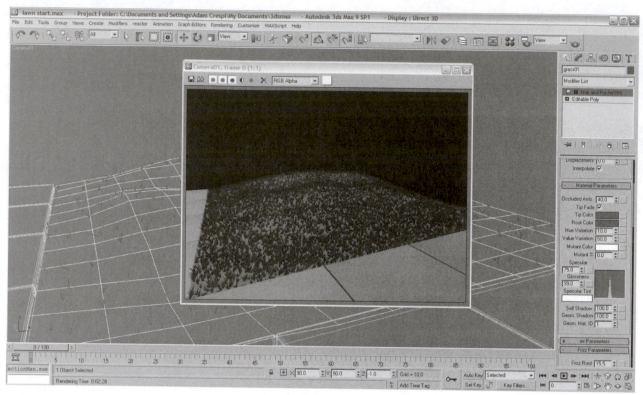

FIGURE 11.6

The rendered hairs, showing the lawn beginning to look correct.

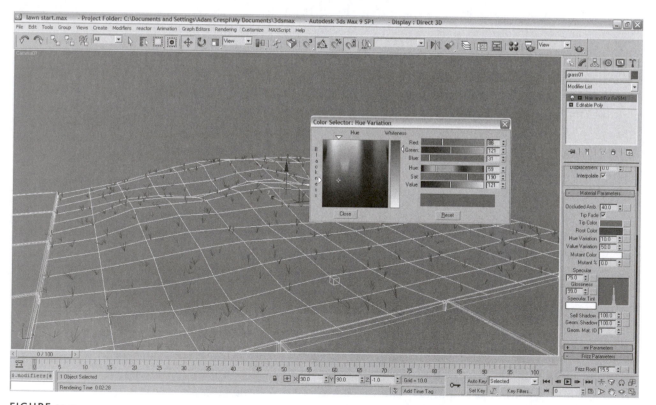

FIGURE 11.7

The changed root and tip colors.

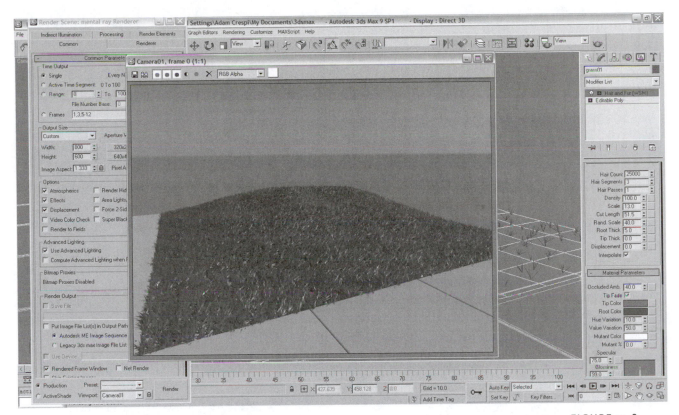

FIGURE 11.8

The rendered grass after the increased hair count.

8. Finally, before we increase the hair count, change the Tip Thickness in the General Parameters to 1 to add a little width to the tip of the hairs. This will shape them closer to blades of grass.

9. Increase the Hair Count to 25000 and test render again. The hair, or grass in this case, should fairly fill the lawn and have a reasonable though not excessive variation in color, size, wave, and direction (see Figures 11.8 and 11.9).

10. Since the grass coverage on the hill is still somewhat sparse in places, despite the increased count and multi-strand clumps, increase the Tip Thickness to 0.375 or 0.5. Hair has a root and tip thickness, allowing the hairs to be straight, tapered, pointed, or flat on the ends depending on the parameters used. As this is cut grass, we can increase the tip thickness so that each hair is broader and hides more of the ground (see Figure 11.10).

11. At the moment, the hair covers the hill nicely, with good edge randomization and an organic feel. Once the hair is growing correctly and covering properly, now is the time to experiment with reducing the hair count to save rendering time if possible. Try reducing the hair count to 20000 and test rendering again (see Figure 11.11). If it looks too sparse or mangy, bring the number back up in increments of 1000 until you are satisfied. As with lighting and materials, you need to experiment with hair to get the right look. Parameters given here are a general target; play around with it until it looks right.

FIGURE 11.9

*A larger rendering
of the grass on
the hill.*

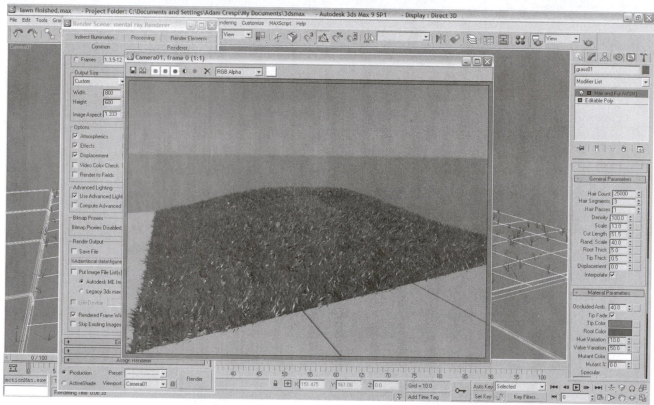

FIGURE 11.10

The rendered hairs with increased tip thickness, showing the nearly complete ground coverage.

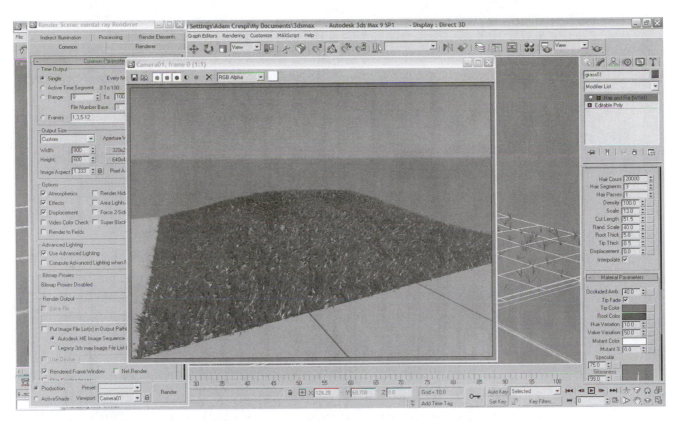

FIGURE 11.11

The hair rendered with a count of 20000.

FIGURE 11.12

The final grass on the hill.

12. At this point, the hair, or grass as it seems to be in the rendered images, is complete (see Figure 11.12). If you wish, continue to experiment with different parameters, such as length and color, to make alternative types of grass. In the next tutorial, we will continue to refine our hair techniques, using maps to control density, color, length, and many other parameters.

EXERCISE 2:   Controlling hair with maps for a non-uniform look

In this exercise, we will use maps to generate irregular hair for a stylized look, in this case on a modern shag rug as might be found in a well-designed home or private executive office. The Hair and Fur modifier allows control of almost every parameter with a map. Most of these maps can be grayscale, with black being the 0% or None condition, and white being the 100% or All condition, much like bump maps. We will also explore hair generated as a mental ray primitive, rather than as a post effect in the buffer. As you may have noticed, the grass in the previous exercise was generated after the rendering, although the shadows were created during the rendering.

1. Open the *Office start.max* file from the Assets folder for this chapter. This is a simple scene for quicker rendering times while experimenting, and as such it is missing much of the detail and additional furnishings that would normally be found in a space like this (see Figures 11.13 and 11.14). If you are creating hair for a rug such as this, it is always better to hide the other objects in the scene or create the rug in a new scene and then merge it in to reduce rendering time. (Notice in Figure 11.13 that there is no geometry in place for the rug yet, as we will create it as part of the exercise. Also notice the sexy sunbeams reaching across the floor and up the wall in Figure 11.14; the rug will be seen in those.)

FIGURE 11.13
The starting scene, ready for the rug.

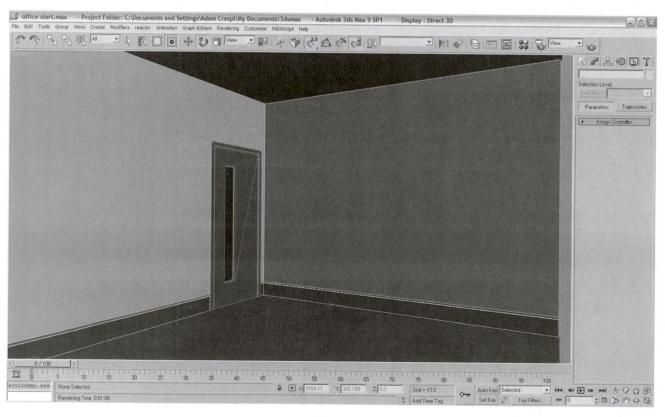

FIGURE 11.14

The starting scene rendered.

2. This will be a 5′ × 7′ rug with a soft shag, rectangular, and full with a pleasing messiness to the shag. Start by creating a Chamfer Box on the floor, roughly in the view of the camera, with a length of 60, a width of 84, a height of 0.6, a fillet radius of 0.25, and 2 fillet segments. Additionally, give this Chamfer Box 5 length segments and 7 width segments (see Figure 11.15).

3. Add a UVW Mapping modifier to the rug, using the default planar map.

FIGURE 11.15

The Chamfer Box in the scene.

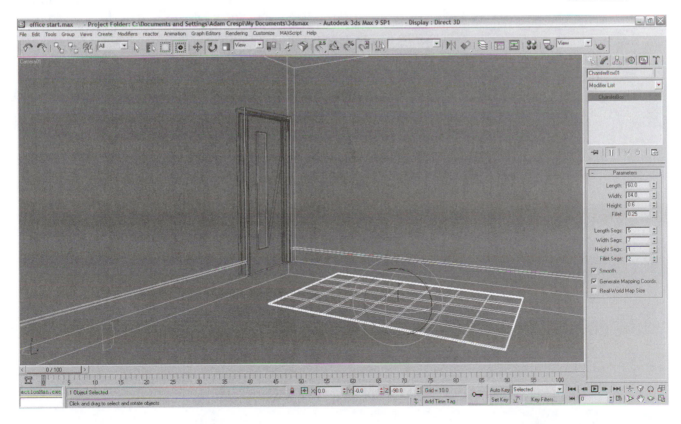

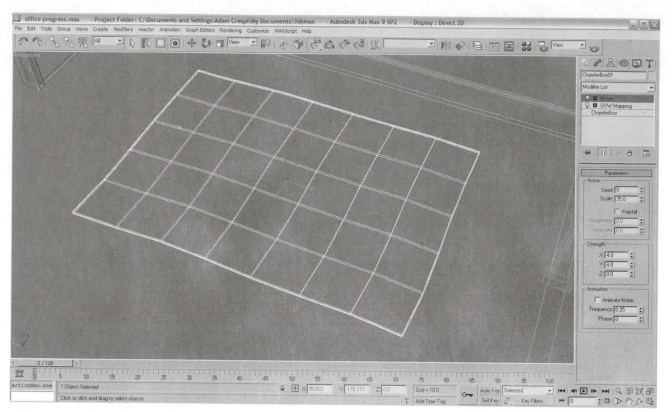

FIGURE 11.16

The Noise modifier applied to the rug.

4. Add a Noise modifier to the Chamfer Box, with an X and Y strength of 4 and 4, and a scale of 35 (see Figure 11.16). This will add a subtle wave to the rug, deforming both the geometry and the mapping coordinates.

5. Apply a Hair and Fur modifier to the rug. Click on the Polygon button in the selection rollout, select all of the rug polygons, and then deselect the bottom polygons (see Figure 11.17). Click on the Update Selection button when you are finished. This will constrain the hair to grow only from the selected polygons, and exclude it from growing into the floor. Also, this will concentrate the number of hairs over a smaller area, allowing a fuller look without as many hairs.

6. In the General Parameters for the hair, dial the Scale back to around 8, the Segments to 3, and bring the Tip Thickness up to 3 from 0 (see Figure 11.18). This will yield shorter, thicker hairs, which look much like those found on a shag rug of this type.

7. At this point, before adjusting any parameters such as density or hair count, we will change the hair to a mental ray primitive and apply a material to both the hair and the Chamfer Box. Pull up the Environment and Effects dialog by pressing 8 or choosing Rendering > Effects from the File menu. In the Effects section, click on the Hair and Fur effect.

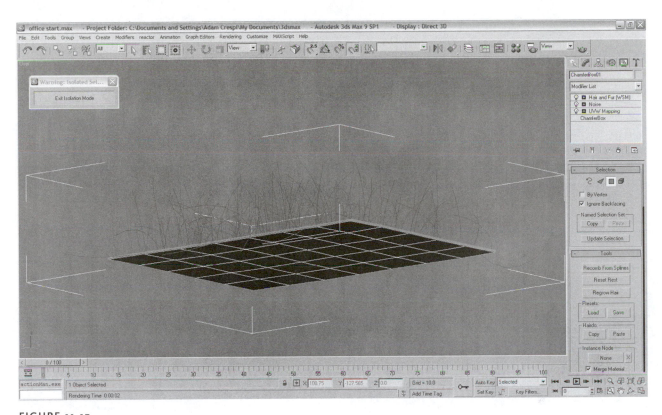

FIGURE 11.17

The isolated rug, showing the deselected polygons and the resulting hair growth.

FIGURE 11.18

The shorter and thicker hair.

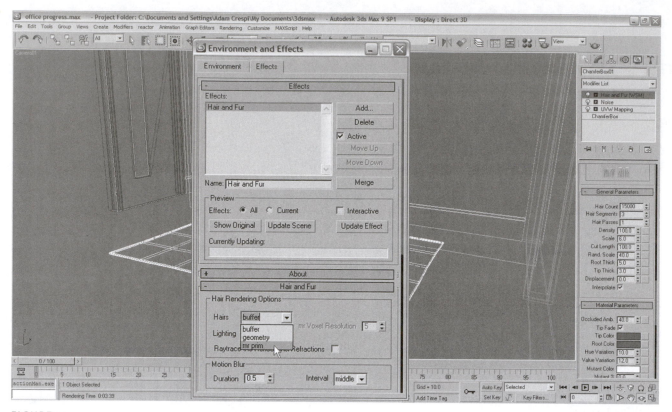

FIGURE 11.19

The hair changed to a mental ray primitive in the Effects dialog.

8. With the Hair and Fur selected, drop down the Hairs menu in the Hair Rendering Options rollout, and choose mental ray primitive, shown as mr prim (see Figure 11.19).

9. By changing the hair to a mental ray primitive, it will render with the scene rendering, not as a post effect. Additionally, this allows us to apply a mental ray material to the hair, such as the Arch & Design material, for a more realistic look. In this case, since we want the color of the rug to be consistent and not show the backing, we will apply the same material to the Chamfer Box and the hair. In the previous tutorial, we left the dirt under the grass as a dirt material, for contrast and realism in that situation. Press M to engage the Material Editor.

10. Click on any available slot, and change the material type to Arch & Design.

11. Change the template for the Arch & Design material to a Matte Finish, and increase the roughness to 0.75.

12. Change the Diffuse color of this material to a deep bronze/brown, with an RGB of around 0.25,0.2,0.15 (see Figure 11.20).

13. Drag this material onto the Chamfer Box to assign it.

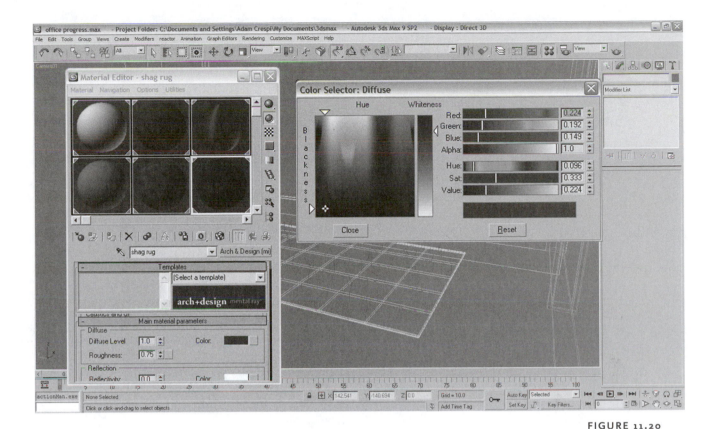

FIGURE 11.20
*The new Arch &
Design material,
purposefully
made darker and
rougher than the
final because it
will be seen in
bright sunlight.*

14. On the Modifier panel, scroll down until you see the mr parameters rollout. Check Apply mr shader and then drag the rug material across to the slot on the Modifier panel, cloning the material as an instance (see Figure 11.21). Using the mental ray material in conjunction with the mental ray primitive hair allows the color to be rendered correctly in the scene, even in a strongly lit daylight system such as the one in this scene. It also provides an opportunity for post houses or other facilities to custom code shaders for the hair as needed.

15. Test render the rug again. It should be consistent in color within each stripe, and look fairly shaggy (see Figure 11.22).

16. At this point, the rug can be used as a solid-colored, fairly uniform shag rug if desired. However, to add a little more randomization to the rug, we will use procedural maps to vary the length and scale of the hair. Click on the map slot next to the length in the Hair modifier, and choose Noise from the Material/Map Browser.

17. Drag this Noise map across to the Material Editor as an instance for editing.

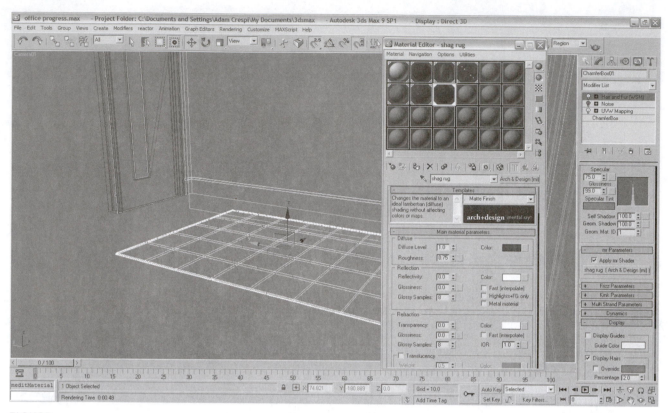

FIGURE 11.21

The rug material cloned across to the Modifier panel.

FIGURE 11.22

The rug rendered with materials applied to the Chamfer Box and hair.

FIGURE 11.23
The Noise map controlling the scale of the hair.

18. Change the Noise colors to white and 50% gray, with a size of roughly 15. This will vary the length of the hair, but will be multiplied by the scale percentage. Increase the scale to around 30 and test render (see Figure 11.23).

19. The last touch for this rug is to brush the hair down, as the pile of a rug like this is generally not stiff and standing on end. In the Tools rollout, click on the Style Hair button. This will turn on the styling tools, the default of which is the brush. Brush the hair down and to the side, sweeping it over and adding messiness to it (see Figure 11.24).

20. When you have brushed the rug to your liking, test render again (see Figure 11.25). Continue to refine and style the rug if you wish, or add more maps for further control.

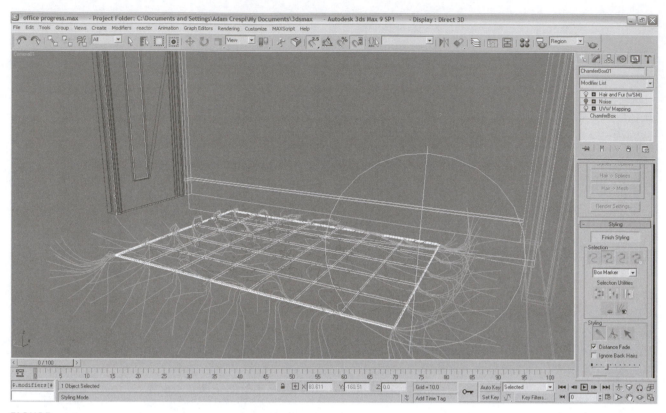

FIGURE 11.24

Styling the rug. Orange guide hairs show the general direction of styling.

FIGURE 11.25

The finished styled rug in a rendering.

SECTION B: CONCLUSION

Looking effortless is a constant concern in the visual world we live in, whether in clothing, hairstyles, work, sports, or architectural visualizations. Witness the tousled hair look of any given rock star, the layered casual ease proffered by dozens of fashion magazines, and the perfectly arranged pictures leaning against walls in countless interior design photos. These various looks took, of course, much longer than the five minutes they want to suggest; they are the result of meticulous attention to detail and a rigorous study of the elements of casual design.

We as visualization artists, of course, do not throw together anything in five or even ten minutes for a rendering. Every move, every object or *objet,* is the result of painstaking work and time invested. Thus, if there is any opportunity to turn up the casual filter or strategically mess up a few things in a rendering, we should and need to jump on it. The Hair and Fur modifier gives us just this ability, letting the randomness within set ranges found in a particle simulation manifest as natural lawns and shaggy rugs, and even pillow fringe should you so need. So go on, mess up your hair a little bit.

CHAPTER **12**   Cloth in 3ds Max

SECTION A: SEWING VIRTUALLY

One of the biggest challenges facing the visualization pro is crafting the randomness found in real life, even in precisely positioned architectural or interior design renderings. As shown in the chapters on painting textures, what we strive for is apparent randomness within a given parameter set. Standing on the shoulders of pioneering visual effects firms, we now have cloth simulation on the desktop. This allows us to simulate the draping of cloth in a physically correct manner as needed, rather than modeling every fold in a duvet or slipcover.

This method of simulation may be somewhat foreign to the traditional animator who is used to crafting a version of reality not necessarily bound by the laws of physics or tailoring. However, thinking in terms of fabric stiffness, warp and weft, panels and seams allows the architectural or interior designer to tap and repurpose existing knowledge. Design in virtual cloth as you would in the real world; it is a language of stuffing, backing, frames, ties, tension, and flow.

There are a number of methods to creating cloth. There is the pure route, creating and stitching flat panels into a volume, such as a sofa cover, and then solving the draping over the sofa. In the context of cloth simulation, solving the cloth refers to the settling of the cloth on an object or objects in the scene, and possibly over many frames in an animation. If cloth is not solved, it does not interact with objects and forces in the scene, such as wind, but instead appears as its rather stiff component panels or base model.

Alternatively, the shape can be modeled using polygon modeling techniques, then solved as cloth over another object. Finally, there is a hybrid approach, setting out the initial flat panels, partially solving the cloth, then converting to an Editable Poly for further editing and final solving.

The common thread in all cloth simulation then is the simulation of the cloth over, under, or onto other objects. This involves two phases, Local Simulation and Simulation. These two steps exist as a result of the pipeline in animation and visual effects. Characters are often modeled in a skin pose, a neutral stance with arms straight out at the sides, legs slightly spread, and a neutral facial expression. The skin pose may also be referred to as the da Vinci pose, after the famous drawing. In this neutral pose, clothing is tailored to the character, and then simulated locally, or solved to sit on the character. After the character is animated in the scene or scenes, the clothing is then simulated to follow the underlying model. For our purposes, this simulation may only reach the first phase, the local settling. Objects like slipcovers, tablecloths, bedspreads, and so forth rarely need additional animation; we are looking for accurate local draping. Where visualizations enter the second phase is in the application of forces or animation to the cloth, such as wind blowing curtains, opening or closing drapes. Additionally, "temporary" animation can help solve cloth on a model requiring gathering or bunching, then be deleted once the cloth is set.

EXERCISE 1:   Simulating a tablecloth

In this exercise, we will create and solve a simple tablecloth over a standard-sized restaurant table. Our work will provide a foundation for additional cloth simulation and design.

1.   Start 3ds Max or choose File > Reset from the top menu to begin with a clean scene.

2.   Press T to switch to the Top view.

3.   On the Command panel, click on the Create tab, then the Geometry button, and finally drop down the menu that reads Standard Primitives, and choose Extended Primitives.

4.   Click on the Chamfer Box button, and then click and drag in the viewport to create a Chamfer Box.

5.   Click on the Modifier tab, and then enter these dimensions for the Chamfer Box: length 30″, width 48″, height 1.5″, and fillet radius of 0.5″ (see Figure 12.1).

Note:
Why use a Chamfer Box? Cloth simulation is the act of conforming hundreds if not thousands of polygons into a shape that a piece of real cloth might assume. When cloth is draped over a box, such as a tablecloth over a table, it naturally forms small radii over the table corners. In order to do this in the virtual world, we would need to increase the polygon count of the cloth to a ridiculously high level, most of which would be wasted after solving. The cloth would simulate and drape, leaving many of the polygons roughly coplanar and hence wasting rendering time. A better solution in cases like these is to add small radii to the

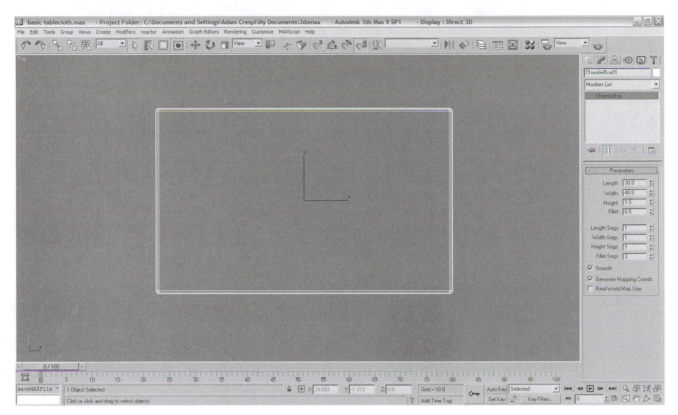

FIGURE 12.1
The Chamfer Box
in the scene.

collision object, the table. The cloth can then have a lower polygon count, take less time to simulate, and use lower rendering overhead.

6. Press Ctrl + RMB and choose Plane from the Modeling quad menu. Create a Plane roughly centered over the Chamfer Box, with a length of 54″ and a width of 72″, with 108 Length Segments and 144 Width Segments.

7. On the Main Toolbar, click on the Align button with the Plane selected, then choose the Chamfer Box to align to. In the Align dialog, align the Center of the Plane to the Chamfer Box on all axes.

8. Press W or right-click and choose Move from the quad menu. In a Front or Left view, move the Plane above the Chamfer Box by an inch or two (see Figure 12.2).

   Really Important Note:
   When preparing to simulate cloth, make sure that the objects are not colliding, coincident, or coplanar. If they are, this will cause either an excessive simulation time or a flowery polygonal explosion stretching across the viewport.

9. On the Modifier panel, add a Cloth modifier to the Plane.

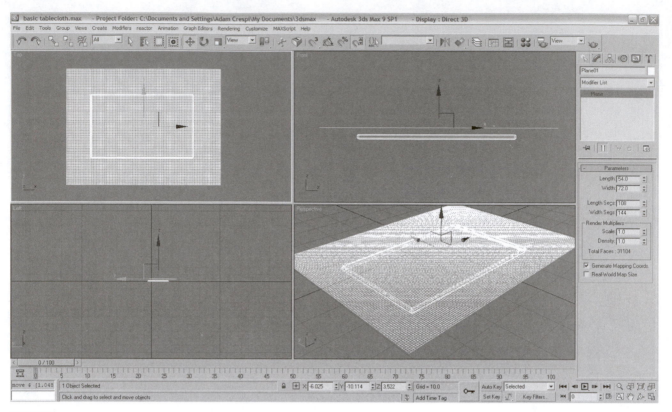

FIGURE 12.2

The Plane positioned over the Chamfer Box, showing the Plane's parameters.

10. In the Parameters for the Cloth modifier, click on the Object Properties button at the top. Cloth performs a localized simulation on objects registered as Inactive, Collision, or Cloth, and ignores everything else in the scene (see Figure 12.3).

11. In the Object Properties dialog, the Plane will be listed in the Objects in Simulation field on the left and set to Inactive by the radio button on the top middle. Click on the Plane in the Objects in Simulation field, and then change it to a Cloth object by selecting the radio button next to Cloth.

12. In the Cloth Properties section, pull down the menu of templates for cloth presets (see Figure 12.4). As this is a tablecloth, choose Cotton, which is a rather loose cotton, or Starched Cotton if you require a bit more stiffness. I use Starched Cotton in more formal settings, such as upscale restaurants, and Cotton for a more casual feel in houses. Alternatively, Silk works very well for tablecloths that are shorter, or for accent panels lying diagonally across the tablecloth.

13. Back in the Objects in Simulation field, click on the Add Objects button. This will allow you to add any unhidden objects in the scene to the simulation. Choose Chamfer Box and click OK.

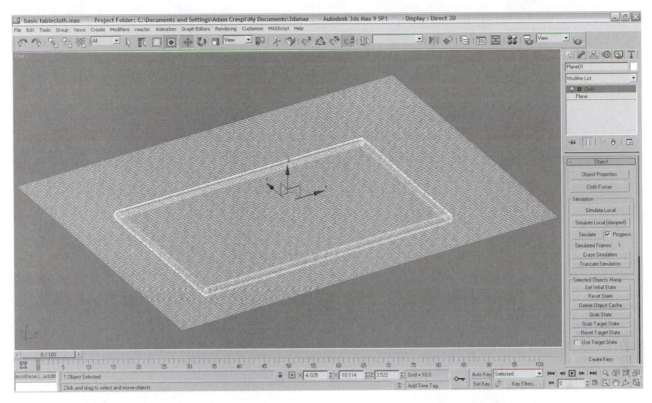

FIGURE 12.3

The Cloth modifier applied to the Plane.

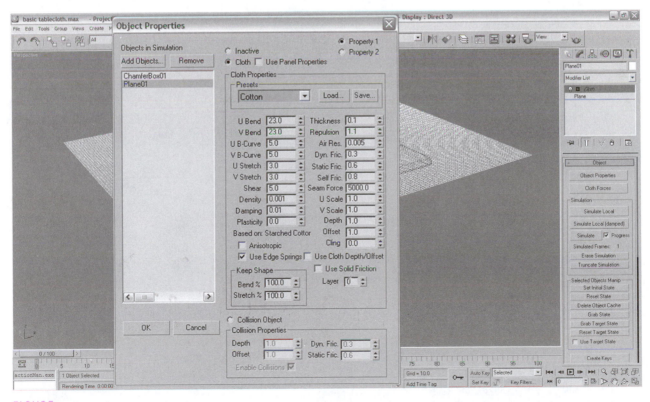

FIGURE 12.4

The Object Properties dialog for the Plane.

14. With the Chamfer Box selected in the Objects in Simulation field, click on the Collision Object radio button. Any cloth in the simulation will drape over and possibly slide off this collision object, and the object will not fall with the gravity that will affect the cloth.

15. In the Collision Object Parameters, the offset determines the distance at which the cloth will sit above the collision object, measured in scene units. For this tablecloth, reduce the offset to 0.125 so that the cloth sits on the table and does not appear to be floating (see Figure 12.5). Click OK to close this dialog when you are done.

16. Back on the Modifier panel, press Simulate Local to settle the cloth. This simulation occurs within frame zero, before there is any animation.

17. The tablecloth should drop onto the Chamfer Box, flap a few times, and settle (see Figure 12.6). When the simulation is at the stage of twitching, click on the Simulate Local button again to stop the simulation.

FIGURE 12.5
The Object Properties dialog for the Chamfer Box as a collision object.

18. The tablecloth is now complete and ready for material application and use in the scene. If you don't want to feature any further animation on the cloth, you can collapse it to an Editable Poly to reduce file size. If animation will be a part of the visualization, do not collapse the cloth.

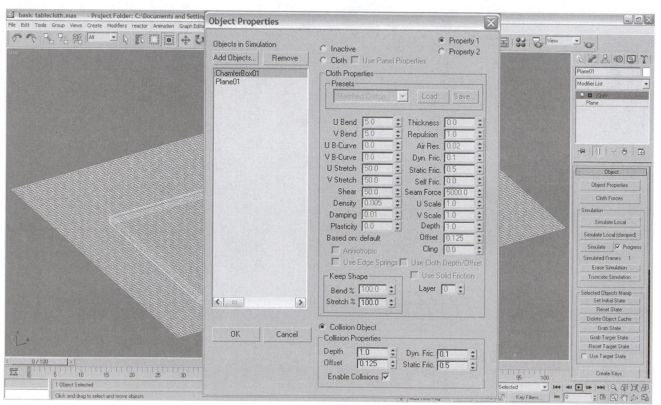

CHAPTER 12 : CLOTH IN 3DS MAX

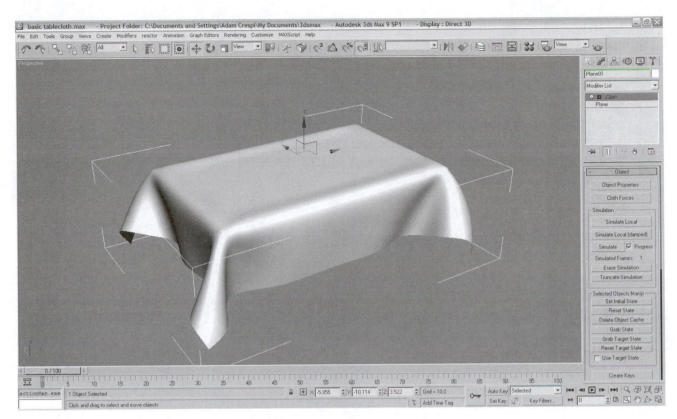

FIGURE 12.6

The local simulation, allowing the plane to drape over the Chamfer Box.

BONUS EXERCISE: Alternative tablecloths and cloth on cloth interaction

---

1. Try adding another layer on top of the tablecloth, such as a smaller accent cloth turned diagonally (see Figure 12.7). You will need to perform a multistep simulation, first simulating the bottom tablecloth, and then making it a collision object for the second layer.

2. Instead of a full tablecloth, use a long narrow Plane to create a table runner along the length of a table (see Figure 12.8).

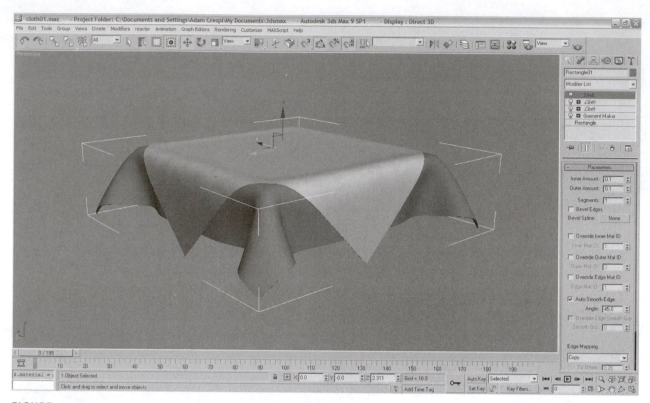

FIGURE 12.7

A layered tablecloth.

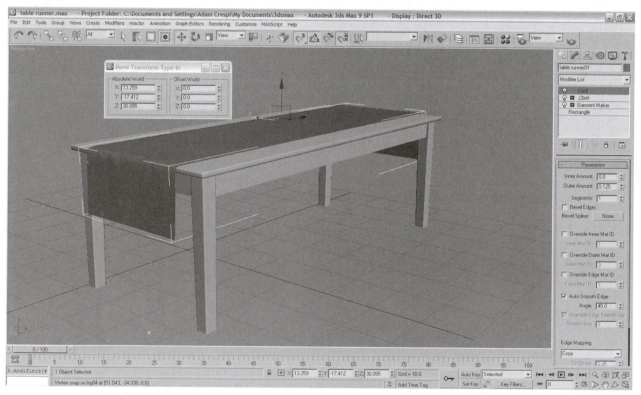

FIGURE 12.8

A table runner draped over a long table.

SECTION B: SLIPCOVERS

EXERCISE 2: Creating a chair slipcover

In this exercise, we will utilize the Garment Maker modifier on a collection of splines to craft a slipcover for a dining chair. The Garment Maker modifier allows the positioning and stitching of panels of fabric, as well as specific density and properties per panel in a cloth object.

1. Load the *slipcover_start.max* file from the Assets folder on the CD. This file contains a simple chair for which we will construct a slipcover.

2. In a Top view, we'll create the panels for the slip cover using splines. It is important to create the panels in a Top view and then rotate them into place in the Garment Maker modifier, as gravity inherently pulls down in the scene. On the Command panel, go to the Create tab and then into the Shapes section. Click on Rectangle and then draw rectangles over the chair to start the panels. Begin by drawing one over the seat, roughly 17″ × 17″ and one over the top of the seatback, roughly 4″ × 17″ (see Figure 12.9).

FIGURE 12.9

The rectangles over the seat and top of the back.

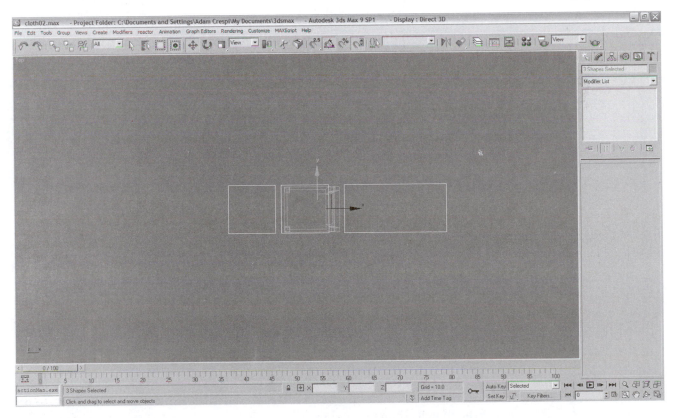

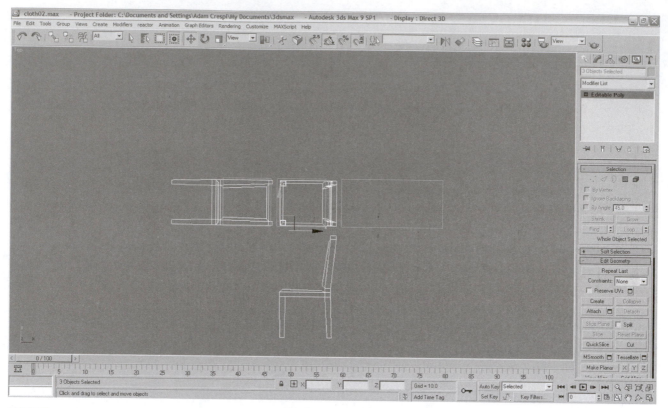

FIGURE 12.10

The chair clones for use as templates.

3. For the side, front, and back panels, I typically rotate and clone the chair so that the panels can be drawn in a Top view using the side and front of the chair as a template. Right-click and choose Rotate from the quad menu, press A to engage the Angle Snap, hold Shift, and rotate the chair on the X axis by 90 degrees, cloning as an instance.

4. Repeat this rotation on the Y axis as well so the front of the chair is facing up in the Top view (see Figure 12.10). We'll delete these clones after making the panels; cloning them allows us to use the real chair to align with as well.

5. Move the cloned chairs to the front and side of the real chair so you have room to work and see all of the panels laid out.

6. Finish creating the other panels as rectangles, using the cloned chairs as templates. For the sides, create two panels, one large pane for the seat and skirt, and one for the side of the back (see Figure 12.11).

7. Once you have drawn one set of side panels, select them and click on the Mirror button on the Main Toolbar. Mirror them on the Y axis as a copy, using the Offset to move the cloned panels to the other side of the chair. Alternatively, mirror and clone the panels, then move them into place.

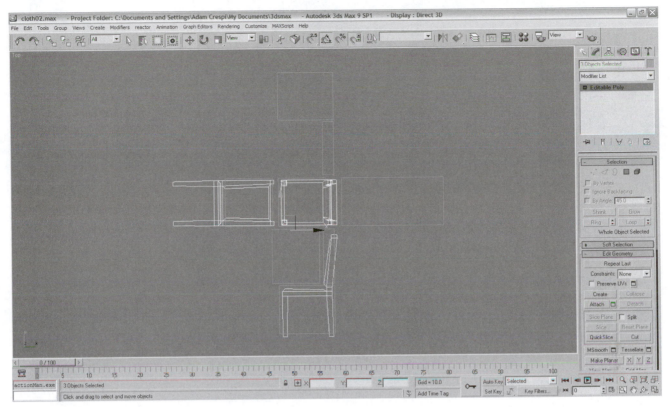

8. For the back, depending on the kind of slipcover you are making, create either one panel that goes from the top to the floor, or two panels that meet at the same place as the two side panels.

9. When all of the panels are finished, move them into place in the Top view around the chair, and delete the cloned template chairs (see Figure 12.12). Make sure that none of the panels are overlapping when you position them. Place the front panel for the seatback next to the seat panel.

10. Select any one panel, right-click, and choose Convert to Editable Spline from the quad menu.

11. Right-click again and choose Attach from the quad menu, and then click on each of the other panels to attach them together. Right-click to stop attaching when you are done.

12. Right-click and choose Refine from the quad menu. Remember that 3ds Max is context- and tool-sensitive, so you do not need to change to Vertex before refining; Refine is inherently part of the Vertex toolset and hence can be chosen from the Top Level.

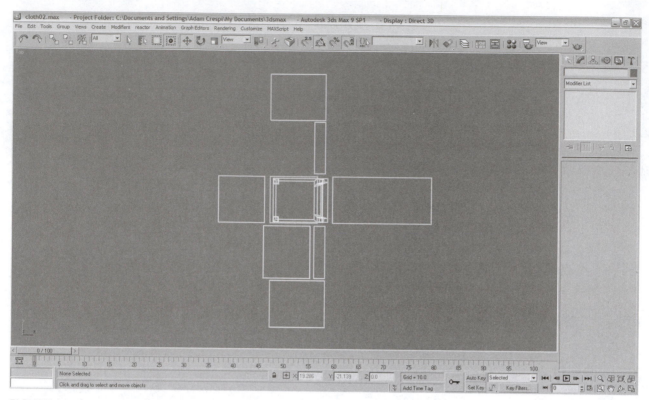

FIGURE 12.12

All of the panels created and placed in the Top view.

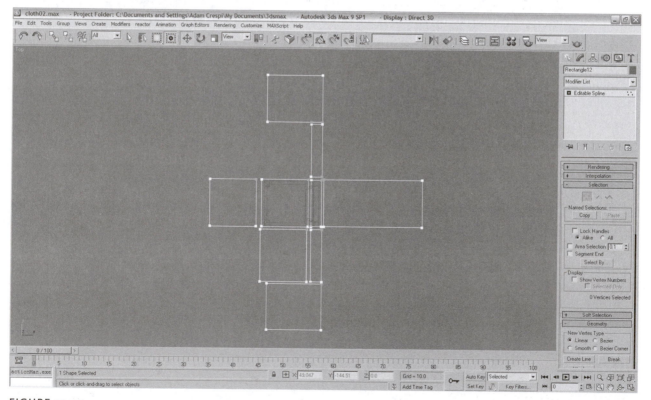

FIGURE 12.13

The additional vertices inserted into the lower side panels.

13. On each of the big lower side panels, use Refine to insert a new vertex aligned with the inner bottom corner of the slim side panel (see Figure 12.13). Right-click when you are done to exit the Refine tool.

14. The panels are almost ready for rotating into place and stitching using the Garment Maker modifier, but we need to do one more thing. In order to make separate seams that will stitch correctly, we need to break the vertices of the panels so that individual segments will form seams. If we do not break the vertices, the Garment Maker will run the seam completely around each panel, and we will be unable to join them. In this case, since all of our panels will be joined to other panels on three or four sides, we can break all of the vertices. If this was not the case, we would not need to break all of the vertices, only those at the ends of the seams. Select all of the vertices, right-click, and choose Break Vertices from the quad menu.

15. Right-click and choose Top Level from the quad menu once all of the vertices are broken.

16. On the Modifier panel, drop down under Modifier List and choose Garment Maker from the Object Space modifiers. The Garment Maker modifier will use the splines to guide a Delaunay mesh to create the fabric panels (see Figure 12.14). The Delaunay mesh is a triangle-based mesh that will produce fewer artifacts in

FIGURE 12.14
The Garment Maker modifier applied, showing default meshing.

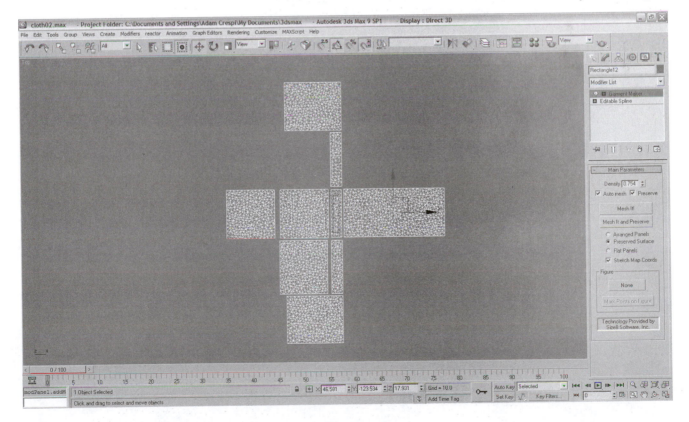

the cloth than a quad-based mesh. It does this by triangulating to maximize the minimum angles of each triangle, avoiding slivers or long thin triangles. Because we broke the vertices at the corners, the Delaunay mesh will continue to the corners; if we had not done this, a low mesh density might result in clipping some of the corners. The Density setting for this mesh determines the size of the triangles, which should default for this construction to about 0.75. For this simulation, the default should be fine as this will be a relatively stiff slipcover. If you are working with softer, floppier, looser, or stretchier fabrics, increase this density as needed.

17. In the Garment Maker modifier, there are sub-objects for Seams, Curves, and Panels. First, position the panels in roughly the right places around the chair. Right-click and choose Panel from the quad menu.

18. Select each panel and rotate and move it into place around the chair, making sure that they are not colliding. Leave a little space between each panel, but don't space them too far out. Additionally, make sure that the panels on the bottom are not passing through the floor plane; it is fine if the slipcover panels are assembled and floating slightly above the chair (see Figure 12.15).

FIGURE 12.15
The panels rotated into place around the chair.

19. Seam creation is where we tell the panels how to stitch together. If we did not add seams, when the cloth was simulated all of the panels would simply fall onto the floor. Right-click and choose Seams from the quad menu.

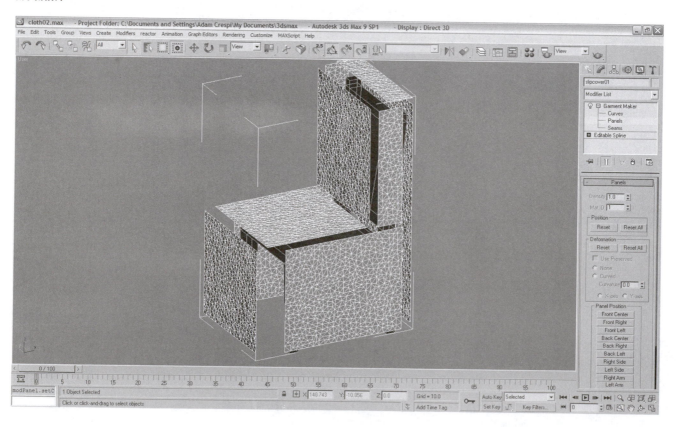

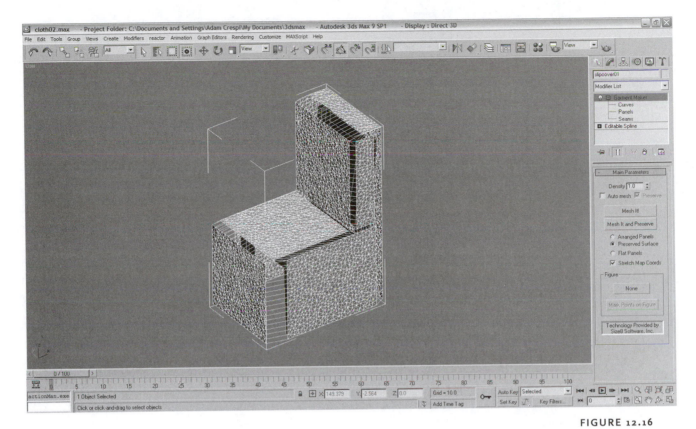

FIGURE 12.16

*The seams created
between the panels;
connecting lines
are sewing springs.*

20. We can make two types of seams, simple two-part seams and multi-segment
     seams. Simple seams are just that, two panel edges joined together. Multi-segment
     seams allow the joining of three or more edges with common corners, such as
     where top and bottom side panels meet the back panel. Another example of a
     multi-segment seam would be the joint of a shirt's sleeve, front, and back panels,
     or the inseam of a pair of pants. Select two adjacent seams, which should high-
     light in red, and click Create Seam on the Seams rollout on the Modifier panel.
     Work your way around the chair, creating seams for the slipcover except for the
     sides and back seam (see Figure 12.16).

21. When you create a seam, you should see sewing springs connecting the seam
     edges, and these should run reasonably straight from panel to panel. If the sew-
     ing springs twist, or come to a pinch in the middle of the seam, select that seam
     and click on the Reverse Seam button. (Notice that selected seams and sewing
     springs are red, and unselected ones are green.)

22. Now for the multi-segment seams connecting the back panel. Multi-segment
     seams involve an extra step in their creation but are not terribly difficult. To start
     the first one, select rear seams of the top and bottom right side panels, and click
     on the Create Multi-Segment Seam button on the Modifier panel. Nothing vis-
     ible will change; however, if you deselect and then reselect the Multi-Segment
     Seam, clicking on either piece will select both edges (see Figure 12.17).

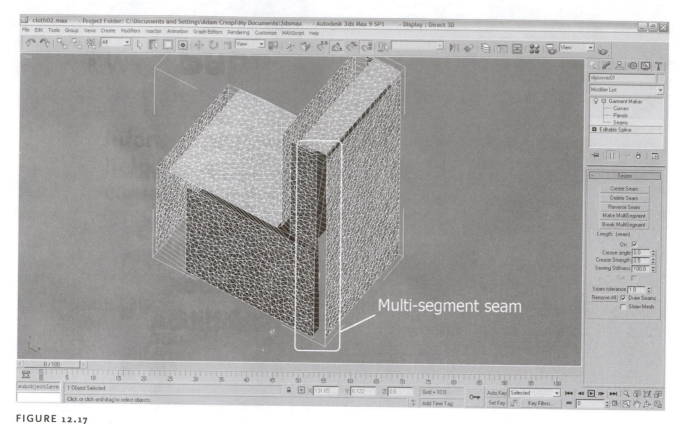

Multi-segment seam

FIGURE 12.17

The multi-segment seam selected, and then the seam created with sewing springs.

23. With the new multi-segment seam selected, hold Ctrl and select the adjacent corner edge of the back panel, and click Create Seam. The sewing springs should connect all three edges. Repeat this procedure for the other side of the chair.

24. At this point, you should have seams connecting all of the panels of the chair to each other. It is important to create the multi-segment seams last; otherwise you may get a Seam Topology error. On more complex constructions, this may require some trial and error before all of the seams are solved. Right-click and choose Top Level from the quad menu.

25. On the Modifier panel, drop down under the Modifier List and choose Unwrap UVW from the Object Space modifiers. Using the Edit dialog, arrange the panels to fill the extents of the map boundaries (see Figure 12.18).

    Note:
    Unwrapping mapping on a Garment Maker–generated cloth object is quite easy, because transformations made to panels as part of the modifier do not register in the default unwrap. Thus, all of the panels are flat and in the starting arrangement from before the Unwrap was applied.

26. Make sure that the slipcover is still selected and apply a Cloth modifier to it.

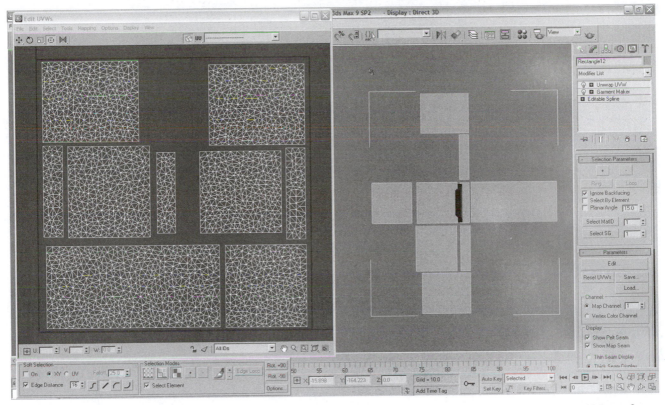

FIGURE 12.18
*The slipcover
panels unwrapped
for texture.*

27. On the Modifier panel, in the parameters for the Cloth modifier, click on the Object Properties button.

28. In the Object Properties dialog, make the slipcover a Cloth, using the cotton template. Add the chair and the floor plane as collision objects, with the chair having an offset of 0.5 (see Figure 12.19). Click OK when you are finished.

29. Press the Simulate Local button to settle the cloth and observe where fixes will need to be made. Some of the most common items requiring attention are torn seams, overly stretched panels, and inadequate mesh density.

30. When the local simulation is barely twitching, press Simulate Local again to stop it. At this point, we can do several things to fix some of the errors that may have shown up.

31. Once the cloth has done a local simulation, click on the Reset State button to return to the pre-simulation state (see Figure 12.20). When the cloth is reset, we are ready to fix problems with the simulation.

32. *Problem: Seams are not closing fully when simulated.* Right-click and choose Seams from the quad menu. Select one or more of the nonclosing seams, and increase

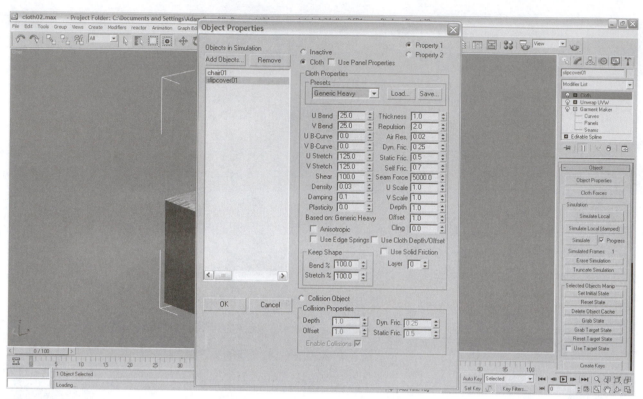

FIGURE 12.19

The slipcover with Cloth applied, and the Object Properties set for simulation.

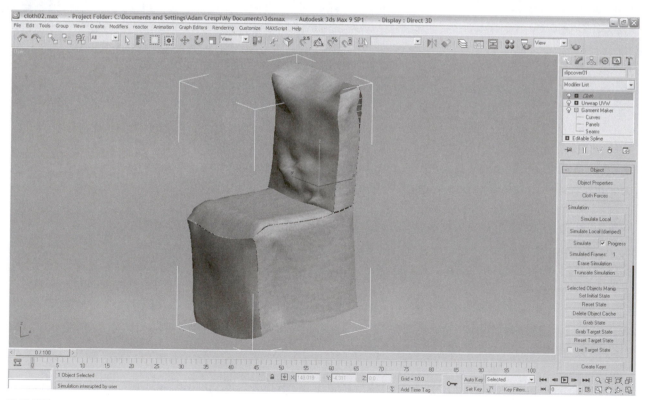

FIGURE 12.20

The cloth after local simulation over the chair.

the sewing stiffness in the Seams Parameters. Run the local simulation again and see if this worked. You may want to return to the Seams Parameters and adjust the Crease Stiffness if the stronger seams are causing creases in unwanted areas.

33. *Problem: Seams are still not closing fully when simulated.* If the seams are still not closing when simulated, reset the state again and then scroll down the Simulation Parameters rollout. Uncheck the box next to Use Sewing Springs. This will force 3ds Max to create geometry between adjacent panels rather than bringing them together with the springs. When you simulate again, the cloth may pass through the chair before settling (see Figure 12.21). The downside to this is that the sewing springs are gone once this is done; to get them back, delete and reapply the Cloth modifier.

34. *Problem: The seams are fine, but the cloth is draping too much over the chair.* Go back into the Object Properties dialog, and change the template type for the slipcover to a stiffer fabric. Within that dialog, U and V Bend control the stiffness of the fabric; a higher number means more resistance to bending. Additionally, the U and V Stretch numbers control the stretchiness of the fabric; a higher number there means more resistance to stretching. You may need to customize your fabric to fit the look you want.

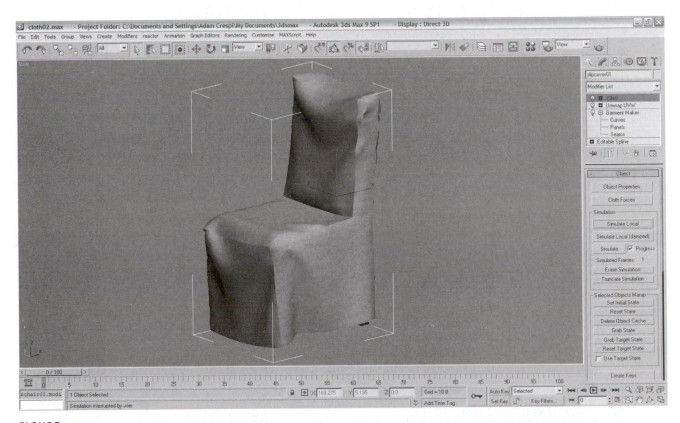

FIGURE 12.21

The cloth simulated without using sewing springs.

Note:

Why are the Object Properties of cloth objects so loaded with U and V values? Fabric has both warp and weft threads, which may add variable stiffness or flexing depending on the axis of tension or compression. U and V values allow you to customize the fabric to represent an anisotropic weave, and to create fabrics cut on the bias versus straight of grain.

35. *Problem: The cloth falls off the chair in places, or the chair pokes through the cloth.* Reset the simulation, and scroll down to the Simulation Parameters rollout. The number next to Collision is a sample, with higher values adding a finer sampling quality to the simulation at the expense of more time and processing power. Try increasing this number to 1 or 2 and simulate the cloth again. Alternatively, delete the Cloth modifier and drop down in the Modifier stack to the Garment Maker modifier. In the Garment Maker Parameters, increase the Density of the mesh. You may need to unwrap again if you do this, as well as reapply the Cloth modifier, set up, and simulate again. If the cloth simply falls off the chair or does not interact with the floor, go back into the Object Properties dialog and verify that the chair and floor are both collision objects, then simulate again.

36. *Problem: The cloth is passing through itself.* Reset the simulation and scroll down to the Simulation Parameters. Check Self-Collision and then simulate again. This will be a slower simulation, but it will force the cloth to interact with itself and detect and solve collisions.

37. Once the cloth has been settled, it is ready for positioning and additional detail. Now is the time to soften the look of the cloth or add thickness as desired. If the slipcover has settled and simply needs to look thicker, add a Shell modifier to it. Drop down the Modifier List and choose Shell from the Object Space modifiers. Usually an inner thickness of 0.1″ or 0.125″ will look fluffy enough. Use the Shell modifier if you will be seeing both sides of a piece of cloth, such as skirts on a sofa, a thin throw or blanket, or if the cloth object is draped over a reflective floor and the underside will show in the reflections.

38. If the cloth does not need thickness but shows some artifacts from the simulation, add a TurboSmooth or HSDS modifier to it. TurboSmooth will increase the polygon count but will reduce artifacts caused by smoothing across single vertices or flat areas.

39. The slipcover is complete. Using the UVW Unwrap template, you will want to apply a fabric color and texture as part of a material to the cloth. Be sure to orient any grain in the fabric in matching directions from panel to panel; this holds for any color variation as well (see Figure 12.22).

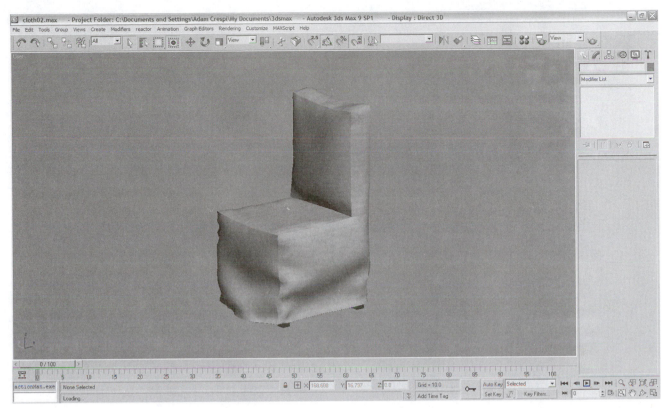

FIGURE 12.22
The finished slipcover with material applied.

BONUS EXERCISE: Adding welting to the slipcover

Welting is the sewing or stitching of a cord or rolled piece of fabric along a seam. This both serves as a cover for the seam and a detail to highlight workmanship. Additionally, welting can serve as a contrasting line or color in a design to emphasize a silhouette or shape.

1. Turn on the Object Snap by pressing S or clicking on the snap toggle on the Main Toolbar. Make sure the 3D Snap is engaged.

2. Press Shift + RMB in the viewport to bring up the Snap Overrides quad menu. Check Vertex and uncheck Grid Points if they are not configured to that already.

3. Press Ctrl + RMB and choose Line from the Modeling quad.

4. Snapping to the vertices at the seams of the slipcover, draw lines along the slipcover's corners. For this slipcover, add lines around the seat and around the back panel (or more if you wish).

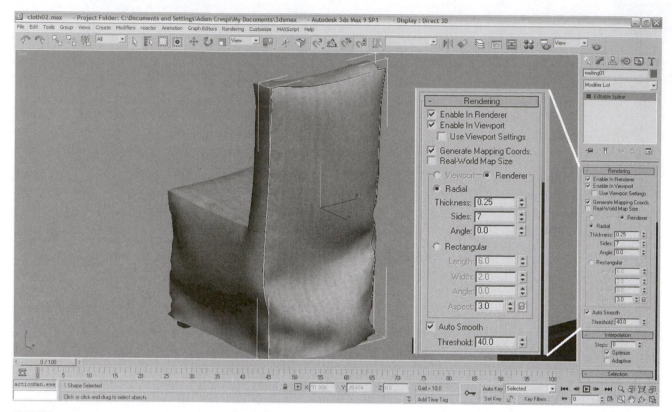

FIGURE 12.23

The welting, viewable and renderable.

5. On the Modifier panel, open the Rendering rollout in the Line's parameters. Check Enable in View port and Enable in Renderer, and use a thickness of 0.125″ to 0.25″ for the welting (see Figure 12.23).

6. In the Rendering rollout, set the number of sides of the renderable line to 7. For objects this thin, as long as it looks reasonably round in a rendering, we can reduce the amount of geometry considerably.

EXERCISE 3: Using darts to tighten fabric

---

1. Open the file *slipcover start with darts.max* from the Assets folder on the CD. Darts are openings cut in fabric panels that when sewn together will draw the fabric tighter around something, such as at the back of a dress around a lady's waist, or in this case at the back of the slipcover at the base of the seatback.

2. For this exercise, the slipcover's panels have been created and arranged around the chair. Note that in the middle of the back panel, there are two almond-shaped splines that will form the darts (see Figure 12.24). When using the Garment Maker, any splines inside the splines that comprise the panels will become holes or slits in

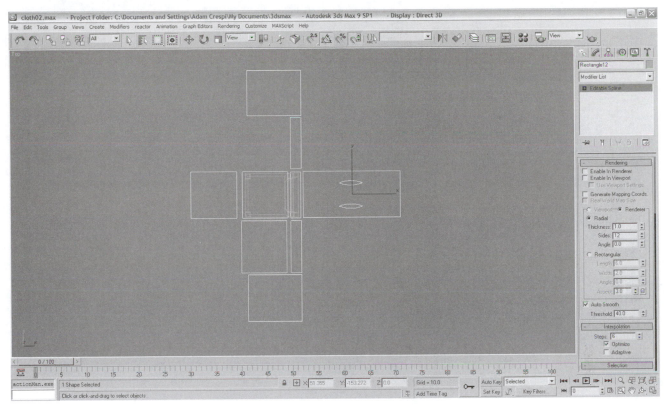

FIGURE 12.24
The slipcover with additional splines for darts.

the cloth simulation. Closed shapes become voids, while open lines are cuts in the fabric. They can then be stitched with sewing springs if desired. Select the object Slipcover02 and apply the Garment Maker modifier to it.

3. As with Exercise 2, go into the Panels sub-object on the Garment Maker modifier and move and rotate the panels into place around the chair. This slipcover is of a slightly different design than the first one, having an additional vertex along each side of the bottom panels. These vertexes will allow the slipcover to be fitted around the seat but flow in loose skirts around the legs of the chair.

4. Once the panels are positioned, switch to the Seams sub-object on the Garment Maker modifier. Create seams at all of the panel joints as before, including multi-segment seams at the joint between the side and back panels (see Figure 12.25). Do not create seams at the lower segments of the side and back panels as these will form the skirts.

    Note:
    For this design, the side and back panels and the skirts are cut from one piece of fabric, then stitched and hemmed as needed. As an alternative, the skirts could be separate panels, stitched to the side panels only at their tops.

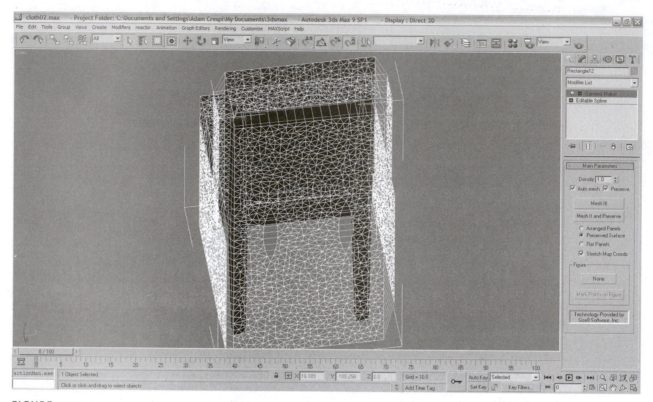

FIGURE 12.25

The slipcover with the seams created.

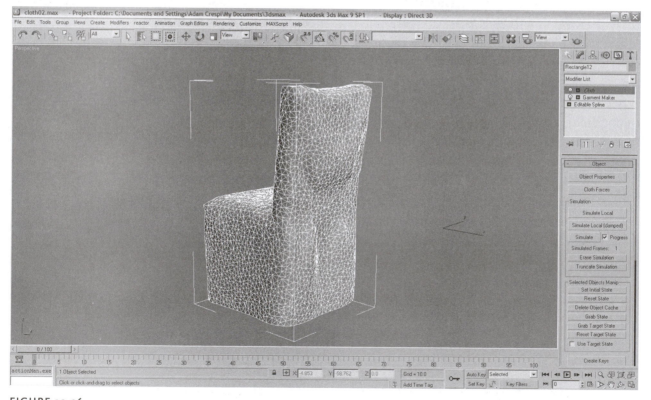

FIGURE 12.26

The finished slipcover with material applied.

5. On the back panel, the two sides of each dart opening are separate splines; their vertices were broken as before. Create a seam across each dart from one side to the other.

6. Simulate the cloth as before. The darts will close, pulling the back panel tight around the seatback (see Figure 12.26).

SECTION C: CURTAINS

EXERCISE 4: Using animation to simulate cloth

To this point we have created and simulated cloth using panels and the Garment Maker modifier, conducting the local simulation of cloth at frame zero. The cloth is inherently static and will not react to anything that animates in the scene. This exercise will use animation and Cloth sub-objects to deform the fabric in a natural way. After the animation is simulated, you can either collapse the cloth to delete the animation, or render an animation after the range of simulation.

In this exercise, we will construct a simple straight curtain, pin it to a rod, and then animate a tieback pulling the curtain open. We will see the cloth deform in a natural way in folds and wrinkles.

1. Start 3ds Max or choose File > Reset from the top menu to begin with a clean scene.

2. Press F to switch to the Front view.

3. Press Ctrl + RMB and choose Plane from the Modeling quad menu. For this simulation, we will use modeled geometry; you could construct the curtain from shapes and use the Garment Maker modifier as well. Create a Plane with a length of 96″ and a width of 60″, with 96 Length Segments and 60 Width Segments.

4. Press L for Left view.

5. Press Ctrl + RMB and choose Cylinder from the Modeling quad menu. This will be the curtain rod, a collision object in our simulation. Create a Cylinder with a Radius of 1″ and a Height of 60″, with 16 Sides and 1 Height Segment (see Figure 12.27).

6. In the Front or Top view, position the Cylinder over the Plane.

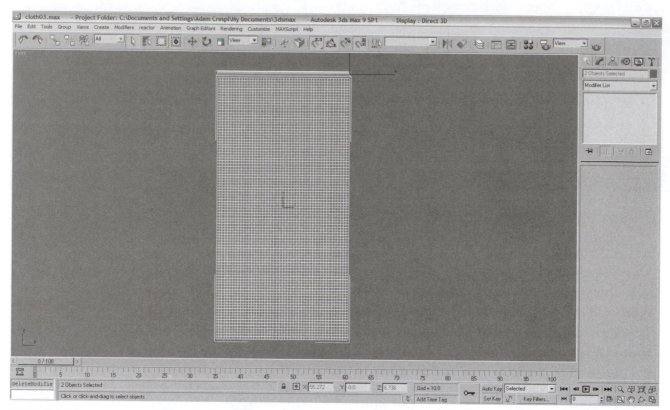

FIGURE 12.27

The Plane and Cylinder in position.

7. In a Top view, create a Tube primitive near the left side of the Plane. Make the Tube with radius 1 of 4″, radius 2 of 3.5″, height of 4″, and with 16 sides. Additionally, turn on the Slice parameter for the Tube, and slice from 225 to 315 degrees. This will open the tieback to scoop the cloth.

8. In the Front view, position the Tube roughly one third up from the bottom edge of the Plane (see Figure 12.28). Alternately, an extruded spline can be used as shown.

9. Because we will use animation over many frames to drive the cloth simulation, we need to animate the tieback first, and then perform the simulation. (Yes, I realize that the book has not covered much on the topic of animation; other books cover animation in great detail. Stay calm. We will use a simple animation that you should have no problems with.) For the purpose of this simulation, we will use the default frame count of 100, which at the default frame rate of 29.97 frames per second (fps) is just over 3 seconds of animation. More complex simulations may require additional frames to settle properly; these may be added in the Time Configuration dialog accessed by right-clicking on any of the playback controls on the bottom of the screen. Press the Auto Key button below the Timeline. Drag the Time Slider to 100 frames, and then select the tieback and move it about halfway across the curtains roughly horizontally.

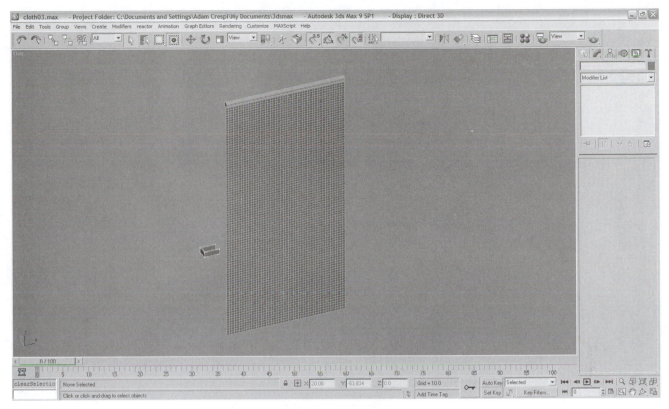

FIGURE 12.28
The Tube positioned as a tieback.

10. Turn off Auto Key mode by clicking on the Auto Key button again. If Auto Key mode is on, everything you change will animate over time.

11. Select the Plane and apply the Cloth modifier to it.

12. Go into the Object Properties dialog and make the Plane a Cloth object, using a soft fabric such as terrycloth or satin.

    Note:
    Stiffer fabrics will require longer times to simulate properly, along with higher mesh densities and increased subsampling in the simulation.

13. Add the Cylinder and the Tube into the simulation as collision objects in the Object Properties dialog. Close the dialog when you are done.

14. We need to do one more thing before simulating the cloth and that is binding it to the Cylinder. For this simulation, we will fix the cloth to the curtain rod and use the tieback to cause bunching. Alternatively, you might construct a curtain from either a polygonal model or a system of panels, and let the Simulate Local drape it over the rod. The animation of the tieback would cause similar gathering and folding, with secondary folding at the top around the curtain rod as well. How

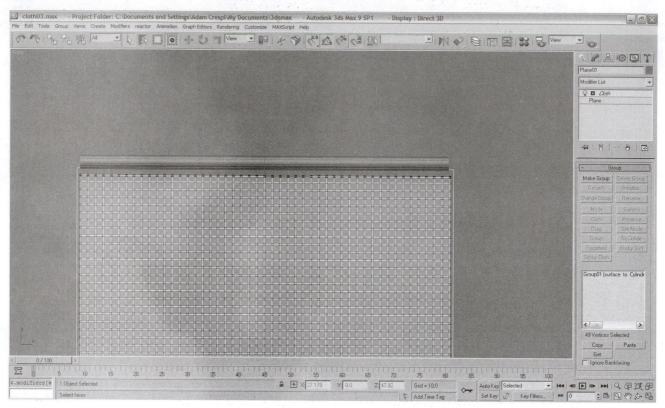

FIGURE 12.29

The top vertices of the curtain selected to make a group.

you simulate and construct depends on your design, as always. With the Plane selected, right-click and choose Group from the sub-objects on the quad menu. The sub-object Group allows you to select one or more vertices of the cloth, make them into a group, and then bind the group to other objects, make it drag or slip, preserve the original shape, and so on. Select the top row of vertices and click on the Make Group button on the Modifier panel (see Figure 12.29).

15. Now that the top of the cloth is a group, the other buttons around Make Group on the **Modifier** panel will be available. Click on Surface, and then click on the Cylinder to select it as the surface. In the list below the buttons, it should now read Group 01 (surface to Cylinder01). A piece of cloth can have multiple groups, each with a different function, serving to Surface, Preserve, Drag, or add stickiness to the cloth.

16. Right-click and pick Top Level from the quad menu. Get ready to simulate!

17. Start by clicking on the Simulate Local button to settle the cloth. There won't be too much settling, but it will let the cloth stretch a bit and hang more naturally. Turn off the Simulate Local button when the cloth is settled (see Figure 12.30).

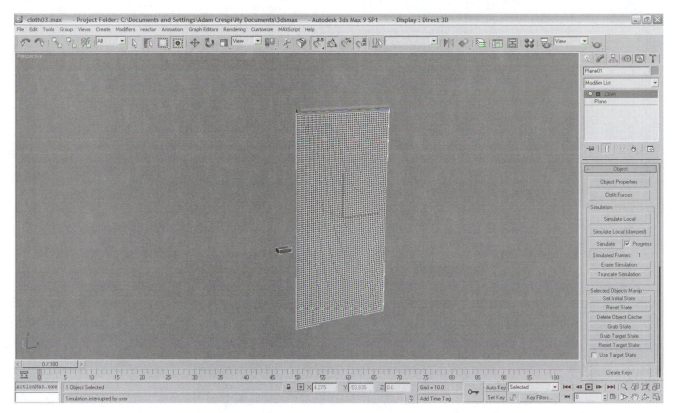

FIGURE 12.30
The cloth after local simulation.

18. Click on the Simulate button, which simulates the cloth reacting to the animation in the scene. By default this simulation is set to the scene range of 100 frames; down in the Simulation Parameters you can set a Start and End as desired.

19. After 100 frames of simulation, the Simulate button will turn off automatically. The cloth should have been swept up in the tieback, with folding and bunching in it, while staying pinned at the top. To reset the simulation, click on the Erase Simulation button on the Modifier panel. This will return the cloth to the settled state.

20. Scroll down to the Simulation Parameters, and click on the Self-Collision check box, then simulate the cloth again. This should reduce the clipping and bunching, although the simulation will take longer.

21. The curtain is done! You may want to adjust the density of the cloth, the depth and offset of the collision objects, and the type of fabric used to refine the simulation. Remember, getting natural results with Cloth is a matter of experimentation and tweaking subtleties as well as inventive approaches, but the results are worth it (see Figure 12.31).

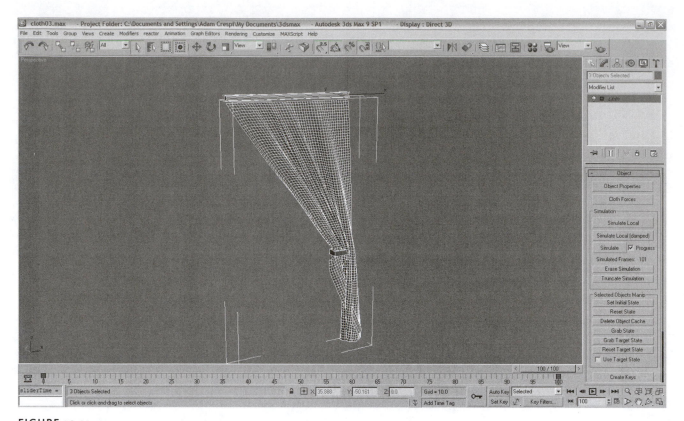

FIGURE 12.31

The simulated curtain, pulled back by the tieback over 100 frames.

SECTION D: CONCLUSION

The real world is full of messy occurrences no matter how regular we try to make it; the virtual is the opposite. It is far too easy to make a perfect scene, with none of the variation we expect to see in the real world. Using a physics-based simulation of cloth allows us to insert an element of randomness and irregularity within given parameters in our visualizations. The softness provided by this randomness goes a long way to enhancing the detail and mood of the visualization, as well as adding further proof in the client's mind that we are the professionals he is paying us to be.

SECTION A: INTRODUCTION TO COMPOSITING

Compositing involves combining two or more images in some fashion, the result of which is called a composite. You see composites all the time on TV weather reports. The meteorologist is videotaped in front of a blue or green screen, then the screen is removed in a process called keying. That video, now transparent around the meteorologist, is then composited or superimposed over a map of the nation, state, or local area. The movie industry uses compositing to insert digital characters into real footage in any number of movies. In all three *Lord of the Rings* movies, thousands of digital orcs, men, and other creatures were composited with real backgrounds and actors. In this case, rather than filming real people in front of a blue background that was then removed, the digital characters were generated with a transparent background, known as an Alpha channel. Many layers of images were then combined in a compositing program to produce the final image.

There are many ways to composite an image or animation, ranging from simply brushing on highlights in Photoshop to employing purpose-built compositing software such as Adobe Systems' After Effects, Autodesk Combustion, eyeon's Fusion, or Apple's Shake. Many people make a very good living as compositors, doing everything from removing wire or microphones from footage to seamlessly combining hundreds of elements into a highly believable image. Since our focus is on visualization using 3ds Max, we will skim over vast areas of compositing as a field and concentrate on a few key areas that will instantly add polish to your images. We will explore four main areas in compositing: camera effects, post effects, backgrounds and matte paintings, and color correction. Beyond that, I leave it up to you to play with the compositing tools on your own.

For this book, we will use Autodesk Combustion, as it is a natural partner with 3ds Max. Combustion supports full floating point images, with trillions of colors available per channel of the image. Additionally, Combustion has full support for the OpenEXR and RPF formats, with all of their attendant metadata, or arbitrary image channels. These include Z-depth, transparency, object and material ID, velocity, and many more. We will push many of the artistic decisions normally done in camera, or at the time of photographing a real building, into the post process where we have greater flexibility and lower rendering time than in 3ds Max.

EXERCISE 1:   Setting up the scene in 3ds Max

In this exercise, we will set up the 3ds Max scene for maximum flexibility in the postproduction process. This will involve setting both material and object IDs, as well as correctly formatting the rendered images. I try to set up my scenes for maximum compositing flexibility as a general rule. That way, if I find an unplanned something that needs attention, I can fix it, perhaps saving valuable time by not rerendering the image.

1.   Open *Retail Renovation Finished.max* from the Assets folder for this chapter on the accompanying CD.

2.   First, set unique object IDs for as many items as you can think of that might need to be selected individually in Combustion. As an example, the polished concrete floor may need some individual color correction, and the store logo on the cash/wrap desk is a candidate for a post effect glow. I usually separate which objects and materials get unique IDs beforehand and keep an Excel spreadsheet of where each ID is assigned. Objects such as the many plaster walls, which are all white, may be more efficiently selected by using a material ID, which we'll do in step 6. Select the concrete floor by clicking on it in any of the camera views, or select by name by pressing H and choosing int concrete floor from the listed objects.

3.   With the floor selected, right-click and choose Object Properties from the Quad menu.

4.   The Object Properties dialog governs items such as visibility to the camera and reflections, how objects appear in the viewport, and G-Buffer Object IDs. Most compositing and post effects plug-ins or software use either 0 or 1 as a default, so set the object ID to 2 for the floor (see Figure 13.1). An object ID simply provides a unique method of selecting a specific object or objects in a scene from a rendered image; hence the actual number can be anything you wish, from 2 to 99999. In practice, I have found that I can use about a dozen if I really try hard, so running out is not an issue.

5.   Repeat steps 3 and 4 for the store sign on the cash/wrap, the chandelier in the center, and the glass tile backing at the accessory display. Use a unique object ID for the glass tile backing and the sign. As the chandelier is made from many tiny glass beads, select the group Chandelier, and assign the whole piece a unique object ID.

6.   On the Material Editor, below the sample spheres, there is a 0 on a button between the buttons for Put to Library and Show Map in Viewport. With the white plaster

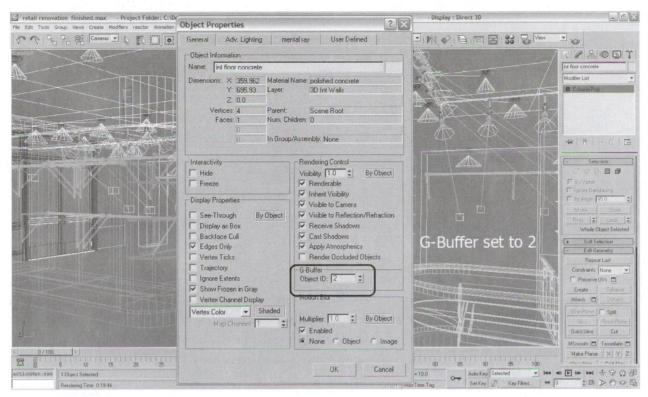

FIGURE 13.1

Setting the G-Buffer in the Object Properties dialog.

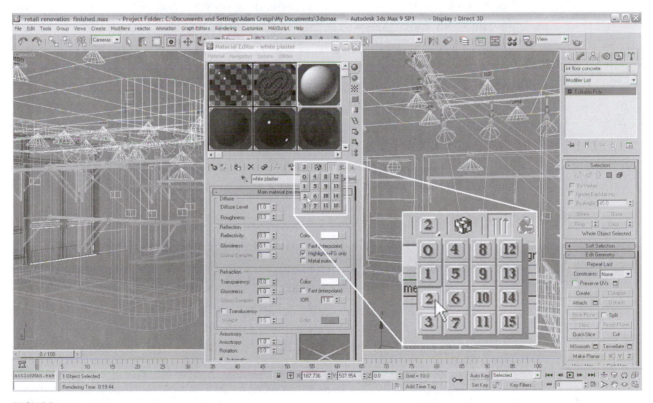

FIGURE 13.2

Setting the material ID for the white plaster in the Material Editor.

material selected, click on the 0, which is the material effects ID channel, and choose 2 (see Figure 13.2). As with the object IDs, there is no hierarchy in the numbers; 125 is not better than 3. They are simply unique identifiers for that material. By assigning a unique material effects ID to the plaster, we can select and color correct all of the plaster in the rendered image at once. In Combustion or After Effects, material and object IDs are traveling mattes; that is, the selection will travel with the portion of the objects visible in the image, and change shape as the view of the object changes.

7. Repeat step 6 for the padauk, the gloss black paint, and the brushed steel. With the object and material IDs set, we can select objects or materials by their unique ID and adjust them as needed later.

8. For this exercise, we'll assume that this is a single-pass rendering, where only one image is rendered in 3ds Max for use in Combustion or After Effects. At other times, you may wish to do a multi-pass rendering, or render elements that will form a composite; see the Bonus Exercise at the end of this section for suggested stylizations requiring multi-pass rendering. Press F10 or choose Rendering > Render from the File Menu to pull up the Render Scene dialog.

9. On the Common tab on the Render Scene dialog, set the Output Size to NTSC-DV using the drop-down template. (For this exercise, you can adjust the number of frames you wish to work with depending on your computer's CPU speed and available memory. We will set up the rendering to do a range of frames as this camera is animated in the space. However, if you are limited by time or a wheezing machine, you can render a single frame or only a few frames and still complete the tutorial. Rendering more frames allows you to see the post effects travel with the images as well as change based on luminance changes as the camera moves.)

10. Set the Time Output to Active Time Segment if you are rendering the full animation; this will render 150 frames, or 5 seconds of animation (see Figure 13.3). If you are rendering only a few frames, select Range, and set the range from 0 to 30, as an example. For single frames, select Single.

11. Scroll down on the Common tab to the Render Output section, and check Save File. Then click on the button labeled Files . . . and browse to the directory where you wish to save the images. By default 3ds Max will save these in My Documents\3ds max\renderoutput\, but you may place them wherever you wish as long as you can find them again. In the Render Output File window that pops up, name the image or images *Retail_store,* and set the file type to RPF using the Save as Type drop-down list.

12. Click on the Save button in the Render Output File window. Another window will pop up that allows you to set the metadata options for the RPF. Check all of the boxes for the metadata (see Figure 13.4).

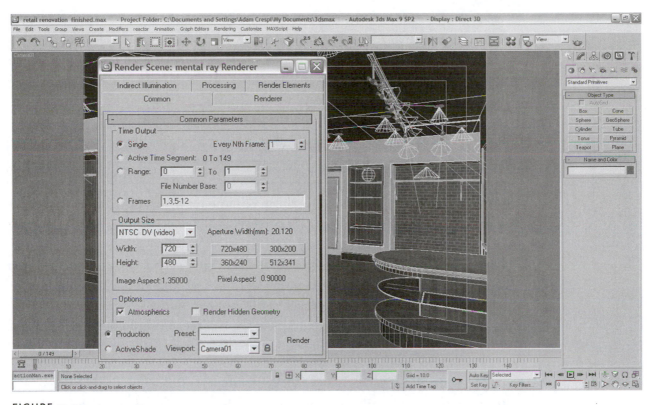

FIGURE 13.3

The Render dialog set to render the animation.

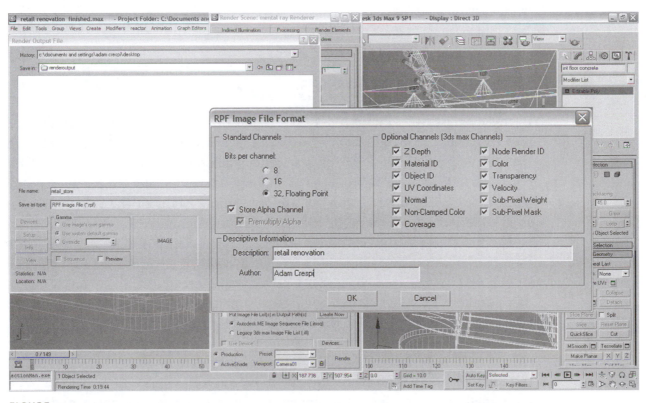

FIGURE 13.4

The RPF file dialog with metadata options.

Note:

The RPF format includes all sorts of metadata, from Z-depth to transparency, velocity, and so on. I usually check all of the boxes as insurance; it is better to take the disk space hit than be missing something important later, such as velocity for adding motion blur.

13. Set the color depth of the image to the following bit depths.

Combustion	After Effects 6.5 or 7	After Effects CS3
32-bit or floating point	16-bit	32-bit or floating point

Remember, for compositing, use the maximum bit depth possible so that there is maximum flexibility when color correcting.

14. Click on the Render button to render the image or image sequence. As you may have noted, we have not mentioned Final Gather, Global Illumination, or Sampling Quality in this exercise. The file as saved on the CD has these parameters set already for this rendering; look at the Indirect Illumination and Renderer tabs if you feel so inclined.

15. Depending on whether you chose to render one or many frames and the speed of your computer, this might be a good time to sip a cup of coffee or get lunch. What you should have when all is said and rendered are a collection of sequentially numbered RPF images, which both After Effects and Combustion will regard as an animation.

EXERCISE 2: Applying post effects

In this exercise, we will use Autodesk Combustion or Adobe After Effects to add post effects to the images we've created in the previous exercise. If you did not do Exercise 1, the first ten RPF images are included on the CD accompanying this book. The idea of the post effect is a slippery one, especially for people familiar with traditional still or motion picture production. Many of the things we treat as a post effect, after rendering, in the computer-generated (CG) world are in fact in-camera effects in the real world. As an example, depth of field in a real-world camera comes from a combination of the focal depth, aperture, available light, and lens chosen. In generated imagery, depth of field is created after the image is rendered and can be manipulated at will. In a similar vein, while photographers may take great pains to minimize the amount of bloom or flaring of light sources in a picture, in CG there is no flare until we add it. Hence, I find it quite common to use assigned material or object IDs to add a bit of flare or glow to objects such as the can lights found in this retail store to heighten the impression that the bulbs are actually giving off light. Remember that in this exercise, and by extension this chapter, we are pushing the final artistic decisions to a place where the ability to adjust the final output comes at a significantly lower cost of rendering and more than justifies the use of yet another program in the pipeline.

1. Open Combustion and go to File > New Workspace. In Combustion, a workspace is a container to place footage and effects in, and may have effects of its own applied. When the New Workspace dialog comes up, we will need to set a few parameters.

2. In the New Workspace dialog, set the workspace type to Composite. In the Format Options section, drop down the template list and choose NTSC-DV from the selection. This will match the rendering standard we used in 3ds Max, 720 times 480 times 0.9 at 29.97 frames per second (fps). In Combustion, whenever there is a light blue entry field, you can either click and drag the number up or down, or simply click once and key in a number. Click once in the Duration field and enter the number of frames you rendered in Exercise 1 of this chapter. Set the Bit Depth to Float and click the OK button at the bottom (see Figure 13.5).

Note:
The default Combustion interface has a charcoal color scheme; however for ease of viewing in print, I have switched to the platinum color scheme. To change the colors, choose File > Preferences from the File menu. In the Preferences dialog, select Colors and choose the scheme and colors of your choice.

FIGURE 13.5
The new Combustion Workspace parameters.

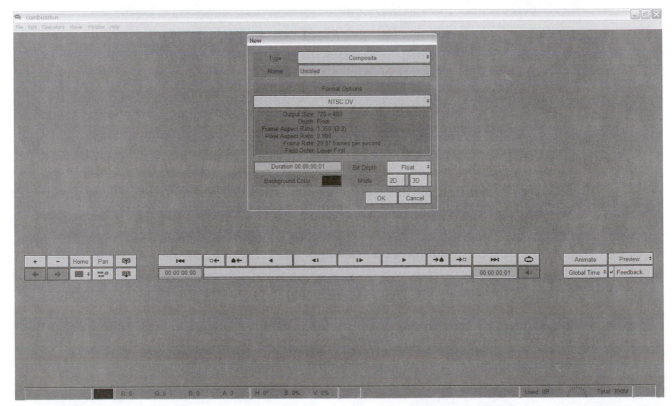

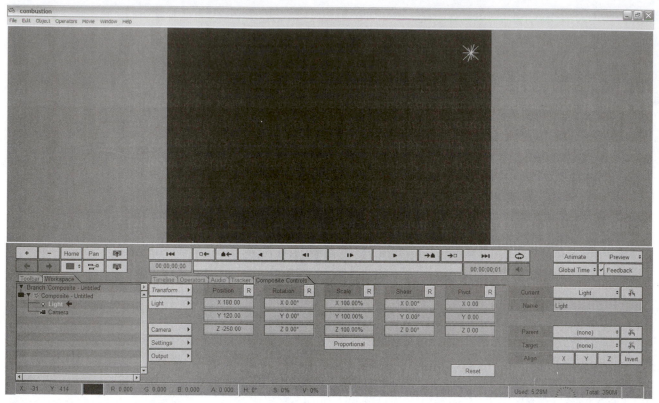

FIGURE 13.6

The Combustion interface ready to import footage.

3. The new workspace will be created with exactly nothing in it, just a blank black canvas and the interface. Figure 13.6 provides a quick overview of the Combustion interface. On the lower left is the Workspace and Tools section; this provides a tree view of any footage and effects, as well as the context-sensitive tools for the action in progress. In the center is the Tab menu, which has the constants of Transform, Operators, Audio, Tracker, and Composite Controls, plus additional tabs that will appear as functions are needed. On the lower right are the link and key frame controls, necessary for animation. In the middle is the Timeline, expressed as either frames or SMPTE timecode, and complete with playback controls. The upper half of the screen is dominated by the viewport, which can be configured to use one, two, three, four, or more views as needed.

4. Go to File > Import Footage, or press Ctrl + I (see Figure 13.7). When the Import Footage dialog pops up, browse to the My Documents\3dsmax\renderoutput directory and select the *Retail_store* RPF sequence. By default, the Collapse button is checked, which shows sequentially numbered images as one animation for ease of import. The footage should show up as RLA/RPF footage, with a duration shown at 30 fps. Click OK when you are done.

5. The store footage should now show up in the viewport as well as the Workspace section on the lower left of the interface. If the Workspace tab is not visible, click on it to bring up the composite tree. Now we will add on effects, called Operators

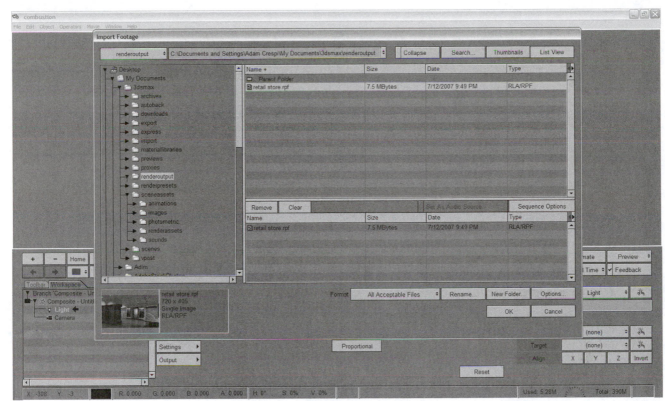

FIGURE 13.7
*The Import
Footage dialog in
Combustion.*

in Combustion, and Effects in After Effects. If the animation of the store is not highlighted in the viewport and the Workspace in yellow, click on either one to select it (see Figure 13.8).

Note:

In Combustion, the spheres to the left of the footage or composite name in the Workspace section turn off and on that particular element when clicked. To select an element, click on its name.

In After Effects, clicking on the name of the footage or the footage in the Monitor will select it; the visibility for each track is denoted by the eye icon on the left side of the timeline.

6. Now it is time to add operators or effects to the footage. In general, I try to add the 3D post effects first, such as depth of field, then the 2D effects, such as color correction. On the File menu, drop down the Operators menu and choose 3D Post > Depth of field (see Figure 13.9). If the footage is not selected, you will get an error message stating that the operator cannot be applied. When the operator is applied, the Workspace window should now show the Composite, with the container *Store_retail* in it, inside of which is the actual store footage and the operator. Think of it this way: we are using a series of containers to compartmentalize what we are doing, much the same way we use groups and layers in Photoshop.

7. The Tab menu in the center of the interface should now contain a new tab for 3D Depth of Field Controls. The interface is context-sensitive and will configure as

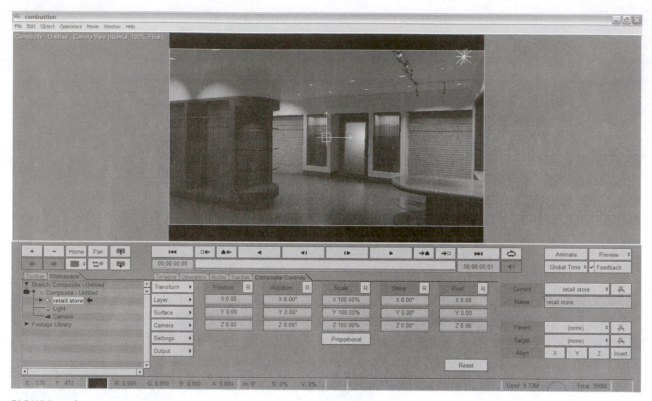

FIGURE 13.8

The imported animation, selected in the Workspace window and viewport.

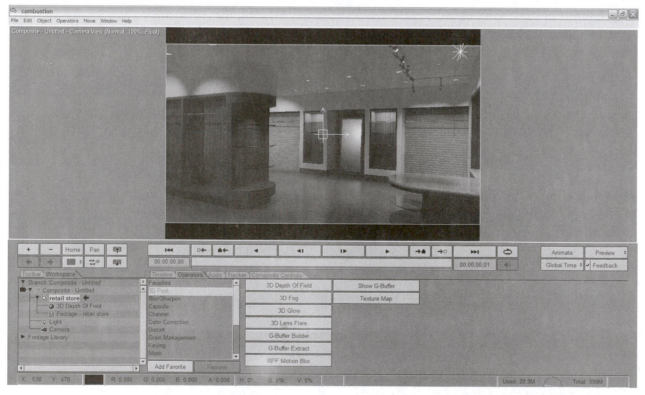

FIGURE 13.9

Adding the 3D Depth of Field operator.

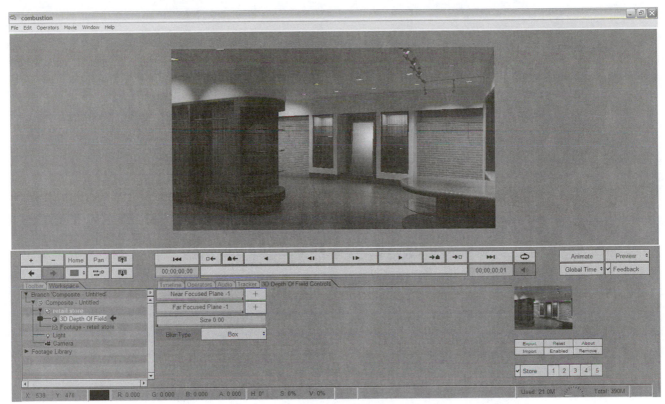

FIGURE 13.10

The Depth of Field parameters.

needed automatically. Click on that tab, and double-click on Depth of Field in the Workspace window (see Figure 13.10).

8. The Depth of Field Controls have only three parameters, Near Focus, Far Focus, and Blur. To set the focal depth and planes, simply click on the plus sign next to the Near slider, and then click on the image where you want to set it. For these images, pick the counter on the right side of the image.

9. Click the plus sign for the Far Focus Plane and set the far plane on the brick wall by the front entry, on the left side of the image. The Z-depth channel of the RPF allows us to simply pick the focal depth at will and easily.

10. Increase the Blur Amount to 3 and see how it looks. Depending on where you placed the focal nodes, you may want to increase or decrease it slightly. Alternatively, you may need to move the focal nodes as well. When you are finished, the scene should have a subtle blur in the extreme foreground and background, focusing attention on the display in the center (see Figure 13.11).

11. With the Depth of Field set, now is the time to add other optical effects. Now we can put some of the other metadata to use, such as the material IDs on the can lights. With the Depth of Field operator still highlighted in the Workspace window, choose 3D Glow from the Operators menu, in the 3D Post section.

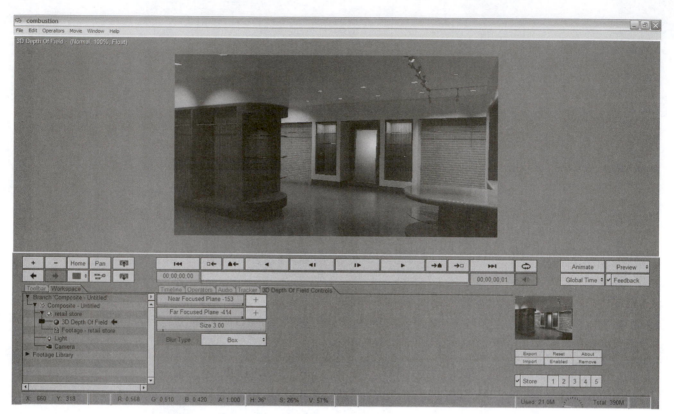

FIGURE 13.11

The Depth of Field applied to the footage.

12. The 3D Glow operator allows the compositor to choose glow application by material ID, object ID, and render node ID. The last, render node ID, is a failsafe, assigning a unique ID to every object in the scene; this is good for select items but hard to deal with when many items are concerned. On the 3D Glow Controls, change the type to Material ID using the drop-down menu. Click on the plus sign next to the Material ID slider, then click on the image above to select the can light bulbs (see Figure 13.12). Alternatively, key the exact material ID number you assigned in 3ds Max into the slider.

13. Increase the Radius to 2.5 or so. The can lights should have a small glow around them. You may need to increase the Luminance Boost by 5–10% if the glow is not strong enough; alternatively, the Minimum Luminance slider will clamp the glow to a set luminance percentage or above. This will make sure that the glow is planted on the most visible can lights, and not accidentally glowing on the ones nearly tangent to the view.

14. Repeat steps 12 and 13 to add a soft glow to the white plaster as well, but keep the radius very low (see Figure 13.13).

15. One of the major uses of a post program such as Combustion in a context like ours, with completely generated footage, is to add depth of field in a method far less rendering intensive than adding it in 3ds Max. Selecting unique materials or objects

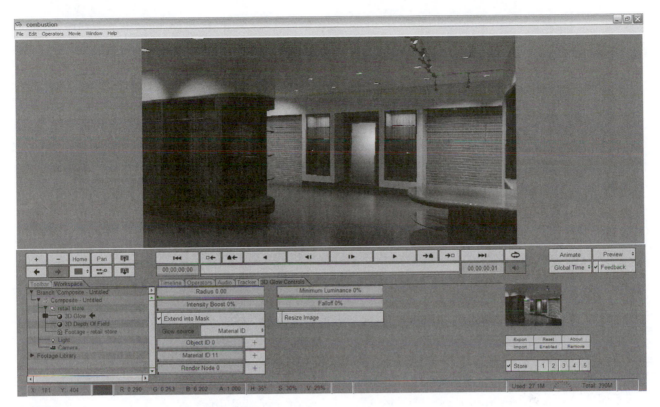

FIGURE 13.12

Applying the 3D Glow operator and setting the parameters.

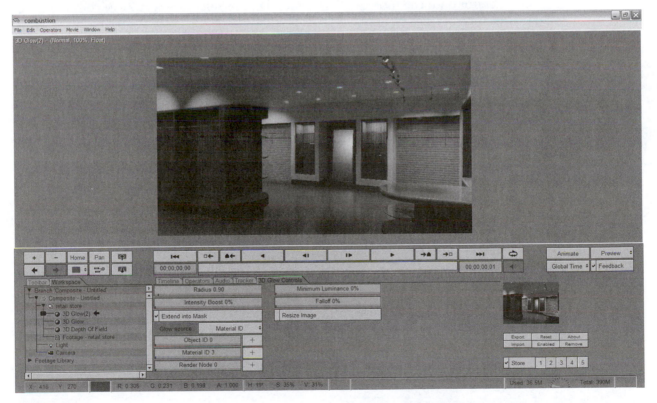

FIGURE 13.13

The Workspace window, showing the additional 3D Glow operators.

and modifying them independently of the rest of the image is the other major use of 3D post effects. With the 3D Glow operator still selected, add a G-Buffer Material Selection operator; this can be found under the Selections operator section. On the G-Buffer Material Selection, as with the other 3D operators, you can click on the plus sign next to the Material ID slider, and then click on the image to select the material ID. For this exercise, we'll brighten and whiten the plaster walls and add a little glow to give them a clean, luminous appearance. Click on one of the plaster walls to select them by material ID.

16. The walls should be selected by a marquee around their perimeter (see Figure 13.14). If you cannot see the marquee, double-click on the G-Buffer Material Selection operator in the Workspace window. When you do this, you will see a small gray rectangle next to the G-Buffer Material Selection operator. This is the Show in Viewport icon, which shows the current footage or operator as well as everything below it. Add a Brightness/Contrast operator on top of the G-Buffer Material Selection operator. You can find Brightness/Contrast in the Color Correction section of the Operators.

FIGURE 13.14
The G-Buffer Material Selection applied, with the plaster walls selected.

17. Increase both the brightness and the contrast by 10%. This should make the plaster luminous while preserving the corners' visibility.

18. In order to deselect a buffer in Combustion, we need to add a Remove Selection operator onto the footage. This is found in the Selection section of the operators.

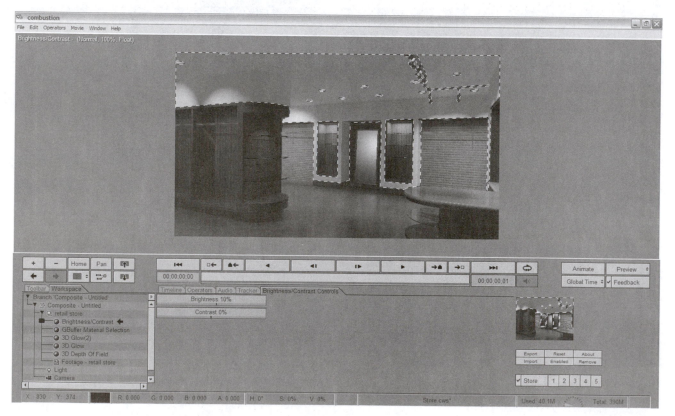

19. At this point, the footage is somewhat stylized and ready for the 2D effects and final polish. Double-click on the Composite in the Workspace window to make sure all effects are being applied. In this exercise, we have taken this image or animation to the point of being a complete offline file, ready for final post work either on its own or in concert with other footage. Save your workspace by pressing Ctrl + S or choosing File > Save Workspace from the File menu.

SECTION B: FINAL POLISH

What effects you add on at this point depend on how you wish to stylize the image or animation. As an example, one of my clients wanted to add glamour to his presentation of a new high-end woman's clothing store and asked for black and white renderings. We warmed up the shadow tones while leaving the midtones and highlights neutral, knocking the client's and his financier's socks off. For another client, I constructed and rendered several model home interiors, leaving them in full color but adding a soft honey-toned glow on the midtones and highlights for a warm and inviting feel.

In the postproduction world, offline refers to work being done on files that are not the final resolution, color space, or format. Online files, work, or finishing refer to the final editing and color correction, done in the final color space, and output to the final format for display. As an example, the animation from the previous exercise was an offline composite, needing further work such as final color correction, glow, grain, and rendering. If it was part of a sequence of camera animations to showcase the space, there are two ways this might be done, depending on the editing and output needs. Typically in architectural visualizations, the editing needs are fairly minimal, and sound is reduced to a background music track or voice-over narration. Thus, the editor (in my shop, me, of course) will not have to deal with syncing soundtracks to lips, J-cuts, or even worrying about cutting on action. Editing becomes a matter of sequencing the clips in the right order, adding any dissolves, and syncing the soundtrack. If the editing needs are minimal, such as simple cuts, I will sequence the footage in Combustion. If the editing needs involve more complex dissolves, additive dissolves, or additional export to a proprietary compressed format, such as Windows Media HD, or MPEG-2 for DVD, I will edit in Adobe Premiere. Beyond these simple finishing needs, as an example, if I am mastering to a higher resolution, such as some flavor of high-definition DVD, I have a working arrangement with a video editor to finish on an Avid editing system and render the final from there. My editing needs, and yours, will scale up depending on the quality and resolution of final output, and the final format.

If the finishing involves another program, such as Premiere, I typically render out uncompressed QuickTime movies for import, using a 10-bit color space. The goal is to try to preserve the color fidelity as far through the process as possible, scaling or compressing colors only once at the end. Combustion is designed as a single shot effects package, made to composite and render one animation at a time for export to an editor. Only if the final edit is something that I can do perfectly and easily in Combustion, and if the clip will go either to a compressed Web format or into a DVD authoring program will I assemble multiple clips for finishing in Combustion. If I am using After Effects, usually the same rule applies. Although there are many people that use After Effects for finishing, I prefer to use a tool for what it is designed for and hence export to an editor.

EXERCISE 3: Online work and finishing

We will treat the footage in this exercise as a single effects shot, destined for export in an uncompressed format to an editor. However, the final color correction and post work will be done in Combustion, assuming that the online edit will be exported at a lower color depth than the floating point we are using. This exercise will focus primarily on color correction and the tools available for it. Additionally, we will add film grain and other 2D finishing effects. As with the previous exercise, what we are doing here can be replicated in After Effects, or any other compositing program for that matter.

1. Begin with either the workspace from the last exercise or open the *Retail_store. cws* file from the Assets folder on the CD for this chapter by pressing Ctrl + O or choosing File > Open from the File menu.

2. The workspace as it is currently has the store footage and its operators as part of a composite. The finishing effects will sit on top of this composite and hence be applied to everything in it. If this was a multi-shot animation, the footage would be sequenced in the composite, and the finishing effects applied on top would affect each clip. Click on the Composite in the Workspace window to select it; it should be highlighted in yellow.

3. Choose Operators > Color Correction > Discreet Color Corrector from the Operators tab or from the File menu (see Figure 13.15). The Discreet Color Corrector has its roots in the superb color correction tools found in the high-end Autodesk products of Inferno, Flint, and Flame, used for movie work.

4. The Color Corrector starts with a color wheel and buttons for Color, Basics, Histogram, Curves, and Ranges, all found in the Color Correction tab. Each button then has controls for Master, Highlights, Midtones, and Shadows. In online color correction, we want to correct the footage to a particular mood to effectively sell the image. Rather than simply tint the entire image, which produces flat colors and may compromise depth in lighting, we need to think about the color and pronounce it in three parts, highlights, midtones, and shadows. For this animation, we'll start by deepening the shadow tones, but adding warmth,

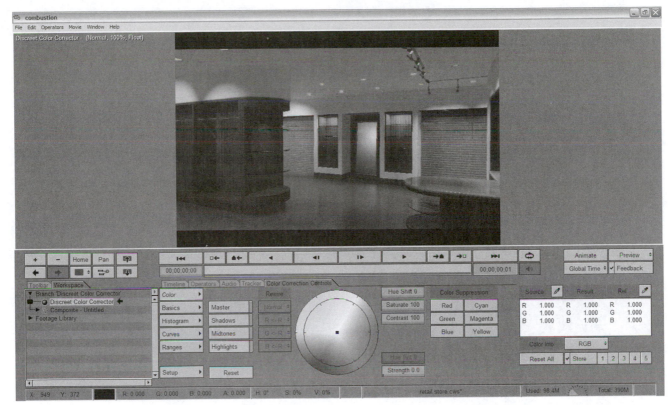

FIGURE 13.15
The Discreet Color Corrector applied to the Composite.

whitening the midtones for a crisp look, and then adding yellow to the highlights to emphasize the bright warm lighting. The color wheel has an inner and outer section, the inner representing the original colors, and the outer the remapped or shifted colors. Start by clicking on the Shadows button and swinging the wheel around counterclockwise so that the Hue Shift slider to the right is around −12 (see Figure 13.16). This will add yellow orange to the shadow tones, which are the lower third of the image luminance.

5. Below the Hue Shift slider is the Saturate slider; click and drag this down to about 80. In combination with adding yellow orange to the shadows for warmth, we will want to desaturate them so that the yellow is more visible, rather than being swallowed by the red in the image.

Note:

People are finicky when it comes to color. Color is subject to display device limitations, color space or bit depth, program constraints, and whether Mercury is rising relative to the potato chip consumption in Rhode Island. (Okay, the last one was a little over the top, but not by much. I have had clients freak out over two points of red and that their coffee was too dark; everything affects the subjectivity of color and how we see it.) It is important to learn how to mix colors for subtlety and mood. I personally have a lot of experience drawing colors of paint for houses and buildings; I think that looking at and trying to pronounce

FIGURE 13.16

Using the Color Corrector to modify the shadow tones.

the distinctions between close swatches is a great place to start. As an example, yellow plus blue makes green, but yellow plus black makes bronze. Bronze appears colder than brass because of the black component, which reads toward green; bronze plus red swings toward brass, which we perceive as warm. Hence in the image we are correcting, because so much of the red brick is part of the shadows component, if we added yellow straight out it would feel orange. By desaturating the shadows and letting the black and charcoal tones come out, the yellow mixes to head toward bronze. However, this is balanced by the red component, which swings the deep tones toward brass, producing warmth without oversaturation.

6. For the midtones, we will use the Basics section of the Color Corrector. The Basics section allows control over each channel of the image, both in amount and brightness of color, as well as saturation and contrast control for each luminance range. Start by clicking on the Basics button, and then increasing the Value to about 115 (see Figure 13.17). This will make the midtones a little bit brighter to start.

7. Next, add a little blue to the midtones by pushing the blue Gain slider to about 120. The blue will neutralize some of the warm yellow light bounce on the plaster and floor, giving the walls a crisp look and slight ethereal translucency.

8. Finally, we'll warm up the highlights by adding red and green. Switch to the Histogram section and make sure to click on the Highlights button.

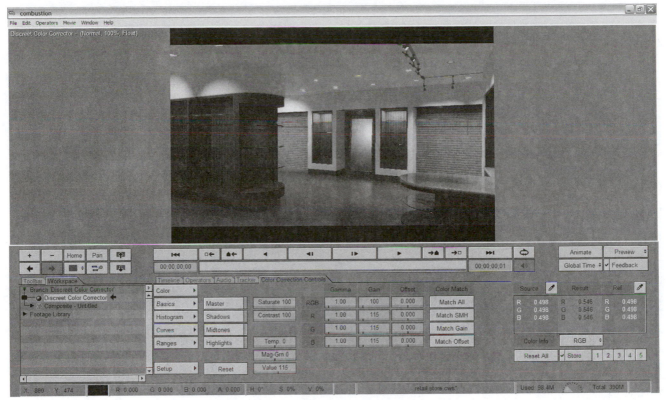

*Using the Basics
section to alter the
midtones.*

9. In the Histogram, click on the Red button below the RGB button, and then drag the right side marker down to about 0.9. This will force more red to show in the highlights. Bring the green down to about 0.93, so that the resulting red and green mix has a red bias. This will appear as a warm yellow (see Figure 13.18).

10. With the color correction done, you may want to add an overall glow to the image to enhance the luminous surfaces. As you may have noticed, we bounced around between the sections of the Color Corrector to shift the colors. The exercise was designed this way to expose the versatility of the toolset. However, in practice you could use just one of the sections to do the color correction. Choose the tool that works for you and run with it. Finally, make sure that the Color Corrector is selected in the Workspace window, and then add a Glow operator from the Stylize section to the composite.

11. The Glow operator is a luminance-based brightness and blur effect, similar to the 3D Glow we used in the previous exercise, but lacking the 3D capabilities. This glow will add a little extra punch to the light fixtures and bloom from the display case lights and reinforce the brightness of the plaster. Set the Radius to about 1.3, and the Minimum Luminance to 20% (see Figure 13.19). These parameters will subtly add glow to the bright areas, while keeping the shadow tones crisp.

Section B: Final Polish   **329**

FIGURE 13.18

Using the Histogram to change the highlights.

FIGURE 13.19

The Glow operator applied on top of the Color Corrector.

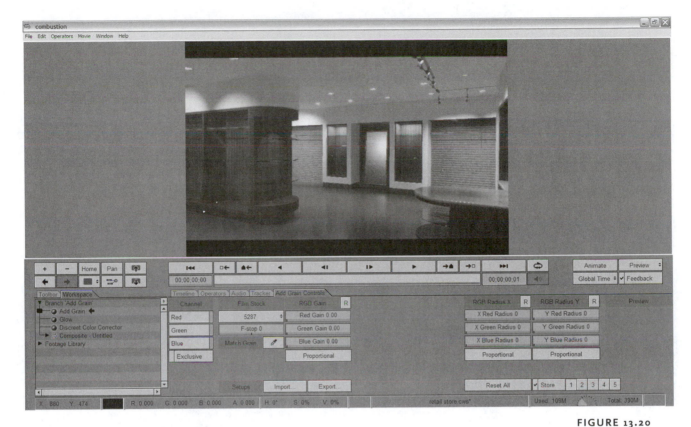

FIGURE 13.20
The Film Grain operator applied over the glow.

12. From the Operators menu, add a Film Grain operator from the Grain Management section. This will add the finishing touch, giving this animation the warmth we perceive of film.

13. The Film Stock templates allow you to choose different movie films, with the option to import custom grain setups or sample an existing image if needed. For architectural visualization, we usually want a fine-grained look; try the 5287 or another one of the higher numbers (see Figure 13.20).

14. Increase the Amount to about 1.2 for red, green, and blue. These channels should be proportionally locked by default.

15. With the grain added, the finishing is complete. Save your file, and then choose File > Render from the File menu.

16. In the Render dialog, set the file type to QuickTime, and then click on the Options button to set the compression type. For this example animation, use the Sorenson Video 3 codec set to best quality (see Figure 13.21).

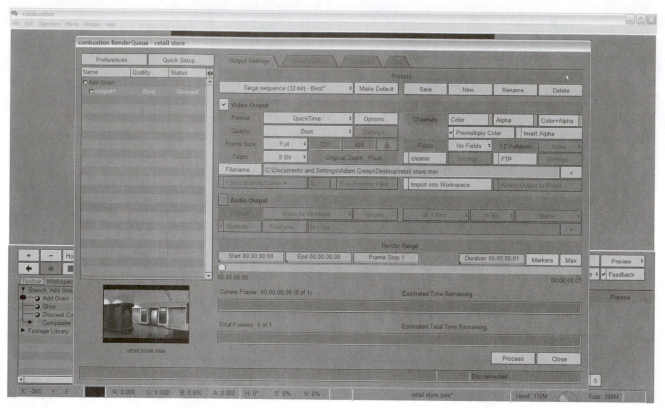

FIGURE 13.21

Setting up the Render dialog to render the footage.

17. Click on the File button to set the output filename and path to a directory of your choosing, then click Process to render the animation.

BONUS EXERCISE: Further stylization ideas

Using the techniques from this chapter, try to simulate the following stylizations in your animation.

1. Black-and-white photography in the style of Julius Shulman, the noted architectural photographer: the images should feature rich blacks, bright whites, and crisp lines, with glowing surfaces if they are in full sun.

2. Soft focus portrait photography: the images should have rich colors and warm shadow tones, with a welcoming, warm softness that does not obscure crucial detail.

3. Cool modern photography: the images should be cool toned, with indigo shadows and crisp whites, featuring true black only as tiny accent areas.

SECTION C: CONCLUSION

What is rendered from 3ds Max is not and should not be the final image or animation presented to the client. Compositing and post effects in a program made expressly for that purpose adds a polish to the image that today's clients demand, if not outright, then indirectly by the absorption of the mass media. We have become so accustomed to commercials, films, print ads, products, and toys with brilliant, well crafted renderings and imagery that we expect to see similar quality imagery in associated fields such as this. By using proper finishing techniques and effects, we are further raising the status of our image in the eyes of the viewer; we have truly arrived as visualization professionals when our image can be mistaken for a well-taken photograph or well-shot video of the actual building, invisible as a generated work.

Index